| Oxford Shakespeare Topics

Shakespeare and the Romantics

T0352074

OXFORD SHAKESPEARE TOPICS

Published and Forthcoming Titles Include:

Oxford Shakespeare Topics

GENERAL EDITORS: LENA COWEN ORLIN,

PETER HOLLAND, AND STANLEY WELLS

Shakespeare and the Romantics

DAVID FULLER

OXFORD
UNIVERSITY PRESS

Great Clarendon Street, Oxford, OX2 6DP,
United Kingdom

Oxford University Press is a department of the University of Oxford.
It furthers the University's objective of excellence in research, scholarship,
and education by publishing worldwide. Oxford is a registered trade mark of
Oxford University Press in the UK and in certain other countries

© David Fuller 2021

The moral rights of the author have been asserted

First Edition published in 2021

Impression: 1

All rights reserved. No part of this publication may be reproduced, stored in
a retrieval system, or transmitted, in any form or by any means, without the
prior permission in writing of Oxford University Press, or as expressly permitted
by law, by licence or under terms agreed with the appropriate reprographics
rights organization. Enquiries concerning reproduction outside the scope of the
above should be sent to the Rights Department, Oxford University Press, at the
address above

You must not circulate this work in any other form
and you must impose this same condition on any acquirer

Published in the United States of America by Oxford University Press
198 Madison Avenue, New York, NY 10016, United States of America

British Library Cataloguing in Publication Data
Data available

Library of Congress Control Number: 2020947114

ISBN 978–0–19–967911–9 (hbk.)
ISBN 978–0–19–967912–6 (pbk.)

DOI: 10.1093/oso/9780199679119.001.0001

Printed and bound by
CPI Group (UK) Ltd, Croydon, CR0 4YY

Links to third party websites are provided by Oxford in good faith and
for information only. Oxford disclaims any responsibility for the materials
contained in any third party website referenced in this work.

In memory of my mother,
Rose Fuller
(1916–1992)

Acknowledgements

I am grateful first of all to the Department of English Studies of the University of Durham, which has supported the research for this book in many ways, not least in providing a subvention which has allowed me to include illustrations. Also to the interlibrary loans service of Durham University Library and its staff, who helped with a great deal of the material needed, particularly for the chapter on the English stage; and to the staff of Durham University Library's Special Collections, who have been similarly helpful with eighteenth-century and Romanticperiod editions of Shakespeare, and with material related to actors and the theatre in the period.

It is a pleasure to thank Dr Fraser Riddell, whose nineteenth-century seminar at Oxford gave me an opportunity to talk through some fundamentals of the book; and Professor Denis Renevey, the host of a visit my wife and I made to the University of Lausanne, through whose kindness I was able to visit the chateau of Madame de Staël at Coppet and see where much of *De l'Allemagne* was written and where August Wilhelm Schlegel worked on the *Vorlesungen über die dramatische Kunst und Literatur*. I also wish to thank the general editors for giving me the opportunity to write about so many great writers on Shakespeare in what is, in my view, a period unequalled in the history of Shakespeare's reception for range, depth, and variety; and particularly to thank Sir Stanley Wells for his generosity in detailed comments on the final typescript.

I am grateful to the editorial team at Oxford University Press – Jacqueline Norton, who was wonderfully patient and supportive with the problems of an extended writing process, and Eleanor Collins and Aimée Wright, who guided the book into production. Nivedha Vinayagamurthy and her colleagues at SPi Global have been unfailingly helpful. Neil Morris saved me from many errors, most notably in my reading of German in gothic type. Dr Michael Baker prepared the index with punctilious negotiation of its attempts to direct the reader to recurring themes.

I am above all grateful to my wife, Corinne Saunders, who has read every part of this with the most intense attention and suggested improvements throughout. Twenty years ago I dedicated my part in the Clarendon Press edition of Marlowe to the memory of my father, whose punctiliousness as a coffin-maker was, I hoped, in some way present in that work. At the time I proposed to myself a dedication to the memory of my mother. I share the view of Pater that a fundamental issue in criticism is 'temperament'—a view my own version of which I have explained in relation to Shakespeare criticism in the preface to my *The Life in the Sonnets* (Shakespeare Now! 2011), and in essays in *Shakespeare and I*, ed. William McKenzie and Theodora Papadopoulou (2012; 'Reading from the Passions'), and *Thomas Mann and Shakespeare*, ed. Tobias Döring and Ewan Fernie (2015; 'A Kind of Loving: Hans Castorp as Model Critic'). My hope is that the temperament I shared with my mother is active in the inflections of this book, since that temperament, as I understand it, has a particular suitability to the book's subjects.

Contents

List of Illustrations

Note on Texts

Where standard translations from French and German are available, these have been used and details are given in the notes. Where no translations are referenced, translations are my own. Except where indicated, references to and quotations from Shakespeare are from *The Riverside Shakespeare*, ed. G. Blakemore Evans (Boston: Houghton Mifflin, 1974; 2nd edition, revised J. J. M Tobin, 1997), a modern text which prints the plays in the forms in which Romantic-period readers knew them, as many contemporary editions do not.

1

Introduction

Making it New

'Literary criticism', said T. S. Eliot, 'is an instinctive activity of the civilized mind.'[1]

The instinct is manifested in different forms in ancient, medieval, and early modern civilizations. Many of its contemporary forms, however, are Romantic-period inventions. Before the Romantic period criticism tends to be general poetics, perhaps applied to individual works—praising beauties, deprecating faults, eliciting patterns sometimes later hardened into 'rules'. Rarely is it an exploration of individual works, with all the ramifications of this that explode in so many new directions in the late eighteenth and early nineteenth centuries. For better and worse, the Romantic period brought into being many of the modes of Victorian, modern, and contemporary criticism: for better when they retain characteristics of their originary forms—investigative, fluid, intellectually inventive, responsive to the sheer difficulties of understanding and reporting on aesthetic experience and seeing that experience in meaningful contexts. In many ways Romantic criticism was engaged with the forefront of intellectual and social currents of the time. It was nevertheless characteristically—albeit not invariably—tentative and modest in its pretensions. The fundamental change it embodies is from criticism as judgement by accepted criteria derived from classical literature to criticism as exploration by new criteria discovered through the works themselves—a trust that where there is an intuition of meaning and coherence, often at odds with the terms in which these were expected, an aesthetic works; and following through that intuition to discover the terms in which it

Shakespeare and the Romantics. David Fuller, Oxford University Press (2021). © David Fuller.
DOI: 10.1093/oso/9780199679119.003.0001

can be given form and the principles that lie behind it. It was often written in interaction with what appeared new possibilities of life in a social world born again on new bases. It was an exciting and an alarming world, and the best of its literary criticism is often engaged with that.

Shakespeare is the central writer of this development, which took place at different times in England, Germany, and France. There are major common elements, but these take different forms, based in different histories and cultural circumstances. In Germany and France, where social changes produced by the French Revolution and the Napoleonic Wars were more radical than in England, literary criticism developed as part of a broad programme about the place of the arts in intellectual, spiritual, and social life; about understanding the past and creating the future. English Romantic criticism starts from the focussed problem: how to understand Shakespeare. For some writers—Coleridge most obviously—this spills over into issues of literary theory: how to understand all imaginative writing. But for England, which already had a diverse literary tradition, Shakespeare, though hugely important, is a less crucial figure than he is in Germany and France. In the eighteenth century Germany as a political entity did not exist. 'Germany' was a collection of independent states, some of them loosely held together as part of the Holy Roman Empire. It did not have a national literature—or at least its national literature was too far in the past to constitute a living tradition on which to build. In the middle of the eighteenth century some writers argued that it should develop a national literature by adopting French neoclassical traditions, to which Shakespeare was antithetical—a 'German' writer, that is, broadly from northern European culture, not southern, not based in Greece and Rome. In this broad sense 'German', in the later eighteenth century Shakespeare became a contested model for modern writing and a major source of new ideas about the cultural functions of imaginative writing and the nature of criticism. France was different again. It had a long national history and a prestigious cultural tradition, but this culture was elite, aristocratic, and by the late eighteenth century, in a revolutionary period, it belonged to a past that had been uprooted. In France Shakespeare became an even more contested figure, central to post-Revolutionary cultural politics and ideas about writing and criticism. Together German and French criticism took the first steps in placing Shakespeare in a European, and later international, canon of great writers which, insofar as it existed at all beyond writers of classical Greece and Rome, consisted of writers in educated elite forms—Dante, reinventor of epic, and Petrarch, inventor of the most fecund of 'modern' forms, the sonnet. Adding Shakespeare to this canon, a writer addressing a socially eclectic and variously educated audience in the popular theatre, was a new step.

One foundational perception of Romantic criticism common to all three cultures is of Shakespeare's artistic judgement in the shaping of his materials: Coleridge's 'Multëity in unity . . . in which the *many*, still seen as many, becomes one'; August Wilhelm Schlegel's 'all in all at one and the same time'; Victor Hugo's master criterion of the 'grotesque', the inextricable intertwining of opposite qualities, the antithesis of neoclassical unity by limitation. Along with a new sense of the relativity of all cultural judgements to historical circumstances, emanating primarily from Herder in Germany, this prompted the overthrow of the universal decontextualized application of an entire system of neoclassical aesthetics; the end of Johnson, of Gottsched, and above all of Voltaire. From these new perspectives everything is seen afresh, especially the relation of parts to the whole—of Mercutio and the Nurse to Romeo and Juliet; of Falstaff to Lancastrian politics; of the gravediggers to Hamlet; and generally the juxtapositions of subject, mode, and style offensive to neoclassicism. Not everybody is wholly converted: even the enthusiast for Shakespeare, Goethe, rewrote *Romeo and Juliet*, drastically reducing the roles of Mercutio and the Nurse; the neoclassical adaptations of Jean-François Ducis continued to be performed at the Comédie-Française long after the polemics of Stendhal and Hugo had changed educated opinion; Coleridge continued to believe the Porter in *Macbeth* an interpolation. But fundamentally it was understood that the heterogeneity of Shakespeare's work—in its materials, its forms, and its language—is an immense strength, and that a major task of criticism is to understand how this works and to explore the profound reorientation that recognition of this brings into being.

Beyond this, Romantic criticism proposed a wide-ranging programme. It stressed the importance of dramatic form, showing the unity of effect invisible to neoclassical criteria; the importance of understanding literary conventions, and so (as in Lamb's *Specimens*) of seeing Shakespeare in the context of contemporary drama; and of understanding in historical context. Here Coleridge's focus is, like A. W. Schlegel's, European and literary; the scholar-editor Edmond Malone's is English and material—a mode of criticism developed in the twentieth century to read Shakespeare in opposite ways, as both reflection and critique of Elizabethan orthodoxy. Coleridge's emphasis on attention to the precise articulations of poetry ('practical criticism') passed into the twentieth century in a decontextualized form, narrowed from the lateral interconnectedness of Coleridge's speculative intellect into the verbal emphases of New Criticism. Coleridge's highly diverse interests, which hardly admit of being brought together under a single heading, are often formal, Hazlitt's political, those of Keats poetic and anarchically pleasure-seeking. German interests, from the philosopher and theologian Johann Gottfried Herder and the eccentric polymath Johann Georg Hamann in the 1760s, again highly diverse, characteristically take a theoretical turn, though this ranges from theories of history to theories of textual meaning. In the context of growing national self-awareness and post-revolutionary social disruption a political perspective, often explicit, can regularly be felt. While this nationalist perspective can be seen as problematic—and was so seen by the poet Heinrich Heine in the 1830s in what would later appear astonishingly prescient predictions of Nazism—German criticism's consistently theoretical turn has been positively influential in modern and contemporary criticism, in which the interest in multiple and unfixed meaning has been especially taken up since the 1970s. In France, many of the main figures, from Germaine de Staël and François Guizot in the early years of the century to Victor Hugo and his translator son François-Victor in the mid-century, are engaged in practical politics and write with a political or broadly social perspective.

The Romantic period was also a great age of translation. Both Germany and France already had substantial translations of Shakespeare dating from the 1760s, but the Romantic period produced translations that were to become standard in both countries into the late twentieth century, establishing Shakespeare as a major cultural figure for the reading public and in the theatre. The work of translators supported and enabled the work of critics and cultural commentators, making Shakespeare increasingly naturalized into German and French cultures, in which, since the Romantic period, his work has been regularly read and performed.

Finally, the Romantic period also occupies a significant position in the transmission of Shakespeare's text, the construction of the canon of his works, and the assumptions about authorship underlying that canon's construction. Precisely how this is seen, in relation to the past on which it built and the futures it enabled, is debated. The position of Edmond Malone is, in any account, central. His development and consolidation of eighteenth-century practices of editing and annotating Shakespeare led to the early twentieth-century 'New Bibliography' which dominated the editing of Shakespeare into the 1970s. He restored the non-dramatic poems to the canon, with critical consequences for the way in which Shakespeare is seen as a poet in the plays. With others, he placed new emphasis on the study of Shakespeare's sources, and he raised new issues about Shakespeare as a collaborative dramatist. Malone's immediate predecessors, George Steevens, Edward Capell, and Charles Jennens, variously active in relation to these same topics, also gave more attention to problems of variant texts which have been taken in new directions by contemporary editing. Twentieth- and twenty-first-century textual studies, and studies of theatre and performance history, are all implicit in Romantic-period scholarship.

Broadly the legacies of Romantic-period Shakespeare criticism in England, Germany, and France were developed in different waves: those that were immediately carried forward, and created the terms in which Shakespeare was discussed into the early twentieth century; and those that were not taken up by the following period, but have been revisited variously by twentieth-century and postmodern criticism. These include ideas about reading in context (contexts of political, social, intellectual, and literary history), ideas about multiple meaning, unfixed perspectives, and unstable irony, and issues concerned with criticism and creative form which contemporary criticism is only now beginning to explore again.

Some aspects of Romantic Shakespeare, which passed into Victorian Shakespeare, have not, in their original forms, been revived. Theatrical productions with elaborately realistic scenery were gradually superseded from the 1890s by other kinds of production, which also had their origin in Romantic-period developments—the critique of

Shakespeare in the theatre by Coleridge, Hazlitt, Lamb, and others; the researches into the structure and working conditions of Elizabethan theatre by Malone; the experiments with quasi-Elizabethan theatrical structure by the poet-translator Ludwig Tieck. Romantic practices of realist presentation, banished from the modern theatre, have, however, been revived and extended in Shakespearean cinema. Romantic productions are also interesting in giving a wider perspective on Shakespeare and the battle between those whose love of the work as created deplores what it sees as mutilation and those whose love of theatre sees the work as a legitimate 'quarry' for modes of making what is permanently interesting more evidently amenable to contemporary concerns.

One primary legacy of Romantic to Victorian criticism, regularly caricatured later as unsophisticated, is the study of character, based in the recognition that, especially in the tragedies, Shakespeare is in some sense profoundly lifelike. Anybody whose fear of appearing unsophisticated has managed wholly to repress this recognition is unlikely to write good criticism of Shakespeare. The idea was not a Romantic-period invention. On the contrary, Pope—a writer who can scarcely be regarded as worm-eaten with Romanticism—exalts Shakespeare in this above Homer—a judgement that, as a great poet, editor of Shakespeare, and translator of Homer, he was well qualified to make. Romantic criticism saw the obvious problems of this, that a fictional character is a literary construct, not a human being. Coleridge puts the issue clearly: 'It is a mistake to say that any of Shakespeare's characters strike us as portraits: they have the union of reason perceiving, of judgement recording, and of imagination diffusing over all a magic glory.'[2] Romantic critics also saw that literary constructs— especially dramatic characters whose existence lies in actions as well as words: actions that can be variously embodied, words that can be variously inflected—have part of their power to resonate in the imagination from an implied existence not precisely limited to their textual being. Now that the twentieth-century phase of distinguishing 'modern' sophistication from the supposed errors of Victorianism is historic, it is possible to see criticism focussed primarily on character with a more just recognition of its strengths. A. C. Bradley's *Shakespearean Tragedy* (1904), a direct heir of Romantic concerns, has remained in print for over a century because it is the superbly intelligent articulation of a permanent point of view which has its origins in Romantic criticism's development of the idea that part of Shakespeare's greatness lies in the human depth of his creations. In a longer perspective, the danger that this might confuse art and life, in any case exaggerated by anti-Romantic polemic, may be preferred to professionally sanitized criticism that keeps reference to lived experience at a safe distance.

Though the Romantic period invented many of the modes of modern criticism, its characteristic forms of those modes are antithetical to the predominant modern assumption that criticism should present arguments about issues demonstrably present (in a text, in a context) in an impersonal voice. The major Romantic-period commentators are mostly not professional critics but writers. This is obvious with Coleridge and Keats, Goethe and Heine, Stendhal and Hugo, but it is variously true with all the major commentators. Hazlitt was an essayist and political journalist, Herder a historian-philosopher, Hamann a theologian; the Schlegels were polymaths; de Staël was a novelist and cultural commentator, Guizot a historian and politician, Stendhal a writer in many forms, Hugo a writer in every form. For all of these, literary criticism is one aspect of a broad intellectual and often social programme. Their address is to a readership looking to enjoy its pleasures more deeply, with more intelligent awareness; people who think of literature, and especially theatre, as an instrument of social cohesion and positive social change; people looking simply to lead their lives more fully. Real reading is understood as a creative negotiation between the reader and the work, not limited to the kinds of meaning endorsed by the pseudo-objective procedures promulgated by institutions of education. It is a context wholly different from that of a professional clerisy addressing a clerisy of fellow professionals, supported by a readership whose reading habits are shaped by that same clerisy. The characteristic modes of Romantic critical writing reflect this difference of context, writer, and audience. They are professedly engaged, written in a personal voice from more or less declared points of view which shape literary experience and the emphases of interpretation. Romantic criticism maintains the possibility of an unmediated encounter with aesthetic experience that is not simply the product of cultural circumstances. From this point of view the critic who cannot believe in such a possibility evinces inadequate libidinal contact with art, has no basis from which to speak, no business to fill the world with words. The antithesis of the Romantic point of view is what Hazlitt called criticism as 'stenography': insert material, apply formula, extract result: simulacrum of meaning produced; real contact with art avoided. Opposite to stenography (again Hazlitt's term) is 'gusto', giving 'truth of character from the truth of feeling . . . power or passion defining an object'—not (in Matthew Arnold's famous phrase) showing the object of criticism 'as in itself it really is' but, rather, showing the object as it appears to passionate attention attuned to its perception.[3] On this view criticism highlights elements genuinely present in the work, but given prominence and emphases coloured by individual predispositions brought to the reading—not predispositions that sit on the surface of the mind and will change as fashions change, but predispositions which are settled tendencies of the whole being.

These individually inflected voices are sometimes those of downright social and political polemic, as with Victor Hugo before and during his exile, for whom Romanticism in art meant liberalism in politics, and for whom literary criticism was a mode of political action. Overt polemic apart, Romantic criticism accepted that writing is from a cultural and personal situation, and that a pretence of quasi-scientific commentary is what Heine called the new historiography of his contemporary Leopold von Ranke that claimed to show 'how things actually were' (*wie es eigentlich gewesen*): an arid lie (*eine trockene Lüge*). The historian or critic is situated, culturally and personally, and his or her writing, insofar as it is honest and full, reflects the nature of that situatedness. While one characteristic expression of this is the fragmentary, immediate perception unqualified by any attempt to accommodate its precision to some pattern of perceptions, even where some overall argument is presented, as in Hamann's wryly entitled 'aesthetics in a nutshell', it is often undermined by a play of perspectives that keeps the reader an active interpreter—a creator not a receiver of meaning. 'Only then do I show that I've understood an author: when I can act in his sense, when I can translate him and transform in diverse ways, without diminishing his individuality' (Novalis, *Athenaeum Fragments*, 287). Understanding art is active: it can be translated by the reader, and can transform the reader, in diverse ways. It permeates the whole being: it shapes who one is.

One aim of Romantic criticism is therefore a *fermenta cognitionis*—Lessing's phrase, taken over by Friedrich Schlegel: provoking independent thought, nurturing attitudes of mind that stimulate the reader's own reflections. More mastering kinds of discourse occur, as in A. W. Schlegel's *Lectures on Dramatic Art*, influential in England through Hazlitt and in France through de Staël; but even here Schlegel is at odds with himself, presenting magisterially a view of Romantic art and its supreme exemplar, Shakespeare, which is the obverse of magisterial: 'the expression of the secret attraction to a chaos which lies concealed in the very bosom of the ordered universe'. System building and anti-system building are both characteristic of Romantic art and criticism. System falsifies the chaos of reality: anti-system is intellectually vulnerable if not defenceless. 'I must create a system or be enslaved by another man's' is the cry of Blake's personi-fication of the Imagination (*Jerusalem*, 10.20); but Blake constantly fragmented and dissolved his own systems. Similarly with Herder, who aimed to combine the antithetical methods of the analyst, stand-ing apart, and the rhapsodist, recreating from within. Similarly with Friedrich Schlegel: 'It is equally fatal for the mind to have a system and to have none. It will just have to decide to combine the two' (*Athenaeum Fragments*, 53). In form, nevertheless, Coleridge's often chaotic lectures are more characteristic than those of A. W. Schlegel— the ultimate 'fragment', unpredictable, delivered extemporaneously from a collection of fragments, which might or might not on the occasion of delivery reach some temporary coherence, but never given final form, existing often in almost comically multiple witnesses (notes, contemporary transcriptions, later reconstructions, diary and newspaper reports) which may or may not represent accurately what Coleridge said: uncompleted structures created with characteristics of ruins. Even Coleridge's isolated observations on Shakespeare similarly exist only as notebook jottings, marginalia, or (as with Goethe), recorded conversations ('table talk'), less intentionally fragmentary than the polished fragments of Friedrich Schlegel, but if anything even more so. Compared with much of this the Schlegelian fragments, teasing and open to multiple readings as they often are, are at least stable forms of words. In their incompletion as delivered, compounded by their indeterminacy as preserved, Coleridge's Shakespeare lectures are exemplary forms of Romantic critical utterance—suggestive, open-ended, for the reader to germinate.

A more intentional use of creative form in criticism is also charac-teristic. This is at its most obvious in Goethe's use of the novel

(*Wilhelm Meister's Apprenticeship*) to situate critical discourse in contexts of character and situation which comment in variously interpretable ways on its meanings. The critical fragments of Friedrich Schlegel and his circle are similarly interpretable, open-ended, inviting the reader as active creator of meaning. Likewise Schlegel's *Dialogue on Poetry*, contemporary voices, stylized versions of members of the Schlegel circle, debating critical issues, but with no resolution of their debates—or, at most, with implied resolutions for the reader to elicit. Similarly the personae of 'Stendhal'—Henri Beyle (Napoleonic soldier), Henry Brulard (subject of his 'autobiography'), in polemic 'The Romantic', representative but destabilized by scepticism and dissidence. Even more amenable to open interpretation are forms of criticism as recreation, what Tieck presented as the creative artist as commentator—Fuseli, Berlioz, Delacroix, Chassériau, recreations of Shakespeare in visual art and music even more open to different understandings than Goethe's critical discourse, textual adaptation, dramatic production, and art–life interaction presented in fiction. All of these are modes of 'creative' criticism—formally experimental, individually expressive, amenable to a variety of constructions.

Beneath the issue of critical methods, of central importance though these obviously are, there is an underlying attitude in Romantic-period criticism to all methods, a scepticism about tools and techniques, which recognizes that a human being employing a technique may imperceptibly become a technician, a quasi-mechanical instrument through whom a technique is applied: that critical methods may—as the workings of intellect are prone to do—become separated from the experience of the aesthetic which is their alpha and omega. Hence the experimentation with critical conceptions and with modes of expression evident throughout Romantic criticism.

As Friedrich Schlegel insists in his discussion of *Wilhelm Meister*, 'poetic criticism'—criticism that is, like Goethe's novel, overtly creative and experimental in form—is not a separate category. All real criticism is creative and experimental. Criticism may deploy methods, even tools, but a report on real aesthetic experience is, like a report on any kind of complex multilayered experience, necessarily creative, in part a naked encounter, albeit conducted on a basis of sophisticated preparation. Tolstoy illustrates the issue in Nikolai Rostov's account of his first engagement in battle (*War and Peace*, Book 1). What Tolstoy's account shows as chaotic (I.ii.19), Nikolai's report radically falsifies (I.iii.7), because he knows what his listeners expect to hear, which is in any case all he can find words for: an account conforming to conventions of expectation which profoundly misrepresent the reality of what happened to him. Hence Ezra Pound's slogan, 'Make it New' (Canto LIII), an injunction not confined to modernism but a permanent truth about expression, garnered by Pound from ancient China via Confucian sources. A more obviously neo-Romantic expression of the same fundamental idea is drawn from Picasso by Wallace Stevens: 'say of what you see in the dark / That it is this, or that it is that, / But do not use the rotted names' (*The Man with the Blue Guitar*, XXXII).[4] This is the problem of the new: however real and intense the perception at its point of origin, without constant pressure of experiment its articulation will be imposed on by conventions of expectation. This is why Romantic-period criticism, of which Shakespeare is the central figure, cannot, in all its multiplicity, be represented finally only in terms of characteristic methods but must also foreground a characteristic underlying all method: emotional and imaginative openness to experience searched with intellectual inventiveness of expression.

England

Genius with Judgement

English Romantic criticism of Shakespeare begins with Coleridge (1772–1834). Nobody is without forebears. In the movement from Samuel Johnson's *Preface to Shakespeare* (1765) to Maurice Morgann's *Essay on the Dramatic Character of Sir John Falstaff* (1777) and other late eighteenth-century Shakespeare criticism it is possible to find adumbrations of the preoccupations of Coleridge and his contemporaries, just as it is possible to argue that the Romantic critics exaggerated their difference from eighteenth-century criticism to establish their own claims to originality.[1] Inherent in literary history is a tendency to find forebears. Inherent in new literary movements may be a tendency to exaggerate novelty. But whatever forebears can be found, whatever polemical exaggerations can be identified, on Shakespeare Coleridge is new.

'Perhaps the greatest single figure in Shakespeare criticism down to the present day': so T. S. Eliot judged Coleridge in 1934.[2] But Coleridge published almost no Shakespeare criticism: he completed just two short pieces, a chapter of *Biographia Literaria* (1817; ch. 15) on Shakespeare's narrative poems as exhibiting exemplary 'symptoms of poetic power', and an essay on method, published first in the *Encyclopaedia Metropolitana* (1818) and revised for his periodical, *The Friend* (1818, essay IV). Everything else exists only as notes for lectures (of which, between 1808 and 1819, he gave about forty on Shakespeare), marginalia, recorded conversations ('table talk'), newspaper and diary reports of lectures, and shorthand and longhand records taken down by audience members (sometimes incorporating

Shakespeare and the Romantics. David Fuller, Oxford University Press (2021). © David Fuller.
DOI: 10.1093/oso/9780199679119.003.0002

much later reconstructions, or with editorial reworkings designed to give fragmentary notes greater coherence). It was Coleridge's declared method as a lecturer, by consulting in the days preceding a lecture all his notes and marginalia—utterly heterogeneous records of his thinking—to fill his mind with all his ideas about a given play, but in the lecture to think these through afresh.[3] Since Coleridge regularly deserted any preconceived plan as his argument drew him along, the lectures thus exhibited the combined processes of thinking premeditated and extempore. This was a process liable to descend into what the diarist Henry Crabb Robinson complained of as 'immethodical rhapsodies' (Raysor, 2.180), a possibility so clearly always present that when preparation worked well and Coleridge developed an argument with relative coherence, his audiences evidently found the results thrilling. Thought alive in the moment was essential: Coleridge knew well that literary experience, however real at its point of origin, was liable to go dead with packaging. But lectures which took off spontaneously in unplanned directions, and were at times extremely difficult to follow as Coleridge characteristically veered away from any plan, defeated attempts to record them even by some skilled shorthand writers.[4] The result is that, apart from fragmentary notes and marginalia, very little of Coleridge's Shakespeare criticism exists as what can be reliably considered his own ideas in his own words: as a critic of Shakespeare he is almost as much a construction of those who wrote down what he said as is Socrates of Plato or Christ of the evangelists. Nevertheless, his elusive words and ideas were profoundly creative for Shakespeare criticism over the following century, and they continue to offer individual insights and general principles from which any reader can learn.

With character, poetry, dramatic form, convention, history—while he does not discuss all of these equally, they are all part of his critical programme—Coleridge invented many of the major forms of Shakespeare criticism of the following century and beyond. His objections to early nineteenth-century staging led to the experiments of the Elizabethan Stage Society (founded in 1895) and William Poel (1852–1943), and thence to the fundamental characteristics of contemporary production, based in the methods of Elizabethan, not eighteenth-century, theatre. His influence passed into twentieth-century criticism more generally through I. A. Richards (*Coleridge on*

Imagination, 1935). His moral and political criticism of Shakespeare reappears in the writings of critics such as L. C. Knights—and though distortions in moral and political readings often appear more obviously as the cultural assumptions on which they are made shift, the impulse to elicit meanings beyond the aesthetic is permanent.

Though Coleridge's presentation of his ideas is often chaotic, though our knowledge of those ideas is largely at one remove, and though what most readily attracts attention is brilliance of detail, nevertheless what emerges fundamentally is a wide-ranging exploration of central qualities of Shakespeare's work, and critical conceptions by which these can be understood that arise from a real and profound sense of intellectual and imaginative life. With Coleridge the reader is constantly in the company of a mind focussed on creative understanding, in dialogue with advanced ideas of his own time, especially the main currents of English poetry, German philosophy (Kant, Schelling), and German aesthetics (A. W. Schlegel, Jean-Paul Richter), and often all the more inviting for the openness of incompletion.

In attempting to come to terms with the variousness and magnitude of Shakespeare's creative achievement, Coleridge's fundamental and most instructive recognition was that criteria derived from non-Shakespearean drama, and particularly the neoclassical criteria by which the eighteenth century had judged Shakespeare, though great, wild, and untutored, were inapplicable.[5] New and more interesting criteria for understanding Shakespeare's aesthetics could be discovered through the works themselves. By these Shakespeare appeared quite differently—as a writer exercising critical judgement that simply could not be recognized by the ready-made criteria of Coleridge's predecessors—'the mere dreams of pedantry that arraigned the eagle because it had not the dimensions of the swan' (Raysor, 1.113–14). It 'has been and it still remains my Object'—Coleridge set this out at the beginning of what proved to be his final series of lectures on Shakespeare—'to prove that in all points from the most important to the most minute, the Judgement of Shakespeare is commensurate with his genius – nay, that his genius reveals itself in his judgement, as in its most exalted form' (Raysor, 1.114). Genius with judgement: Coleridge regarded it as fundamental to his whole sense of Shakespeare. Shakespeare's greatness was above all revealed precisely where for Johnson, for Voltaire, and for neoclassical criticism generally it seemed not to exist. Coleridge looked from 'rules' supposedly derived from Aristotle on Greek tragedy to the fundamental reason for these rules, understanding that coherence and unity of effect were not dependent on the classical unities of time, place, and action but could exist where all of these were violated. It is a critical movement not at all confined to its point of origin. Fundamental are the depth and flexibility of mind that, recognizing in conceptual darkness the power of a work, allow that power to suggest the conceptions by which it can best be understood; also that these conceptions are sometimes involved with the needs and choices of the reader and his or her individual or cultural circumstances. Many of Coleridge's specific ideas are of permanent interest and relevance to understanding Shakespeare, but what he most tellingly exhibits is that search for conceptions that give critical form to intuitive understanding of a work's imaginative power. Typically these were discovered through the plays in which Coleridge's own personal investments were most intense—*Romeo and Juliet*, *Richard II*, *Hamlet* (above all), *Othello*, *King Lear*, *Macbeth*, and *The Tempest*.

It is in relation to *The Tempest* that Coleridge gives the fullest articulation of his most fundamental idea, organic form.[6] In distinguishing between 'what is meant by mechanic and organic regularity' Coleridge describes organic form as 'a law which all the parts obey, conforming themselves to the outward symbols and manifestations of the essential principle' (Raysor, 2.131). He draws an analogy from the natural world: all oaks are oaks; all oaks are different; the myriad differences are relational and interactive. His illustrations of the principle from *The Tempest* (Raysor, 1.113–23) draw together interactions of character, of character and situation, a range of tones and of social levels, and connective transitions between scenes of different kinds: a continuous process of interconnected, mutually modifying, elements. As he expresses it elsewhere, 'organic form . . . shapes as it develops itself from within, and the fullness of its development is one and the same with the perfection of its outward form. Such is the life, such the form' (Raysor, 1.198). Understanding this requires Coleridge's method of what he called 'practical criticism': eliciting unity of effect from diversity of elements by attention to particulars.

Primary is the interdependence of all aspects—what Coleridge referred to as 'Multëity in unity': 'that in which the *many*, still seen as many, becomes one'.[7] The same idea is central to Coleridge's fundamental conception of poetry, his concept of the Imagination, 'the capability of reducing a multitude into unity of effect' (Raysor, 2.63). This is explained most fully in the *Biographia Literaria*:

[Imagination] . . . reveals itself in the balance or reconciliation of opposite or discordant qualities: of sameness, with difference; of the general, with the concrete; the idea, with the image; the individual, with the representative; the sense of novelty and freshness, with old and familiar objects; a more than usual state of emotion, with more than usual order; judgement ever awake and steady self-possession, with enthusiasm and feeling profound or vehement.[8]

It is an extraordinary collection of antitheses. Each one demands meditative absorption, but especially 'judgement ever awake and steady self-possession'—rational self-conscious detachment—in combination with its apparent antithesis, 'enthusiasm and feeling profound or vehement'—intense emotional engagement. This necessary gamut is not easily achieved. It was Coleridge's view that criticism regularly fails to achieve it, typically by placing too great a stress on rational detachment. Coleridge's approach to lecturing, the live occasion with its unpredictable combination of the meditated and extempore, may have helped him in maintaining both aspects; but the fundamental source was loving and impassioned pleasure combined with but not qualified by an intense search for its intellectual realization. With Shakespeare Coleridge saw criticism as aiming to deepen understanding of 'a power and an implicit wisdom deeper than consciousness' (Raysor, 1.198). On this view criticism must engage all the faculties of understanding, intellectual and emotional, at their fullest stretch.

The *Biographia* view of the Imagination derives ultimately from Coleridge's religious philosophy of life: it is the concept of 'the one life within us and abroad' ('The Eolian Harp'), which Coleridge perceived in the human and natural worlds considered under its aesthetic aspect.[9] While much of Coleridge's Shakespeare criticism is concerned with some specific element—character, poetry, dramatic form—his idea of the Imagination and how it functions means that elements isolated by the needs of intelligible discussion, in real understanding—in the experience of the play, whether in the theatre or the study—must be recombined. In the real experience of a work that criticism aims to deepen the separated aspects are reintegrated, and in his practical criticism Coleridge often concentrates on the workings of this integration.

One aspect of multëity in unity, exemplifying Shakespeare's artistic judgement and calculation, is exhibited in Coleridge's account of opening scenes as epitomes of the whole, prefiguring fundamental elements of the plays they introduce—as in *Othello*.[10] What appears at first tangential, as the play develops can be seen as fundamental: the display of Iago's coolness and pleasure in experimental manipulation—his exploitation of Roderigo. It is a prelude to specifically duping him that Desdemona is in love with Cassio (2.1): he rehearses what become his intentions towards Othello on a more readily deceived surrogate (Raysor, 1.47). Similarly, the opening of *Romeo and Juliet* lays before the audience 'a lively picture of all the impulses of the play' (Raysor, 1.5)—Heraclitus and Democritus, the weeping and laughing philosophers, opposite responses to the same error, each with its own validity. Though the Capulet–Montague feud is destructive of civic life and one ground of the tragic action, in his finely invented '*our*-ishness' ('the quality of being connected with ourselves' [*OED*]) Coleridge also registers what is attractive in the 'unhired fidelity' of the feuding servants. Heraclitus-plus-Democritus: the scene is an overture of leitmotifs, a fundamental ground of the play's subject presented in its varied and complex tones. It prefigures tragedy (the lovers) and comedy (Mercutio, the Nurse): the sublime joys and the ordinary delights that are alike destroyed by the action, with one of the forces that destroys them.

The most extended of these opening-as-epitome discussions, in relation to *Hamlet* (Raysor, 1.38–40), is a fine example of Coleridge's 'practical criticism', tracing the dramatic experience moment by moment—gradations of tone (how naturalistic shades into heightened diction), subtleties of characterization (appealing, as usual with Coleridge, to knowledge of real experience), prefigurations of what is to come (Horatio as later praised by Hamlet for his cool rationalism [3.2.63–74]). Even as he was inventing it, Coleridge foresaw the objections to close reading: 'I must not forget in speaking of the certain Hubbub, I am to undergo for hypercriticism, to point out how little instructive any criticism can be which does not enter into minutiae.'[11] But in Coleridge's minutiae there is no hypercritical murdering to dissect because of his evident pleasure in the perception of how in poetic drama intensity of thought and feeling really operate. 'An endless activity of thought, in all the possible associations of thought with thought, thought with feelings, or with words, or of feelings with feelings, and words with words' (Raysor, 1.192): many of his observations on 'minutiae' examine some aspect of what is summarized in this brilliantly cogent and suggestive note.

Unity in multëity, Coleridge saw, could take many forms. He was not interested simply in violation of the classical formulae but in understanding how the complex aesthetic effects he so powerfully perceived really operated—how the attractiveness of a fantastical comedian, for example, may be vital to an effect of tragedy: that in the wit and fantasy of Queen Mab (1.4), as in the exuberant verbal fireworks of his prose, Mercutio is endeared to the reader (audience) as to Romeo; that the reader is accordingly ready to sympathize with the outrage that prompts Romeo's revenge for his death as having a kind of justice; that sympathetic outrage is combined with agonizing irony when Romeo's admirable attempt to prevent harm is the immediate cause of catastrophe ('I was hurt under your arm'). The attractiveness of Mercutio is central: it determines the reader's attitude to Romeo in killing Tybalt and thence to all that follows from that—Romeo's exile, the Friar's disastrous subterfuge, the deaths of the lovers. 'A plague on both your houses': Mercutio's curse shapes the rest of the action; his character is fundamental to how that action is perceived (Raysor, 2.98–9). '*Unity of feeling* ... unity of character pervades the whole' (Raysor, 2.216). What Coleridge so well sees is how what might on a simple view seem poetic excrescence (Queen Mab), or a clash of modes and styles (witty comic prose, romantic tragic poetry), epitomizes ways in which unity of effect is generated by variety of parts.

There are, however, limits to Coleridge's perception of unity in multëity: his rejection of the Porter scene in *Macbeth* as non-Shakespearean (Raysor, 1.67: it was 'written for the mob by some other hand') now seems bizarre (and even as he rejected it, Coleridge acknowledged that some of its phraseology bore the stamp of authenticity). It indicates, however, a more general unease about the place of comedy in tragedy.[12] Coleridge was better able to see the function of comedy when it involved an intensification of tragedy (the Fool in *Lear*, the mode of Samuel Beckett) than when it involved the more complex relation to tragedy of what is usually called 'comic relief'—the effect of which (as in the grim humour of the 'devil-porter' of Dunsinane) is seldom simply to prompt laughter or lighten the tone.

A central thread of Coleridge's Shakespeare criticism—probably the most influential, but also the most problematic—is his discussion of character. As elsewhere his fundamental approach recognizes multëity in unity: 'Shakespeare was pursuing two Methods at once; and besides the Psychological Method, he had also to attend to the Poetical.'[13] That is, effects of character are always involved with the rhetorical and poetic arts of their articulation. Or, even more comprehensively (using an image from Linnaean botany): 'in Sh. – the Play is a *synegesia* [implying interdependence of parts and the whole], each [of the *dramatis personae*] has a life of its own & is an individuum of itself; but yet an organ of the whole – as the Heart and the Brain – etc.'[14] It may be, however, that Coleridge does not always sustain this view in his critical practice. The recognized danger of character criticism is that it may treat a fictional character not as an imaginative construct but as a real person. Coleridge is evidently in danger of this when he comments that Shakespeare's characters have a reality like that of people in real life—that 'Shakespeare's characters are like those in life, to be *inferred* by the reader, not *told to him*' (Raysor, 1.201). This is the danger for which L. C. Knights mocked character criticism in 'How many children had Lady Macbeth?'[15]—a title parodying the appendices of Bradley's *Shakespearean Tragedy*, and through these Bradley's fundamental methods, derived from Coleridge. Muddling real life and fictional characters may be of use to the Stanislavskian 'method' actor in conveying a sense of human depth: it induces confusion in criticism. But there is often a legitimate question about how much background is implied. A play may invoke implications it does not fully spell out, as with Othello's magic handkerchief (3.4.52–76), which implies that the Christian beliefs to which he often refers are adoptions alien to the culture into which he was born. An aspect of Othello presented only obliquely, this is properly part of the audience's idea of his character; but can it be read more specifically as one aspect of an implied Muslim background? So some readers think.[16] Coleridge could be uneasy with a background that he saw as inconclusively inferred, as with that of Gertrude (Raysor, 1.30): did she, as Hamlet accuses her (3.4.27–9), know of her husband's murder? The Ghost indicts her for adultery; she accuses herself—not only to Hamlet (3.4.89–91) but also in soliloquy (4.5.17–20)—of unspecified sins with an intensity for which this may or may not account. Inference is inconclusive—but Coleridge's principle of multëity fully pursued might see this not as a failure of character drawing but as one element, articulated as fully as required, of the murky context of sin and crime with which Hamlet is forced to struggle.

Coleridge's willingness to attend to inference may on occasion make him read more into a character than a play offers. His accounts of Lear and of Edmund illustrate the problem (Raysor, 1.49–52). With both he can be seen as filling out his reading of the play's details by an appeal to knowledge beyond what the text offers—feelings supposed typical of accustomed power and of dispossessed younger brothers. In neither case is this filling-out false to the reading Coleridge is trying to establish from the text: with Lear, despite his faults, a fundamental sympathy; with Edmund, the attractive power of his wickedness because—as Coleridge also argues of Iago and Richard III—his energy of intellect operates with an intensity uncompromised by restraints of conscience. It shows a human possibility at full strength—in content repellent, in manner thrilling. But the readings are established by appeals to knowledge not of the play but of life.

What can be seen as the most developed example of this tendency to read character in terms of inference from beyond the text—and Coleridge's single most famous and influential piece of Shakespeare criticism—is his reading of the character of Hamlet (Raysor, 1.34–7): it shows 'the prevalence of the abstracting and generalising habit over the practical'. Hamlet 'is a man living in meditation . . . the great object of his life is defeated by continually resolving to do, yet doing nothing but resolve' (Raysor, 2.155). It is a reading in which Coleridge disingenuously claimed a degree of personal investment: 'I have a smack of Hamlet myself, if I may say so.'[17] This artless comment made in conversation, so often repeated against Coleridge, was not meant as implying a principle of interpretation: it is an off-the-cuff acknowledgement of a sense of kinship that can scarcely have been meant as other than a mixed compliment to himself. 'My account of Hamlet may be somewhat informed by my own character and preoccupations' would have been a more guarded formulation—less epigrammatic but more true. His contemporaries required no hint from Coleridge on the compatibility of the reader with this reading. Of Coleridge's lecture on *Hamlet* of 1812 the diarist Henry Crabb Robinson recorded: 'Somebody said to me, "This is a satire on himself". "No", said I, "it is an elegy." A great many of his remarks on Hamlet were capable of a like application.'[18] And so it is with many a real interpretation: emphases will arise from the experience and preconceptions of the interpreter. This does not make an interpretation 'purely subjective', or invalid for other readers. As Emerson puts it— less snappily than Coleridge but more comprehensively—*Hamlet* was the play of the age because the 'speculative genius [of the nineteenth century] is a sort of living Hamlet'.[19] It is an admirable comment on the kind of special appeal a work may have for the fundamental biases of a culture, as of an individual reader. Similarly Hazlitt's epigrammatic 'It is we who are Hamlet', 'we' being (on Hazlitt's view) all fit readers; on a severely historicizing view, 'readers of the Romantic period'; on almost any view, 'all readers some of the time'. Coleridge's account of Hamlet was his own; though, as Goethe's independent but similar reading in *Wilhelm Meisters Lehrjahre* implies, it was also a reading for the age. It—and the unguarded conversational remark— need not be taken to impugn Coleridge's reading of Shakespearean characters more generally. If Coleridge's accounts of character occasionally confound art with life and involve some writing about inference that shades into critical fiction, this is an error more readily corrected than sophistication that drains criticism of human content.

Emerson on Hamlet raises another issue about Coleridge's view of Shakespeare's characters. While they are sharply individualized ('life itself does not excite more distinctly that sense of individuality which belongs to real existence'),[20] they are also broadly representative: 'the reader feels all the satisfaction arising from individuality, yet that very individual is a sort of class of character, and this circumstance renders Shakespeare the poet of all ages'.[21] Based on Coleridge's fundamental sense that '*universale in particulari speculatur* . . . is the philosophy of poetry',[22] this view of characters as both individual and representative is one of the most frequently repeated ideas of his Shakespeare criticism.

It is Shakespeare's peculiar excellence, that . . . we find individuality every where, mere portrait no where. . . . [W]e may define the excellence of their method [of his works] as consisting in that . . . union and interpenetration of the universal and the particular, which must ever pervade all works of decided genius.[23]

This view of Shakespearean characters, present in greater or lesser degree in all Coleridge's accounts, may be seen in his reading of Macbeth. In part he offers psychoanalytic accounts of the protagonists: the background of guilty thought evident in the contrast between Banquo and Macbeth in greeting the witches (Raysor, 1.61); the frail self-delusion by which conscience and remorse present themselves to Macbeth's conscious thoughts in pragmatic prudential terms that can be more readily addressed (Raysor, 1.71–2); the comparable evasions of Lady Macbeth, differently explained (Raysor, 2.221–2). These are in themselves both individual and representative—what Coleridge elsewhere calls 'sophistry which is common to man' (Raysor, 1.135). But beyond this he also relates Macbeth to the fundamental personification of evil shown by Milton in the Satan of *Paradise Lost* (Raysor, 1.64). It is characterization showing what Coleridge elsewhere called 'the involution of the universal in the individual'.[24] Lear arraigning Goneril through a personification ('Ingratitude, thou marble-hearted fiend' [1.4.259]), or seeing Poor Tom as 'houseless poverty' (3.4.26); Macbeth on his way to assassinate Duncan sensing 'wither'd Murther, / Alarum'd by his sentinel, the wolf' (2.1.52–3); Titus presenting his antagonists as Rape and Murder (5.2): these generalizing articulations may be characteristic of the speaker and partial in relation to the play as a whole, but they all point in the same direction. 'Banish plump Jack, and banish all the world' (*1 Henry IV*, 2.5.480): Falstaff's apology for his mode of existence may be self-serving, but what reader does not feel of Falstaff (manner of Walt Whitman) that he is vast, he contains multitudes? While it may be that no reader will describe these supra-individual representations in quite the same way, Coleridge's idea is not to name the issues but to experience the sense of representative value.

Meanings of this kind cannot always be demonstrated by specific textual references. Rather, they are meanings that emerge from all aspects of the presentation taken together, for which specific fragments of text may act as pointers, but they may not. Romeo and Juliet have a supra-individual quality not only because of the power with which their individual characters are articulated in their poetry but because they present a myth of love: a power that is socially disruptive, always potentially forbidden and driven toward concealment. A positive reading of Othello may, similarly, understand the character as embodying a kind of idealism, and Iago as embodying forces that are driven to hate and destroy, whether for the pure pleasure of destroying (Coleridge's account of him as 'motiveless malignity'; Raysor, 1.44), or because by its very existence idealism invalidates cynicism. Is a meaning of this kind implied by the constantly extreme pitch of Othello's idealism as by Iago's riddling devilish self-identification as an obverse of the Christian God ('I am not what I am', 1.1.65; Exodus 3:14)? For Coleridge it is—and would be just as much so without whatever can be extracted from Iago's enigma. Though Verdi and his librettist Boito set about it with an explicitness that is un-Shakespearean, they took a Coleridgean view when, in turning *Othello* into *Otello*, they gave Iago an explicit nihilist creed and Desdemona a traditional Christian prayer (Ave Maria). The opera is thus more explicitly a conflict between representative figures of good and evil than the play; but though its methods are not Shakespeare's, on a Coleridgean view broad meanings of this kind are. It is a kind of meaning that can be seen regularly in operatic versions of Shakespeare, which often use no more than fragments of Shakespeare's text, or in balletic versions, which are Shakespeare without words. With words or without, drama is narrative structure, embodied movement, sequence of tones and tableaux, emblematic stage picture; opera and ballet reveal these symbolic or epitomic aspects of Shakespeare's stagecraft, which are often more powerfully operative in the more evidently stylized media. But these kinds of meaning are equally present in verbal drama. Vide Nietzsche on *Hamlet*: 'the structure of the scenes and the vivid images reveal a deeper wisdom than the poet . . . can put into words and concepts'.[25] Romeo and Juliet, Hamlet, and other Shakespearean characters clearly function as cultural myths for people who have no precise sense of the words in which their meanings are embodied. The meaning of any play as a whole lies not only in the precise words of its text but also in its broad outlines, in the structured sequence of embodied actions, images, tableaux, and all the ways in which these interact with and comment on the words. In his accounts of character as 'all *genera* intensely individualised' (Raysor, 1.122)

Coleridge points to this broader kind of meaning, just as his practical criticism keeps in view the complementary minutiae. The minutiae are essential to a vivid sense of the whole ('how little instructive any criticism can be which does not enter into minutiae'), but minutiae become trivial if they are not complemented, as they are in Coleridge, by a sense of the larger meanings they support.

Dependent on the totality of the work, these larger meanings may be more evident in the broad sweep of theatre than in the study. But not for Coleridge, who 'never saw any of Shakespeare's plays performed, but with a degree of pain, disgust and indignation' (Raysor, 2.230): early nineteenth-century modes and styles of performance drove Shakespeare 'from the stage to find his proper place in the heart and in the closet' (Raysor, 2.230). It is one of Coleridge's repeated themes, but it is misunderstood if interpreted as fundamentally anti-theatrical. Coleridge offers a critique of Shakespearean presentation and performance as he found it in contemporary theatre. The plays were rewritten—as, at the most extreme, in Nahum Tate's *King Lear*, with its happy ending in which Lear and Cordelia live and Cordelia marries Edgar; or in the Garrick ending of *Romeo and Juliet*, in which Juliet wakes before Romeo's poison has taken effect—which Coleridge viewed with especial disgust (it 'produces tears, and so does a blunt razor', Raysor, 2.31). These adaptations were far from unique. 'Scarcely a season passes', Coleridge complained, without a production of Shakespeare 'in which the mangled limbs of our great Poet are thrown together "in most admired disorder"'.[26] Besides mangling the texts, while Shakespeare wrote for a stage in which 'the painting was not in colours but in words', and a theatre which was 'as near as possible a closet' (Raysor, 2.130, 68), early nineteenth-century theatres aimed for an inappropriate realism: excessive scenery and visual effects enforced further cuts and replaced what staging should properly not deflect from but enforce—all that can be suggested to the imagination by the words (Raysor, 2.57, 230). The system of star actors meant that audiences went to see not plays but performances, the celebrated qualities of which Coleridge judged not commensurate with any exalted conception of their role or its part in the play as a whole ('speeches usurped by fellows who owed their very elevation to dexterity in snuffing candles': Raysor, 2.68). And finally Coleridge was pained by the speaking of Shakespeare's verse ('ranting') in theatres too large for subtlety (Raysor, 1.129, 2.57). These objections are not, or are not systematically, to theatre per se but to the theatre of mangled texts, naturalistic illusion, inappropriate acting styles, and a focus on central roles at the expense of the play as a whole. While it may be that some of these problems relate to characteristic corruptions of theatre in any age, they are not objections to theatre in its ideal form. Coleridge's account of the nature of theatrical illusion shows a vivid sense of the importance of the experience of a play in the theatre ideally considered.

For Samuel Johnson, 'a play read, affects the mind like a play acted'.[27] But in all ways? This might with equal truth be reversed: 'a play read does not affect the mind like a play acted'—or does so only rarely. Coleridge's discussions of the nature of theatrical illusion imply that, even for the most imaginative reader, the visible movement of the action properly presented and the physical presence of actors conscious of their place in the whole design—Shakespeare presented as he never was on the stage as Coleridge saw it, but as he could be on the stage as Shakespeare found it—can be a stimulus to the imagination.[28] In these discussions Coleridge is concerned to contradict the Scylla and Charybdis of both French neoclassical theory and Samuel Johnson's answer to it—the view that the audience is fully persuaded of the truth of a theatrical representation, and the view that an audience is never other than fully conscious of theatrical representation as illusion. An audience recognizes, Coleridge argues, that drama is not a copy of reality but an imitation. This allows it to be neither conscious nor unconscious of illusion, but in a middle state, analogous to that of dreams—judgement is not suspended; it is simply not present: 'We *choose* to be deceived', or, as he puts it in another account, 'stage presentations... produce a sort of temporary half-faith' (Raysor, 1.116, 178). It is an understanding of the nature of theatrical illusion which relates it to one of his most famous critical formulations: 'the willing suspension of disbelief... which constitutes poetic faith'.[29] The discussions of theatrical illusion in Coleridge's Shakespeare criticism make it clear that he has in mind the effect not simply of a play as read but of a play acted. The state of choosing to be deceived, accepting the temporary half-faith of theatrical illusion, permits the intellectual-emotional engagement which is his ideal: 'judgement ever awake and steady self-possession, with enthusiasm and feeling profound or vehement'.

One aim of Coleridge's lectures was to 'leave a *sting* behind—i.e. a disposition to study the subject anew, under the light of a new principle' (Raysor, 2.262). Coleridge's criticism contains a great deal that is straightforwardly of permanent value. But beyond this, though Coleridgean principles are no longer new, Coleridge's struggles to articulate real imaginative experience, often in conceptual darkness, have the permanent freshness of all real perception. His lectures, and the notes and marginalia from which they were drawn, can still offer the 'sting' for which he hoped: an impetus to fresh thinking.

William Hazlitt (1778–1830) is Coleridge's antithesis. Coleridge began as a radical, a Unitarian in religion and supporter of the French Revolution in politics, and became a conservative. Hazlitt was by background and remained by conviction a radical. The differences between them show how difficult it is to generalize about any supposed 'Romantic view of Shakespeare'. Despite their differences, however, Hazlitt always viewed Coleridge with a residue of affection: he remembered—and paid tribute to—how, as a young man, he had been inspired and set on his way by Coleridge. But in his main writing on Shakespeare, *The Characters of Shakespeare's Plays* (1817), though he had attended some of Coleridge's lectures on Shakespeare, he ignored Coleridge in favour of August Wilhelm Schlegel, and the view of Shakespeare he presents is substantially different from that of Coleridge in a variety of ways.[30]

'The courage to say as an author what he felt as a man': this was Hazlitt's praise of Montaigne.[31] It was the courage to which Hazlitt himself aspired, a keynote of his writing. For Montaigne, speaking his thought had required courage because his scepticism was in advance of his age and a prophecy of the future—as Hazlitt saw his own political views, especially after 1815 his continuing admiration for Napoleon and the ideals of the French Revolution in a time in which they seemed substantially in defeat. That Hazlitt perceived himself as an outsider is central to his writing.

'We can neither beg, borrow, nor steal characteristic excellences': this too is with Hazlitt a keynote—the validity of the characteristic (Howe, 17.33). No approval by the herd instinct of fashion can compensate for loss of the characteristic. As a self-conceived outsider, Hazlitt read against the grain, or, as it might be better conceived, for his preferences—that is, highlighting elements which, genuinely present in the work, are also given prominence and emphases coloured by the predispositions that he brought to the reading—in Hazlitt's case, often pugnaciously alienated predispositions. In its ideal form, which is often exemplified in Romantic commentary, this kind of coloured engagement can produce excellent criticism: meanings that do not confine themselves to history and otherness, treating art as a subject for scholarly investigation that ignites no real connection; meanings that do not ignore history and otherness, treating art as a catalyst that ignites only what is brought to it. The difficult dynamic of pressure on both sides of this Scylla and Charybdis—which means both attending to the work as it really is and allowing the interaction with that of an idiosyncratic living intellect and imagination—this is what for Hazlitt leads to real meaning, meaning negotiated between the work, the reader willing to probe his or her own reactions, and the wider cultural situation in relation to which new perspectives are revealed. This complex negotiation Hazlitt thought should be, as far as possible, conscious—as it often is with Hazlitt, for example, when he admits how differently he might have viewed Shakespeare's comedies if he had been less 'saturnine' (Howe, 4.316); but also as it seems with Hazlitt sometimes not to be, for example, when he moves back and forth between his contentious views of the historical Henry V and Shakespeare's character, absorbing one into the other, and does not acknowledge how differently he might have viewed Shakespeare's histories if he had been otherwise politically committed (Howe, 4.285–6). Insofar as it can, criticism should understand what it is doing. But self-understanding, seeing from the outside the nature of one's own engagements, can never be more than partial. The reality of reading to experience is more important than the degree of its self-consciousness. Hazlitt's passionately engaged readings—sometimes distortions, more or less easily filtered—are infinitely preferable to the far more deadly distortions of a pretended cool objectivity—the kind of criticism that Hazlitt damned as 'a species of stenography' (Howe, 6.319), mechanical, standardized—thinking by proxy and writing by rote (Howe, 17.137).

The poet and critic Tom Paulin has described Hazlitt's collected works as one of the great Romantic autobiographies. Hazlitt did in fact write an episode of quasi-autobiography in his *Liber Amoris* (1823)—albeit thinly disguised as fiction and published anonymously (but soon recognized as by Hazlitt), a Rousseauesque personal confession of humiliating rejected love. But Paulin is right in pointing to submerged autobiography as an element in all Hazlitt's writings—saying as an author what he felt as a man; criticism as an oblique form of life-writing, a way of saying 'I was, and this is what life meant to me'. While there is much in Wilde's poised aestheticism that Hazlitt would repudiate, on the presence in criticism of the critic's personality he is Wildean *avant la lettre*: 'the more strongly [the critic's] personality enters into the interpretation the more real the interpretation becomes, the more satisfying, the more convincing, and the more true.... Personality is an absolute essential for any real interpretation.'[32] Hazlitt would not have formulated the idea in these terms, but this is a principle on which he wrote. A strong flavour of individual personality is written into everything, in the pugnacity of his opinions and the passion of his rhetoric.

Unlike Coleridge, Hazlitt had a natural enthusiasm for theatre. From 1814 he worked as a theatrical reviewer for a variety of journals. His *Characters of Shakespeare's Plays*, the first critical book on Shakespeare's entire oeuvre, incorporated many of his reviews.[33] These show the intense pleasure he took in the experience of theatre, and how imaginatively he was able to analyse its emotional effects, especially effects derived from the expressivity of an actor's physicality—the kind of effects that are implicit in a text but dependent on performance for their realization. As well as recording successes, his detailed commentaries on expressive effects of delivery or embodiment that might have been achieved but were not show his imaginative engagement with all the actor's resources of body and voice.[34] He regarded theatre as valuable to the individual, giving 'a body to our thoughts, and refinement and expansion to our sensible impressions'. In the sense of community it engenders, he saw theatre as also beneficial to society as a whole, 'a test and school of humanity' that serves 'to reconcile our numberless discordant incommensurable feelings and interests together... and to rally us around the standard of our common humanity' (Howe, 18.272–3). Despite this fundamental enthusiasm, however, Hazlitt found much to say against early nineteenth-century presentations of Shakespeare.

Like Coleridge, Hazlitt deplored the cavalier attitude of early nineteenth-century theatre to cutting and rewriting Shakespeare: it is 'a disgrace to the English stage'.[35] He thought a few plays simply better suited to performance than to reading—*Richard III* ('it belongs to the theatre, rather than to the closet': Howe, 4.298), and (perhaps surprisingly) *The Winter's Tale* ('one of the best-acting of our author's plays': Howe, 4.325). More fundamentally, however, 'The reader of the plays of Shakespeare is almost always disappointed in seeing them acted; and, for our own part, we would never go to see them acted, if we could help it.'[36] Even this—Hazlitt at his most Coleridgean on the inadequacies of theatre—is immediately qualified by praise of Sarah Siddons and Edmund Kean as having 'raised our imagination of the part they acted'. But it is a note struck many times: 'We do not like to see our author's plays acted, and least of all, *Hamlet*' (Howe, 5.237). 'Hamlet himself seems hardly capable of being acted' (4.237)—that is, the character is too complex to be represented in all his aspects. While some of Hazlitt's objections are not to performance per se but to specific failures of performers to realize in stage terms the implications of the character as Hazlitt reads it, there is also an underlying sense that the subtlety of the character can only be fully appreciated by the meditative reader. Similarly with *King Lear*, where the fundamental issue is completeness of imaginative engagement. The passion of the character can only be fully grasped by the engaged reader. 'While we read it, we see not Lear, but we are Lear' (Howe, 5.271, quoting Charles Lamb). In reading we become Lear; the storm that assaults him is our passion, the outward form of an inward rage that completely overturns fundamental emotional anchorings. In this only the reader can fully participate. No stage effect can match the symbol. This is not only a comment on *King Lear*: it is the condition of all tragic drama, and of *Lear* in a special degree only insofar as it is the greatest of tragic dramas. It is only through emotional identification of this kind that the moral value of tragedy for Hazlitt can really be experienced—that the evil shown excites 'our sense and desire for the opposite good'; and that our sympathy with suffering is 'carried away with the swelling tide of passion, that gushes from and relieves the heart' (Howe, 4.272). This kind of reading assumes a total inwardness of identification through words that we read for ourselves. Rather than the assumption of some contemporary criticism of a detached reader interrogating the text, it implies an engaged reader interrogated by the text in the demands it places on his/her capacity for full and concentrated imaginative participation.

With *A Midsummer Night's Dream* Hazlitt mounts a similar attack on representation, not in relation to character but to poetry: 'Poetry and the stage do not agree well together.... The ideal can have no place upon the stage, which is a picture without perspective' (Howe, 5.247). The imagination is prompted by words beyond what can be shown—but here Hazlitt's account makes it clear that the problem lies partly in a mode of representation that attempts to stage the conceptions of imagination rather than, in the theatre's own ways, to prompt them. At least in part, his objection is not to the minimalist actor-voice-body-movement theatre of Shakespeare, or of Peter Brook, but to the elaborate settings, costumes, and props of early nineteenth-century quasi-pantomime. Nevertheless, he points here to a real problem about theatre, embodiment, and imagination—a problem that applies equally to the Witches in *Macbeth*, the Ghost of Old Hamlet, the spirits attendant on Prospero, and much else in Shakespeare in any mode of theatre.

But though, in their subtlety and passion, Shakespeare's characters might be beyond representation, and though the conventions of early nineteenth-century theatre were inimical to poetry, stifling imagination with representation, Hazlitt also saw that performance could be, and with the greatest performers was, a mode of critical exploration—perhaps the supreme mode. 'Actors are the best commentators on the poets' (Howe, 4.256)—not in what they say, but in what they do as actors. Kean as Romeo 'treads close indeed upon the genius of his author' (Howe, 4.256); Kean as Hamlet offers 'the finest commentary that was ever made on Shakespeare' (Howe, 5.188). Similarly, on Sarah Siddons as Lady Macbeth: 'she was tragedy personified.... To have seen her in that character was an event in every one's life, not to be forgotten' (Howe, 4.189–90). As Shylock Kean showed Hazlitt that he had misread the play (on the basis of its performance conventions: actors, like critics, can also be bad commentators). Kean revealed the play afresh: Shylock became 'a half-favourite with the philosophical part of the audience' (Howe, 4.320). Interpretive discoveries of the actor, made in the actor's medium of performance, can be translated into conceptual awareness by the significances the critic extrapolates. Performance can bring out implications of the text which, if present to reading at all, are present only to the most actorly imagination: Kean as Richard III in his satanic temptation of Lady Anne ('like the first Tempter'); or in his death, its meaning extracted from his physical posture ('a preternatural and terrific grandeur'; Howe. 4.299–300).

While it may be, therefore, that 'the stage is not in general the best place to study our author's characters' (Howe, 4.324), a great actor can prompt new and better ideas about a play. Hazlitt's pleasure in theatre led him to see that, despite limitations in part inherent, in part contingent, performance can be a revelatory mode of criticism, and that the embodiment of theatre engaged the emotions in ways that no other experience of drama could match. It is an unusual perception in Romantic criticism.

Hazlitt took the view, however, that the stage at best only rarely presents what can be imagined by a mind fully responsive to the words and capable of envisaging all that is implied by them—the rhetorical shapes, rhythms, and tones in which they should to be spoken, the intellectual and emotional interactions of characters, their implied movement, gesture, and setting, the eloquence of action; effects of structure as drama sets tone against tone, elaborates and resolves complications, moves through conflict and confusion to denouement. But he also recognized that he had learned from great acting; that the reader must be his or her own actor and director; that ideal reading requires the imagination of theatre; and that the imagination of theatre is not to be come by without the experience of theatre—seeing and learning from the work of great actors and directors, reflecting on how poor acting and directing have failed. All this Hazlitt did as a reviewer. And he not only incorporated into *Characters* fragments of his reviews: he wrote on the basis of seeing Shakespeare in the theatre, as performed by John Philip Kemble, Sarah Siddons, and Edmund Kean. It was from those experiences, as well as repudiating what he thought wrong in Samuel Johnson and absorbing what he thought right in A. W. Schlegel, that Hazlitt learned how to read Shakespeare with attention to such a various range of the real sources and effects of his work.

Characters of Shakespeare's Plays begins from the modest ambition of illustrating Pope's view that Shakespeare's characters more than 'hold the mirror up to Nature', that in them Nature speaks through Shakespeare. It is one of Hazlitt's most repeated themes that Shakespeare's 'imagination borrowed from the life, and every circumstance, object, motive, passion, operated there as it would in reality, and produced a world of men and women as distinct, as true and as various as those that exist in nature' (Howe, 4.293–4). And Shakespeare did not observe, he became: 'He seemed scarcely to have an individual existence of his own, but to borrow that of others at will' (Howe, 4.23). 'He was the least an egoist that it is possible to be. He was nothing in himself; but he was all that others were, or that they could become' (Howe, 5.47).

Much of *Characters of Shakespeare's Plays* is accordingly concerned with analyses of dramatic character, particularly where these are contested—with Othello, Iago, and Desdemona, with Hamlet; or where the characters are outsiders with qualities which imply critiques of the society that excludes them—Falstaff, Shylock, Caliban. But there are many other strands—structure, poetry, theme, especially where that is political, relationship to sources, and 'character' in the sense of characteristic qualities—the overall tone, mood, and colour of a work. Hazlitt frequently discusses structure—the multiple strands of *Cymbeline*, unified by their relation of parallel and antithesis to the truth and loyalty of the central figure, Imogen; the 'systematic principle of contrast' operative in *Macbeth*, identifying a range of different kinds of effects which 'account for the abruptness and violent antitheses of the style' (Howe, 4.191); the art with which all the elements of the double plot of *King Lear* are woven together, with effects of detailed juxtapositions; and more generally how Shakespeare complicates, aligns, and resolves strands of the action, particularly (*pace* Samuel Johnson) in comedy. He accepts the view of Schlegel that 'in Tragedy the chief object is the poetry, and every other thing is subordinate to it' (Howe. 5.324). Shakespeare's language is 'hieroglyphical': it 'translates thoughts into visible images' (Howe, 5.55). Hazlitt frequently expounds the hieroglyphic implications: Perdita's flowers, Antony's vision of dissolution, Caliban's poetry of the senses, the hunting of Theseus and Hippolyta (Howe, 4.176, 231, 240, 246); valuing in Shakespeare 'the music of language answering to the music of the mind' (Howe, 5.12) that made Spenser among Hazlitt's favourite poets and prompted antagonistic comment on Wordsworth's 'theory that poetry should be written in the language of prose' (Hazlitt's polemical summary of the preface to *Lyrical Ballads*; 'On consistency of opinion', Howe, 17.25).

But there is no critical formula, explicit or implicit. Hazlitt's observations are dictated by his view of what is most interesting in each play individually. Unlike Coleridge, and unlike his German contemporaries, including Schlegel, on whom in a degree he draws, he is not attempting to discover through Shakespeare general principles of criticism. He is rather on principle anti-systematic. For him, 'original genuine observations are like "minute drops from off the eaves", and not an incessant shower' (*Characteristics* (1823), 180; Howe, 9.194). He is here contrasting a discourse of genuine thought, open and inviting reciprocity, with the thinker who aims 'to get up a thesis upon every topic' and thereby considers 'less what he felt on any point than what might be said upon it'. In this view, the attempt to frame a coherent overall argument is inimical to the expression of genuine perception, which is particular, and which, with works of imagination, whatever their fundamental unity, does not necessarily fit into any overall view. It is by being true to the particular perception that criticism can best be true to the whole work. Hazlitt's criticism is accordingly at times more impressionistic, less analytical, than Coleridge's, as in the evocation of fundamental emotional orientation, the exalting of youthful passion, that introduces the discussion of *Romeo and Juliet* (Howe, 4.248–51).

The most remarkable discussion in *Characters* is that of *Coriolanus*, with its claims that 'the language of poetry naturally falls in with the language of power', that 'the principle of poetry is a very anti-levelling principle' (Howe, 4.214). Hazlitt disliked how he felt the reader is led to sympathize with the hero's contempt for the sufferings of the oppressed, and interpreted that response as showing a problem with the very nature of poetry. It might be argued that the flaming political rhetoric in which this view is expressed—a magnificent expression of the view of a republican and Bonapartist in the aftermath of the Congress of Vienna—is connected only tenuously with the complexities of the play that prompts it; that this is criticism as unconscious autobiography, seeing a fragment intensely in light of the predispositions brought to the seeing, blinded by them to the whole. Coleridge took precisely the opposite view: for him *Coriolanus* showed the 'the wonderful philosophic impartiality in Shakespeare's politics' (Raysor, 1.79); a view he reiterated in relation to *The Tempest*, that Shakespeare 'never promulgates any party tenets' (Raysor, 1.122). Elsewhere, when his politics were not touched, this was the view Hazlitt himself took: 'Shakespeare never committed himself to his characters ... He has no prejudices for or against them. ... He saw both sides of a question, the different views taken of it according to the different interests of the parties concerned' (Howe, 4.225). But *Coriolanus* engaged Hazlitt as the English histories engaged him, with an anti-aristocratic view which with the histories can be seen most fully in his account of King Henry VIII (which strays from Shakespeare's play to the historical figure: Howe, 4.305–6). The same republicanism inflects his view of *Julius Caesar*, where he takes sides in a conflict he sees entirely on the conspirators' own self-justifying terms as liberty against tyranny, with no observation of the hubristic self-righteousness of Brutus or the humane vulnerability of Caesar. In writing about 'the friends of liberty', Hazlitt has more in mind a favourable view of his own party than the play's presentation of Brutus and the conspirators, for whom Shakespeare—in what contemporaries of Hazlitt of a different political disposition might have seen as a prophecy of the French Revolution—invented the ritual of proclaiming liberty by washing in blood (3.1; Howe, 4.198).

However one judges its mixture of penetration and partiality, Hazlitt's account of *Coriolanus* shows him in agreement with Coleridge that life imitates art, that 'character is formed by what we read' (Raysor, 2.106); or, in Hazlitt's formulation, 'What men delight to read in books, they will put in practice in reality' (Howe, 4.216). His response to William Gifford, editor of the Tory *Quarterly*, which reviewed *Characters* unfavourably, shows Hazlitt's mastery in polemic of contempt for and hatred of what he regarded as unprincipled sycophancy to power. Like art, criticism matters because it affects who we are and how we act. In this Gifford and Hazlitt agreed, but what to Hazlitt were principled humanitarian ethics—care of the oppressed; opposition to oppressors—was to Gifford sedition. In responding to the *Quarterly*'s critique, Hazlitt vigorously defended the view that *Coriolanus* shows that there is 'a bias to the imagination often inconsistent with the greatest good, that in poetry it triumphs over principle, and bribes the passions to make a sacrifice of common humanity' ('A Letter to William Gifford'; Howe, 9.37). Whatever its partiality, this is criticism that challenges the reader to consider Shakespeare with full seriousness, criticism that engages with art as it affects individual and social life.

Hazlitt's rejection of Johnson was quite different: Johnson he admired, but thought limited—'without that intenseness of passion, which . . . produces a genius and a taste for poetry' (Howe, 4.176).

'Energetical passions' are essential: they 'electrify the whole of the mental powers' (Howe, 4.173; Hazlitt is here quoting Schlegel). It is a typically Romantic view of passion—as not at odds with intellect but providing a fully humanized intellect with material from which to create. If, therefore, as Hazlitt concludes from his account of *King Lear*, 'the greatest strength of genius is shewn in describing the strongest passions' (Howe, 4.271), critical assumptions that exclude passion are fatally disabling. And however unjust Hazlitt is in exaggerating the boundaries of Johnsonian common sense, he does identify a real limitation in Johnson's eighteenth-century aesthetic: his exaltation of general truth is alien to Shakespeare's approach to the general through the particular, which was in tune with—and did much to form—the more comprehensive character of Romantic aesthetics. To Hazlitt one index of Johnson's limitations was his style: the rhetoric of his prose committed him to admirations that can be reflected by the magisterially judicious and balanced—as though not the voice of an individual but the distilled judgement of a culture, supra-individual. While Hazlitt has his own style of rhetorical parallelisms, they are not antitheses of judicious detachment but crescendos of passionate engagement. His mode of constant quotation and sub-quotation implies a mind stocked with words it loves and can scarcely think without. His frequent and striking misquotations imply a mind taking wing, headlong and passionate, that cannot pause for the pedantry of rummaging in books. Trained on highly various modes of journalism, from the colloquial fictional persona of 'The Fight' to the personal despair of thinking and writing paradoxically probed with cogency, learning, subtlety, and eloquence in 'The Indian Jugglers', Hazlitt's style embodies the individuality, range, and engagement that Johnson's decorum excludes. His view of prose as having 'more life, spirit, and truth' when there is a 'flow of expression . . . something akin to *extempore* speaking' (Howe, 12.62) meant irregularity and indecorum: complementary to calculations of art, spontaneities of on-the-hoof journalistic composition, which are another aspect of 'the courage to say as an author what he felt as a man'. The implications of this go beyond a critique of Johnson. Johnson is scarcely alone in observing a stylistic decorum that suppresses individuality and excludes passion: there are many modes of criticism that do this as totally as the style of Johnson ever did, without the compensating pleasure of his rhetorical power. Hazlitt's critical innocence has a freshness belonging to the dawn of Shakespeare criticism that is irrecoverable. But his individuality and passion exemplify qualities for which polish and sophistication can never be a substitute.

Much in the views of Shakespeare of John Keats (1795–1821) can be connected with Coleridge, with Lamb, and above all with Hazlitt, whom Keats knew personally, whose lectures he attended, whose books and essays he read, and whose depth of taste he described as one of 'the three things to rejoice at in this Age'.[37] Many of Keats's central ideas about Shakespeare have some origin in his relationship with Hazlitt—particularly his account of Shakespeare's apparently egoless abilities of imaginative participation. Similarly, the plays that most frequently prompted from Keats comment or allusion were central works for his generation: *A Midsummer Night's Dream*, *The Tempest*, *Hamlet*, and above all *King Lear*. But allusive quotations scattered through Keats's letters, including to some of Shakespeare's least read plays, show that Shakespeare's whole oeuvre was a constant presence lovingly absorbed into his verbal memory. It is clear why: 'I read Shakespeare,—indeed I shall I think never read any other Book much.... I am very near Agreeing with Hazlitt, that Shakespeare is enough for us' (1.143). When Keats thought of 'a good Genius presiding over' him, he wondered, 'is it too daring to Fancy Shakespeare this Presider?' (1.142). He read, thought about, and commented on Shakespeare continually, and the example of Shakespeare was a central stimulus to his own writing.

While Keats's engagement with Shakespeare has much in common with his contemporaries, it is also distinctly different, in substance and in mode. Almost all of his commentary comes from private letters addressed to friends who knew him well, with whom he could rely on a degree of existing understanding, and who did not require explanations. His mode has more in common with the aphoristic fragments of Friedrich Schlegel than the books, essays, and lectures of his English contemporaries. Even his few annotations are unlike those of Coleridge, who often seems to have in view constructing material for a lecture or a theory. Keats wanted rather to observe than to explain or justify. Often he appears to be thinking of no reader but himself. The critic's implicit 'this could [should] be so for you' is almost entirely absent. This is partly contingent on Keats's mode of writing (in private letters). It also has a more profound and inherent relation to his view of reading. Keats's idea of the poetic character, supremely exemplified by Shakespeare, implies an ideal character for the reader of poetry. Keats is a model for a kind of reading that professional criticism, eager to present criticism as a 'discipline', has often sought to avoid—anarchic, seeking pleasure and creative stimulus in Shakespeare's poetic intensity and verbal inventiveness, and willing to take pleasure without worrying where, between the reader and the text, that pleasure has been constructed, even in principle opposed to violating what Keats called 'the Penetralium of mystery' (Rollins, 1.194)—the innermost secret core. Though for the Coleridgean critic and theorist aesthetic effect is always a provocation to explain, Keats's view of the poetic character implies that, as Wordsworth puts it, the meddling intellect can 'murder to dissect', that the urge always to transpose understanding into a more conceptual mode may have less wisdom than the sensibility that 'watches and receives' (Wordsworth, 'The Tables Turned'). Criticism as a discipline is always eager to respond to this view with a confident 'but . . .'. Keats's interest is not in the disciplines of criticism but the pleasures of poetry. For him, as for Blake (in his annotations of Reynolds), 'enthusiastic admiration is the first principle of knowledge and the last'. For Keats, with poetry the alpha and omega is pleasure.

Keats therefore offers a model for a different kind of reading from his contemporaries—a model that accepts intuitive responses involving feelings that cannot be brought fully into consciousness; that understands a drive such as Coleridge's to reason about beauty as coming not always from an admirable desire to comprehend but sometimes from an atrophied ability simply to enjoy. Keats is ready to accept pleasure where he finds it, and to reason about it or not as pleasure suggests. While this view is partly articulated in opposition to Coleridge, it is based on knowledge of Coleridge that was partial. If Keats had seen the naked Coleridge of annotations and lecture notes he might have felt less difference between himself and the searching and at times perplexed theorist of the *Biographia*.

Beauty—a 'yearning passion . . . for the beautiful' (1.404): this is the leading theme of Keats's view of Shakespeare, and of poetry generally. 'With a great poet the sense of Beauty overcomes every other consideration, or rather obliterates all consideration' (Rollins, 1.194); 'I should write from the mere yearning and fondness I have for the

Beautiful even if my night's labours should be burnt every morning and no eye ever shine upon them' (Rollins, 1.388); 'I look upon fine Phrases like a Lover' (Rollins, 2.139). Beauty often had nothing to do with one usual preoccupation of Romantic criticism—understanding character. It could also be independent of dramatic context. It could be purely verbal, as in Keats's citation of lines from *The Tempest* (1.2.326–8; Rollins, 1.133), where context is nothing (Prospero's domination of Caliban with threats of pain), felicity of phrasing everything; or his citation of lines from the Sonnets (12.5–8), among 'so many beauties…fine things said unintentionally' (Rollins, 1.188–9). A review of Edmund Kean as Richard III shows the same attitude.[38] The interest of this review for modern criticism has been predominantly social. Kean is a hieroglyph—the outsider: he stands for Keats. This is plausible, but secondary. It ignores the declared subject of the review, which is aesthetic—an exploration of the proposition that 'a melodious passage in poetry is full of pleasures both sensual and spiritual' (Buxton Forman, 5.229): the spiritual understood in details which 'show like the hieroglyphics of beauty'; the sensual heard in Kean's realization of these hieroglyphics. Keats spells out the implications he hears in imaginative elaborations that are a kind of critical prose poetry indicating the richness of suggestion with which 'the inexplicable mystery of sound' in poetry for Keats actually resonated.[39] The particular meanings are for Keats. Meanings of this kind are for those who have ears to hear. Only the notion that nothing happens in poetry that cannot be brought to the bar of reasoning upon evidence could make the thrilled and imaginative listener deaf to the kind of resonances that Keats heard in Kean's 'power of anatomizing the passion of every syllable'. The critic who would like to see this mode of imaginative interpretation brought, insofar as it can be, to the bar of reason and evidence can consider Keats's annotations of Shakespeare.[40]

Keats leads up to the assertion that for a great poet Beauty 'obliterates all consideration' through the most discussed of his critical ideas about Shakespeare, Shakespeare's *'Negative Capability'*:

that is when man is capable of being in uncertainties, Mysteries, doubts, without any irritable reaching after fact & reason – Coleridge, for instance, would let go by a fine isolated verisimilitude caught from the Penetralium of mystery, from being incapable of remaining content with half knowledge.

(Rollins, 1.193–4)

It is an idea that Keats expressed in other forms: as a truth 'that has pressed upon me lately... [that] Men of Genius... have not any individuality, any determined Character' (Rollins, 1.184); and in his image of the 'camelion [*sic*] Poet' who, capable of taking all forms (equally Iago or Imogen), 'has no self... no character... no identity' (Rollins, 1.387). Shakespeare he saw as the supreme exemplar of this type of the poet, which he defined in part by contrast with its anti-type exemplified by Wordsworth, the poet who impresses his own character and being on his subjects, 'the egotistical sublime' (Rollins, 1.387).[41] It is among the ideas about poetry that Keats developed from Hazlitt, both as a view of Shakespeare, 'the least an egotist that it was possible to be' (Howe, 5.47, 50), a 'ventriloquist... [who] throws his imagination out of himself' (Howe, 5.185), and as a view of Wordsworth, whose 'intense intellectual egotism swallows up every thing' (Howe, 4.113). But where Hazlitt is polemical, and so takes a point of view as part of furthering an argument, Keats (negative capability incarnate) investigates, concerned with understanding his own nature as a poet, but also in line with his view that 'Man should not dispute or assert, but whisper results to his neighbour'. This whole letter to his friend J. H. Reynolds (Rollins, 1.231–3) urges reading based in an active-passive receptivity, accepting difference, not contradicting and combatting, seeing what appears to points of view other than one's own— which will change, the more so if one does not seek artificially to affirm its limitations.

We cannot read straight from Keats's account of the poetic character to its implications for criticism. That the poet 'has as much delight in conceiving an Iago as an Imogen' (Rollins, 1.387) does not mean that the reader is morally indifferent: there would then be no point in Keats's observation on the special character of the poet. It does, however, mean the reader experiences something of that perspective, that there is a supramoral pleasure in the sheer creative exuberance and intensity of conception of characters such as Richard III, Iago, or Edmund. It is a view that separates Keats from the fear of Hazlitt, that 'What men delight to read in books, they will put in practice in reality' (Howe, 4.216). While Keats copied an extended section of Hazlitt's defence of this view into a letter to his brother George (Rollins, 2.71–6), including Hazlitt's unease about 'the sense of power abstracted from the sense of good' in poetry, Keats nevertheless expects the reader to recognize pleasure in creative power for what it is: a pleasure of art, not a guide to life—except insofar as intensity of aesthetic pleasure is a stimulus to every kind of sophisticated enhancement of life.

One of the most frequently cited readings of the idea of 'negative capability' is that of Walter Jackson Bate, who stresses '*irritable* reaching' as though Keats condemns only a particular mode of searching for 'fact and reason'.[42] Bate is not alone in constructing a thesis that evades Keats's opposition to theses. But it is more obviously congruent with Keats's articulation as a whole, including his exaltation of the 'isolated verisimilitude' and the defining counterexample of Coleridge, to understand all searching after fact and reason as a sign of unease with ratiocination and system building. What interests Keats is the specific perception, not distraction into any overall argument it can be made to serve. The whole stance is congruent with the empathetic personal character and the unease with determinate personalities and fixed opinions evident throughout his letters. By his mode of being as much as by his specific ideas Keats articulates the critical equivalent of the poetical character: imaginatively open, speculative, dialogic.

Like Hazlitt and Lamb, Keats stresses reading that is intensely emotionally engaged. The experience of reading *King Lear* is searing ('burn through', 'consumed in the fire'); it is, as a result, also purgative, creatively or spiritually renewing ('new Phoenix wings').[43] It is indicative that, while Hazlitt and Lamb assert identification with characters that they view as general and all-embracing—'It is *we* who are Hamlet' (Hazlitt); 'we are Lear' (Lamb)—Keats's declared identification is more idiosyncratic: 'I throw my whole being into Troilus and repeating these lines [*Troilus*, 3.2.9–11], I wander, like a lost soul upon the stygian Banks staying for waftage' (Rollins, 1.404). Reading that is emotionally engaged is also personal. A deepened sense of *Hamlet* drawing on some experience of sexual feeling about which Keats is tactfully inexplicit makes him feel that we cannot wholly understand a work until we have gone 'the same steps as the Author' (Rollins, 1.279). To avoid criticism that is 'mere wording'—thought such as Hamlet calls 'words, words, words': words with no meaningful content—the reader must connect reading intimately with personal experience. It is a point of view from which some modern attitudes of establishing historical distance from which to 'interrogate the text' would seem sheer madness, the cultivation of spiritual death.

When Keats describes how he will ideally consider exploring a piece of writing, whether 'full Poesy or distilled Prose', his account is various but also precise: 'wander with it, and muse upon it, and reflect from it, and bring home to it, and prophesy upon it, and dream upon it' (Rollins, 1.231). 'Wander with' and 'muse upon'—both undirected, 'with' more remaining in the words, 'muse upon' more taking flight with the subject; 'reflect from'—movement outwards, beyond the self; 'bring home to'—movement inwards, to the self; 'prophesy'—the response of conviction; 'dream'—the response of meditation. Insofar as can be, this is the translation of Shakespearean 'negative capability' into a critical method.

It is an index of the undogmatic nature of Keats's critical sympathies that, along with the polemical style of Hazlitt, he also admired the characteristically more understated mode of Charles Lamb (1775–1834).[44] But Lamb too could be polemical and, in his most famous pronouncement on Shakespeare, was at his most downright: 'It may seem a paradox, but I cannot help being of opinion that the plays of Shakespeare are less calculated for performance on a stage, than those of almost any other dramatist whatever. . . . What we see upon a stage is body and bodily action; what we are conscious of in reading is almost exclusively the mind, and its movements.'[45] Charles Lamb's 'On the Tragedies of Shakespeare considered with reference to their fitness for stage representation' (1811, revised 1818) is his most famous pronouncement on Shakespeare, and some of its statements are unequivocal. Shakespeare is not for the stage. The stage (all surface) is not for Shakespeare (all interiority). Shakespeare is to be read.

Any reader of Shakespeare who goes to see the plays performed will find in him- or herself at some time some such response. Some performances are bad, many no more than good in part; few performances are very good, almost none completely satisfying. But Lamb is not usually unequivocal. Polemic is not his characteristic mode. His usual method, reflecting his critical temperament, is to be anecdotally anti-polemical—to allow a view to emerge by implication, through interpretation; 'by indirections find directions out'. It is the main point of his great essay 'Imperfect Sympathies' (Lucas, 2. 58–64): in opposition to the monocular conviction he humorously characterizes as 'Caledonian', he places the suggestive, lights mutable and shifting, recognition that truth is involved with point of view. And beyond the polemical statements, so it is even here. Even within the confines of this essay, Lamb's objections to the stage, expressed as absolute, are in part contingent. They are contingent on the use of adaptations which seriously misrepresent Shakespeare: Nahum Tate's version of *King Lear*, with its love interest (Cordelia and Edgar) and its happy ending (Lear restored to power); Dryden and Davenant's *The Tempest*, with its parallels to Miranda and Ferdinand, Hippolito and Dorinda (the obverse of Miranda, Hippolito has never seen a woman); Colley Cibber's *Richard III* (including the onstage murder of the princes); and much else in this same vein.[46] Lamb's objections to Shakespeare on the stage are also contingent on the realist mode of early nineteenth-century performance, 'the elaborate and anxious provision of scenery, which the luxury of the age demands' (Lucas, 1.110): slowing the action, this creates a need for yet more cuts; supplying for the eye what the text suggests to the ear, it diminishes imaginative engagement. Acting too has either a 'too close pressing semblance of reality' (Lucas, 1.106) or a 'frozen declamatory style' (Lucas, 1.38), whereas poetic drama requires a flexibility that can combine natural feeling with stylization. Lamb's most extended discussion of a particular performance of Shakespeare, of G. F. Cooke as Richard III, shows two of these errors combined: Cibber's mangled text (with 'miserable additions... producing an inevitable inconsistency of character'); the actor's caricature misconception of Richard, the demon but not the human being. Lamb gives a brilliant account of the energy, wit, eloquence, and aspiration that make Richard's dissimulations convincing to his dupes and delightful to the audience. But Lamb does not describe this conception as unactable, only as not acted by Cooke.[47]

Not all of Lamb's objections to Shakespeare in the theatre, however, are contingent. Given that, as so often in Romantic criticism, his primary focus is character, his discussions of *Hamlet* and *King Lear* raise permanent critical issues about interpretation and performance. Insofar as it is a good test of an interpretation to consider whether and how it can be staged, Hamlet's rejection of Ophelia presents problems even at the level of narrative: should Hamlet be made aware of the concealed presence of Claudius and Polonius; should he act for this audience; should he be presented as supposing Ophelia complicit with it? As Lamb conceives the scene—Hamlet's submerged love for Ophelia as continuously present beneath his violent rejection of her—it is difficult to act because the text will only support Lamb's consistently sympathetic conception of Hamlet on the basis of other parts of the play. If Lamb is right that his interpretation cannot be acted, this might seem a demonstration either that Shakespeare was an incompetent writer for the stage or that the interpretation is untenable. But an actor who accepts Lamb's view has as much chance of conveying it by tone and gesture as a reader has of finding it by reflection. More fundamentally, for Lamb there is an antithesis between performance and the characterization of an introspective melancholic. Hamlet's soliloquies are private communications: they should not, he feels, be spoken before an audience. But this assumes the simple realism he elsewhere deplores. The soliloquies of Iago and of Richard III are addressed to the audience; like many other soliloquies in Elizabethan drama, Hamlet's, overheard by the audience, are meditative communings with himself. An audience accustomed to the convention will not find Hamlet's soliloquizing a violation of interiority—though here it may be relevant that some of Lamb's anti-theatrical polemic seems prompted not by the stage but by the pit, by his view of the callow judgement of audiences.

With *King Lear* Lamb is yet more emphatic: the character 'cannot be acted'; the play 'is essentially impossible to be represented on a stage'. There are problems of representation—how to present the symbolic, a storm adequate to Lear's mental state; how not to submerge the symbolic in the visible, 'an old man tottering about the stage with a walking stick'. For Lamb, no actor can combine the physical infirmities of age with the emotional power of Lear's rage or the mental power of his sanity in madness. Whereas 'while we read it, we see not Lear, we are Lear' (Lucas, 1.107). This is not to be facilely condemned by critics who do not find in themselves Lamb's intense identification with the character. There is great critical writing here—a true sense of the scale of the subject. But there are also problems. The imaginative reader is required to be not only Lear but by turns all the characters. For the imaginative spectator there is potentially not Lamb's polemical caricature of old age but the emotional power of the bodily presence of actors in the physicality of theatre. Lamb implies an untheatrical reading at odds with the stage for which Shakespeare wrote and the ways in which Shakespeare's writing was embedded in the conditions of his theatre—a theatre not of passive spectatorship, as Lamb's discussion assumes, but a theatre in which a great deal was trusted to the audience's imagination. 'On your imaginary forces work': the prologue to *Henry V* enjoins an active spectatorship such as Lamb desiderates in reading—creative engagement with the action through the words. Lamb is persuasive about reading, engagement, and imagination, but questionable about the supposed gulf fixed between this kind of reading and Shakespeare's theatre. Responding in part to the stage conditions of his time, Lamb writes as though the emotional and imaginative engagement for which he argues is impossible in any theatre.

Even in 'On the Tragedies of Shakespeare', however, where Lamb is pushing a point of view as far as it will go, he admits that performance is interpretation, and that a great performance can be a real contribution to understanding. John Philip Kemble and Sarah Siddons 'seemed to embody and realize conceptions which had hitherto assumed no distinct shape' (Lucas, 1.98): they have helped Lamb to see more—or at least to see more clearly. And even as this praise is qualified (even this is a vision 'materialized and brought down... to the standard of flesh and blood'), and Lamb deplores the fame of Sarah Siddons's gestures, he also recalls 'her thrilling tones'—'thrilling' because of her real appeal to emotional and imaginative capacities in the speaking of Shakespeare's verse (Lucas, 1.111). What is not wholly excluded by polemic here is more fully evident elsewhere. Like Hazlitt, Lamb was an enthusiastic theatregoer. His pleasure in plays as texts for meditative reading is complemented by pleasure in the expressivity of performance. 'Stage Illusion' (1825; Lucas, 2.163–5) analyses how meaning in comedy is dependent on understandings tacitly established between audience and performers, subtleties of tone and embodiment, slight but essential degrees of stylization by which subject matter otherwise painful is transformed. 'On some of the old actors' (1822; Lucas, 2.132–41) extends the idea touched on with Kemble and Siddons, of performance as a mode of interpretation. Dorothy Jordan as Viola, speaking the disguised account of her love for Orsino with expressive tone and phrasing by which poetry was carried alive into the heart by passion, is a lesson in 'nature's own rhetoric...altogether without rule or law'. The richly evoked 'Dicky' Suett is the Clown incarnate: 'Shakespeare foresaw him, when he framed his fools and jesters'. His account of slowness of apprehension, the dawning of an idea in the countenance of James Dodd's Aguecheek, is a tour de force. Instruction in playing Iago, fundamental to the whole experience of tragedy in *Othello*, is drawn from the exemplary performance of Robert Bensley: only in soliloquy should Iago let fall the mask of artifice; the audience will sympathize appropriately with Othello only when in dialogue it shares his experience of the consummate deceptions of disciplined cunning. Above all Lamb expatiates on Bensley's Malvolio, a performance which corrects misunderstandings of the role, bringing out the pathos and dignity attaching to a nobly deluded Don Quixote figure: 'a sort of greatness seems never to desert him', and he finally elicits 'a kind of tragic interest' (Lucas, 1.135, 136). Lamb's recreation of the detail by which great acting projects meaning through embodiment indicates how intensely he enjoyed the theatre. And underlying all the detail is Lamb's sense of relation between 'the lesser and the greater theatre', the stage and the world. In passing from his memories of Dodd the actor as Aguecheek to an actual chance encounter with Dodd the man on the verge of the grave contemplating his mortality, Lamb gives a deep sense of the scale on which the pleasures of theatre and of Shakespeare are to be measured. It is the kind of criticism that prompted Coleridge to praise Lamb's 'genius' as a critic, by contrast with what Coleridge judged the more routine performances of Hazlitt (*Table Talk*, 6 August 1832).[48]

Meaning as inhering in verbal detail is one great principle of Lamb's criticism, as in the Empsonian sensitivity to the implications of a 'complex word' through which he opens out a reading of *Richard III*.[49] Meaning as also always contextual is a principle spelled out in a letter of 1801: 'Every thing in heaven & earth, in man and in story, in books & in fancy, acts by Confederacy, by juxtaposition, by circumstance & place.'[50] This is the idea underlying Lamb's *Specimens of the English Dramatic Poets who lived about the time of Shakespeare* (1808). This was in part intended as a contribution to the study of Shakespeare, to show 'how much of Shakespeare shines in the great men his contemporaries' (Lucas, 4.xii), so as to see more fully both him and them. In this Lamb initiated the study of Shakespeare in the context of the drama of his time, proposed but not carried out by Coleridge, which became basic to a whole school of twentieth-century Shakespeare criticism. While much in Lamb's annotations of his selections is superseded, one central strand of his criticism is evergreen—his horror of readers who read 'to be complimented on their own goodness'. In contrasting the 'vigorous passions, and virtues clad in flesh and blood' by which Shakespeare's contemporaries tested their moral suppositions with 'the insipid levelling morality to which the modern stage is tied down' (Lucas, 4.114), Lamb indicates how writings of another age may challenge the present, and also how any age may neutralize the challenge of all imaginative writing if it reads only to find itself and its values approved and endorsed. The sharpness of Lamb's wit in repudiating conformity to the blandness of approved opinion is a permanent intellectual tonic.

In all this Lamb is not simply a critic: he is always also an essayist, a writer. He aims to reveal the work, but also to imply the view of life within which the work so seen has its full meaning. This is particularly clear in 'On the Genius and Character of Hogarth' (1811; Lucas, 1.70–86), an essay which begins from Shakespeare (*Timon of Athens* compared with *The Rake's Progress*) and elicits from Shakespeare central critical principles—great art as implying not stating; the reader as part creator, the interpreter of implication; art as '*imaginary work* [echoing Shakespeare: *Henry V*, Prologue, 18], where the spectator must meet the artist in his conceptions half way' (Lucas, 1.74). Lamb draws the idea from the account, in *The Rape of Lucrece*, of the figure of Achilles in a tapestry of the Trojan War. The figure, part shown, part concealed, Lamb takes as epitomizing the method of art: it is the antithesis of Wordsworth, the poet who exemplifies and explicates, shows and tells—or, on a less sympathetic view, pins down and controls meaning. Lamb's essay exemplifies the principle: criticism, like art, works by suggestion. Lamb's readings of Hogarth engage intensely with the precise articulations of his engravings. By relationship, by context, by interaction with the sympathetic vision through which Lamb attends to them, they also elicit meanings beyond what can be supposed simply objectively present in the designs themselves. It is reader-response criticism, albeit of a more freewheeling kind than modern proponents would accept. In his unselfconscious movement between aesthetic and experiential issues he quietly suggests how these are connected.[51] Undemonstratively, Lamb conveys a way of engaging with art which is also a way of being.

While Lamb's criticism, like Hazlitt's, can be read as oblique autobiography, Thomas De Quincey's 'On the knocking at the gate in *Macbeth*' fully spills over into criticism as a form of what can be more obviously recognized as 'creative writing'. De Quincey (1785–1859) begins from a significant experience of the drama that he felt but could not understand—the effect of the knocking on the gate immediately after Macbeth's murder of Duncan. How was it that this 'reflected back upon the murder a peculiar awfulness and depth of solemnity'?[52] From this powerful though not comprehended experience De Quincey draws the general principle that with works of art intuitive feeling, not conscious understanding, is fundamental; and more than that, that conscious understanding may be so imprisoned by conventions at odds with experience as to be positively misleading. He begins, therefore, from the provocation of Romantic aesthetics in every age: the demand of Nietzsche, in *The Birth of Tragedy* (1872), to speak 'not through logical insight but with the certainty of something directly apprehended'.[53] Criticism is to discover how to articulate real experience of art: it must not be deflected by that perhaps convincing but nevertheless destructive simulacrum, the autoreply dictated by convention. It is a principle of Romantic criticism nowhere more clearly articulated than by De Quincey.

It is especially striking with De Quincey because the key to understanding his experience of the play was an experience from real life— the Ratcliffe Highway murders of 1811, with the knocking on the door of the servant who discovered the crime. The tragedy of *Macbeth* requires that the audience's sympathy be deflected from its natural place with the murder victim on to the storm of passion taking place within the murderer. The sound of ordinary life resuming its accustomed ways (the knocking on the gate) focusses and intensifies, De Quincey realized, the transfiguration of Macbeth and Lady Macbeth that precedes it—the entering into the feelings of the murders that is essential to the tragic effect. The specific reading is magnificent, but also exemplary is the intensity of imaginative response to the drama in all its aspects, and the manner of its articulation. As part of a series of 'Notes from the Pocket-Book of a late Opium-Eater', the essay presents itself as written by a semi-fictional persona, perhaps preternaturally imaginative, perhaps extravagantly fanciful, an effect heightened by having its Shakespearean discoveries reported in part through the teasing and paradoxical persona of De Quincey's later essays discussing murder in its supposed aesthetic aspects as a fine art. It is a combination implying both passional engagement and intellectual control that is an instance, rare in criticism, of the principle of Friedrich Schlegel, 'Poesie kann nur durch Poesie kritisiert werden' (creative writing can only be criticized by way of creative writing; *Kritische Fragmente*, 117). It is the principle enacted by Goethe's discussion of *Hamlet* through the persona of his semi-autobiographical protagonist in *Wilhelm Meisters Lehrjahre*.

While De Quincey's exuberant creativity in 'On the knocking at the gate' was mildly disguised by his essay's modest form, many contemporary commentators felt that the Boydell Shakespeare Gallery appropriated the forms of creative response, but often without its substance. Not consistently notable for the quality of its pictures, the Gallery is, nevertheless, significant for what it suggests about how Shakespeare came to be seen in the Romantic period. Alderman John Boydell's scheme, initiated in 1786, supported by painters and literati including the portrait painter George Romney, Benjamin West, later president of the Royal Academy, and William Hayley, later patron of Blake, was to commission a collection of paintings for a specially built gallery, a collection of engravings from the paintings, and an edition in which the engravings were used as illustrations. The whole scheme was congruent with the ambition of Sir Joshua Reynolds, founder and first president of the Royal Academy, promoted in his biennial Royal Academy Lectures (*Discourses*, 1769–90), to make contemporary England a rival in the arts to the age of Raphael and Michelangelo in Italy. The idea for paintings illustrating Shakespeare was by no means new. Between 1760 and the Boydell initiative over one hundred Shakespeare paintings had been exhibited in the major London outlets.[54] Among Boydell's chosen artists, Henry Fuseli had already illustrated a number of Shakespearean subjects and devised a plan (never executed) for a Shakespeare hall of frescoes modelled on Michelangelo's Sistine Chapel ceiling. But the scale and scope of Boydell's enterprise was unprecedented—the complete works of Shakespeare, illustrated by some of the most respected British artists of the period, the paintings to be housed in a specially dedicated gallery and disseminated in reproductions by the most expert engravers.

The gallery opened in 1789, with a collection of thirty-four paintings, to which a further twenty-two were added the following year, expanding to over eighty paintings by 1796. Subscribers to the projected publication of engravings numbered some 600, rising to about 1400 by the end of the project in 1803. Boydell's example prompted a similar scheme organized by James Woodmason in Dublin from 1792. That the Boydell scheme ended in financial failure, with the collection sold to pay the creditors, had a complex of causes ranging from the quality of the pictures themselves to the difficulties for the art trade created by the Napoleonic Wars and consequent closing off of European markets. Despite its failure, however, the Boydell conception is significant for its implication about Shakespeare as *the* central figure of English arts—placed at the centre of English life in London's Pall Mall, the basis for a renewal of English visual art in the prestigious genre of 'history painting', usually depicting scenes from the Bible or classical literature and mythology. Partly in the selection of painters, this high-status aesthetic scheme was also accommodated to a more middle-class taste for portraiture, and was made democratically available in a contemporary form of mass production (engraving); all this complemented by the intellectual celebrity implied by a multivolume edition of the complete works, with scholarly editing by Samuel Johnson's erstwhile collaborator, George Steevens, and with lavish illustration.[55] In the very comprehensiveness of its ambitions the scheme was perhaps finally incoherent, but it was an aesthetic-cum-commercial-cum-political project on the grandest scale to present Shakespeare as the central figure of English culture.

The results were far from universally admired. Though not directly connected with the theatre, the paintings often envisage a scene as it might be staged—and were therefore vulnerable to the kind of anti-theatrical criticism which sees literal realization as limiting meaning. While Hazlitt straightforwardly recorded the praise of one of its principal painters, James Northcote, who judged Boydell 'a man of sense and liberality, and a true patron of the art' (Howe, 11.216), in a hostile review of a theatrical representation Hazlitt himself judged the pictures 'daubs' with an 'evident tendency to disturb and distort all the previous notions we had imbibed from reading Shakespeare' (Howe, 5.234). Lamb judged similarly, partly on the quality of the pictures, but also on the more fundamental issue of visual representation, which (like Hazlitt) he linked to the theatre:

> What injury (short of the theatres) did not Boydell's 'Shakespeare Gallery' do me with Shakespeare? – to have Opie's Shakespeare, Northcote's Shakespeare, light-headed Fuseli's Shakespeare, heavy-headed Romney's Shakespeare, wooden-headed West's Shakespeare,... deaf-headed Reynolds's Shakespeare, instead of my, and everybody's Shakespeare. To be tied down to an authentic face of Juliet! To have Imogen's portrait! To confine the illimitable![56]

Though, in a less hostile vein, Hazlitt discriminated between what he saw as the more immediately striking paintings of Fuseli and the more fundamentally satisfying work of Northcote (Howe, 12.94), most modern readers are likely to find Fuseli the most interesting of Boydell's painters. While Fuseli's earliest works were theatrically based, influenced by seeing Garrick in London in the 1760s, a move to Rome in 1770 freed him from thinking in terms of the stage to paint imaginative recreations from the text which amount to creative-interpretive explorations remote from any scenic possibility.[57] His *Midsummer Night's Dream* paintings use Titania's infatuation with Bottom-as-ass to imply sexual aspects of the play, with naked, sinister, fantastic beings but also contemporary demi-monde figures, congruent not with the usual Romantic sense of Shakespeare's fairies as mischievous and charming suggested by the famous incidental music of Mendelssohn but with dark readings of the play articulated only in the twentieth century.[58] In one painting Titania is based on Leonardo's Leda (echoing Shakespeare's bestially inflected coupling of human and supernatural) and Bottom on the Barberini Faun (sexually sated animal-human). Fuseli's various Macbeths are similarly unconventional—heroic, in some versions naked, modelled on classical torsos and the stylized muscularity of Michelangelo. Contrary to accounts of the play found in the criticism of Fuseli's contemporaries, they imply the anti-moral, heroic-celebratory reading of Nietzsche—a reading congruent with the Romantic (Blake, Shelley) reading of Milton implied by Fuseli's Satan in his 'Milton Gallery'.[59]

However, with a subject in which he was less personally invested, even the outrageous Fuseli can be absorbed into a conservative counter-reading, as with the Gallery's presentation of *The Tempest*, variously by Fuseli, Romney, Joseph Wright, and Francis Wheatley. This group of paintings can be read as implying a reading suited to reactionary government in an age of revolution: Prospero as the displaced good governor, Miranda as natural virtue, Gonzalo as the danger of idealistic utopianism out of touch with pragmatic realism, Caliban as sans-culotte celebration of undisciplined 'freedom', seconded by opportunist would-be tyrants from the underclass (Stephano and Trinculo), parallel to self-seeking treachery within the governing class (Antonio and Sebastian)—in sum, the dangerous chaos of bad government.[60] But visual images are open to greater latitude of interpretation than verbal texts: how far a reading of this kind depends on the cultural situation not of the early nineteenth-century artists but of the late twentieth-century interpreter is open to question.

In a broad sense more 'political' in its aims, published in the year of the Great Reform Bill, that evolutionary echo of the Age of Revolution, Anna Jameson's *Characteristics of Women, Moral, Poetical, and Historical* (1832), known only much later (and after Jameson's death) as *Shakespeare's Heroines*, is, like the Reform Bill itself, proto-Victorian: it argues for social change in a context of stability, a negotiation for improvements within the scope of current ideals.[61] The book is also post-Romantic. In praising it, Gerard Manley Hopkins associated Jameson with Coleridge, Lamb, and A. W. Schlegel.[62] Though her introduction politicly disavows the connection, the fundamental aims of Anna Jameson (1794–1860) are a muted transformation of Mary Wollstonecraft and the rights of women. Change is in the forefront—hence Jameson's title, with no mention of Shakespeare: her aim is not a better understanding of Shakespeare, and let readers make of that what they will. Her aim is a better understanding of Shakespeare valued for what it can contribute to improvements in the position of women. Jameson's intentions are as political as Hazlitt's, but where Hazlitt's political aims come and go depending on the play he is considering, Jameson's are sustained through all the plays she discusses. Like Hazlitt, she recognizes that interpretation has ramifications not only for how readers read but for who they are and how they act when they take the consequences of seriously engaged reading into the world. Though her specific views have dated more than Hazlitt's, her fundamental polemic has been, if anything, more taken up—and transformed—by modern criticism. In focusing on women Jameson opened up one of the most discussed areas of modern Shakespeare criticism; and while the terms of reference have naturally shifted with changes in society, Jameson's approach engaged Shakespeare with the world around her in ways from which the sophistications of professional criticism, with its etiolating tendency to separate intellectual activity from lived experience, might learn.

Jameson begins with a lively dialogue between Alda (the author) and Medon, a man moderately sceptical about the claims of women, whose nevertheless sympathetic interrogation allows Alda to develop the fundamentals of her argument about sexual politics and answer probable objections. Why not exemplify from contemporary life? Because there women appear only within the constrictions to be overcome. Why not from history? Because there exteriors of behaviour are seen without an understanding of their interior sources. Shakespeare's characters 'combine history and real life; they are complete individuals, whose hearts and souls are laid open before us'.[63] Jameson's basic claim is that

The condition of women in society, as at present constituted, is false in itself, and injurious to them, – that the education of women, as at present conducted, is founded in mistaken principles, and tends to increase fearfully the sum of misery and errors in both sexes.   (*Characteristics*, 49)

The social condition and the education of women are Jameson's subjects. Her method is based on the view that people are more improved by examples of good to aspire to and ills to avoid than by satire; and that Shakespeare's female characters exemplify real-life possibilities beyond the constrictions of modern circumstances. She writes in dialogue with Coleridge, Hazlitt, A. W. Schlegel, and Germaine de Staël—informed by and engaged with the main currents of Romantic criticism in England, Germany, and France; and she takes the usual attitude of that criticism in treating Samuel Johnson as a whipping boy. Through her personal friendship with Goethe's daughter-in-law Ottilie, she knew Ludwig Tieck, collaborator with Schlegel in the later volumes of his translation of Shakespeare (1825–33). *Characteristics* was translated into German almost immediately (1834). Its perspective is European.

Consistent with her purpose of treating Shakespeare's female characters as models of possibility—what women might be if they were able to interact in society with men on more equal terms—Jameson does on occasion lift her subjects from their contexts. It is easy to criticize this approach as tending to mythologize and as confusing art and life, but this, even where it occurs, is the obverse of Jameson's strength in insisting on the interaction of literary and non-literary experience. In any case, she also often shows how context is essential to understanding characters fully (contexts of other characters, of dramatic situations, and of poetry), as in her account of Juliet: how the Capulet–Montague hatred, discord, and artifice are essential to feeling the force of love, harmony, and natural feeling; and how poetry, and apparently disparate elements of dramatic design, cohere into a unified effect.

Jameson's readings can be bland. Portia, though the first example of her most obviously gender-challenging category, intellect, is diminished by being placed in a context devoid of the kinds of complexity to which any modern interpretation will be alive. While aspects of any reading may arise from the critic's culture rather than from the work, it is difficult for a contemporary reader to see Bassanio as a romantic ideal, Antonio as simply a faithful friend, and still more Shylock as the Jew of Venetian stereotyping; but that is the context in which Jameson interprets Portia. Emphasis on the Italian temperament of Juliet, which explains her uninhibited sexuality, unease with the gender challenge of Rosalind's cross-dressing, and with the freedom and assertive wit of Beatrice, are similarly indicative. But Jameson's engagements can also be challenging in ways that transcend their social context.

Her sympathetic account of Lady Macbeth is among the most striking. As elsewhere (though Jameson cites a variety of male misreaders), Johnson is the quintessence of error. Her view is explicitly an extension of Hazlitt's, and, as with Hazlitt, its background is the famous portrayal of Sarah Siddons (*Characteristics*, 361–2, 369). For Jameson, sympathy with Lady Macbeth is essential to grasping the power of the imaginative conception. Judgement depends on not confounding 'the perversion of what is essentially good, with the operation of positive evil' (*Characteristics*, 360). Admitting the character's wickedness, Jameson argues that sympathy is never wholly lost. Her love for her husband mitigates the effects of actions undertaken not for herself but for him; her force of intellect, power of self-command, and strength of imagination perpetually excite, along-side terror, admiration; her intensity of remorse and despair, betrayed involuntarily in her sleepwalking, and so with no compromise of her awe-inspiring strength of will, prompts positive sympathy: Jameson gives the evidence for this original and gender-based reading with a precise tracing of its sources and range of comparative reference that is unusual in the period.

The account of Cleopatra illustrates Jameson's combination of analysis with enthusiasm, not applying to Shakespeare a morality brought to the reading but finding through Shakespeare more comprehensive and, for their time, unusual views discovered by imaginative engagement. Similarly unusual is the account of Constance (*King John*), where again the background of performance by Sarah Siddons is relevant, and where Jameson may have felt an unusual degree of empathetic identification.[64] Consistent with aims that are not primarily literary-critical, Jameson fills in a great deal of historical background not included in Shakespeare's play to interpret 'not the dramatic portrait but . . . the woman herself' (*Characteristics*, 313): it is the dramatic character combined with the strengths and failings of the historical figure that are, from Jameson's viewpoint, instructive.

'In forming our opinions of them [Shakespeare's characters] we are influenced by our own characters, habits of thought, prejudices, feelings, impulses.'[65] The account of Constance is Jameson's most striking example of her principle of personally inflected interpretation. Aware that reading as a woman leads her to construct perspectives not articulated by her male contemporaries, she is explicitly conscious of how perspective actively creates a view of the work of art, and how all criticism, consciously or unconsciously, is perspectival.[66]

Coda: Charles and Mary Lamb, *Tales from Shakespeare*

Charles and Mary Lamb's *Tales from Shakespeare, designed for the use of young persons* (1807) was written for 'the juvenile library' at the instigation of its publisher, William Godwin, and his second wife, Mary Jane Clairmont. Though planned for children, the book's publication history, including a wide range of translations beyond European languages, shows that through the nineteenth century and beyond the book became a conduit for adult knowledge of Shakespeare.[67]

Since the book is now all but unreadable by children, the many twentieth-century editions indicate that it has continued to function as part educational textbook, part introduction to Shakespeare for adults—a Romantic-period legacy perhaps quite as widely influential as much of the period's more acknowledged and prestigious critical writing. The narratives from the tragedies (six plays) were written by Charles, the narratives from the comedies and romances (fourteen plays) by Mary. Only Charles's name appeared on the 1807 title page. Mary's contribution was suppressed, probably as much from a wish not to draw attention to her contribution as from any gender bias in children's publishing at the time. Mary was best known for having, in a bout of insanity, stabbed to death her mother. Her name on a title page would scarcely have been a recommendation to parent purchasers.

Charles Lamb detested the contemporary fashion of didactic writing for children, which he saw as having displaced 'that beautiful Interest in wild tales' on which his own childhood imagination had been nurtured.[68] But his later account of the effect on his childish imagination of just such a wild tale indicates the problem: his terror at the biblical narrative of the Witch of Endor,[69] imaginatively nurturing as it may have been when seen in a long retrospect, could hardly justify terrifying his young readers with an unexpurgated summary of *Titus Andronicus*. When Lamb came to write for children himself, he and Mary attempted to retain the imaginative freedom of Shakespeare's 'wild tales' in a context of didactic adjustment which included more than tempered terrors.

The preface to *Tales from Shakespeare* expresses two fundamental desiderata: 'to give as much of Shakespeare's own words as possible', and to produce narratives that are 'easy reading for very young children', particularly girls, 'because boys are generally permitted to use their fathers' libraries at a much earlier age then girls are'. Much in the mode of the book takes its character from the second desideratum— writing for young children, and especially for girls. As the preface admits, 'the subjects of most of [the plays] made this a very difficult task' (Lucas, 3.1–2). Sex and violence had to be as far as possible avoided—which was in part accomplished by omitting the English histories and the Roman plays. The plays are also held to be 'strengtheners of virtue', which at times requires tendentious moralizing, often based on adaptations of the plots.

One simple aim is to expurgate subjects deemed unsuitable for the intended readership—along with sex and violence, 'low' comedy. Accordingly, there is no Dogberry and Verges in *Much Ado*, Touchstone in *As You Like It*, Sir Toby in *Twelfth Night*, Paroles in *All's Well*, Autolycus in *The Winter's Tale*, nor Stephano and Trinculo in *The Tempest*. Of the combination of low comedy and sex in the bawds and brothels of *Measure for Measure* and *Pericles* there is not a trace—which has the advantage that Lysimachus does not marry the romance heroine having entered the play as a brothel client. In general disruptions associated with festival, carnival, the saturnalian are omitted or reduced. So too is the characteristic melancholy of the comedies: there is no Malvolio, and no Jacques. Female behaviour that might by the standards of the time seem problematically 'forward'—Beatrice's voluble wit, Olivia's professions of love for Cesario—is hedged around with commentary: Olivia forgot 'the maidenly reserve which is the chief ornament of a lady's character' (Lucas, 3.143). There are also less doctrinal reductions of complexity. Subplots are avoided: there are no mechanicals in *A Midsummer Night's Dream*, and no caskets in *The Merchant of Venice*. Omitted characters have sometimes to be reinserted in reduced form where the main plot requires them (Bottom, become simply 'a clown', for the deception of Titania; Aguecheek, unnamed, for the duel with Cesario/Viola). It is instructive to notice where a major character can be entirely written out of the plot: that there is no Nurse in *Romeo and Juliet*, no Cloten in *Cymbeline*. Where possible, vice is punished and virtue rewarded. There are also comments and explanations of a moralizing or interpretive cast, usually supposing a more straightforward and cheerful view of character and action than is now usual. In general, in comedy the characters, in the manner of fairy tales, 'lived happily ever after'. Shakespeare's characteristic dissonances in the final harmony are omitted: there is no recall of the dead Mamillius in *The Winter's Tale*, no reference to the apparent recalcitrance of Antonio in *The Tempest*. The conclusion of *Measure for Measure*—evidently a difficult play to outline for children—though extreme, represents the general drift:

When she became duchess of Vienna, the excellent example of the virtuous Isabel worked such a complete reformation among the young ladies of that city, that from that time none ever fell into the transgression of Juliet, the repentant wife of the reformed Claudio. And the mercy-loving duke long reigned with his beloved Isabel, the happiest of husbands and of princes.

(Lucas, 3.139)

Since in modern productions the textually silent nun-to-be Isabella often, with all the eloquence of action, declines the Duke's proposal, and for most modern audiences neither this transgressive-penitent Juliet nor this mercy-loving duke is recognizable, even the most muted prospect of 'happily ever after' must be improbably confined to the marriage of Angelo and Mariana. Along with the omission of Pompey, Mistress Overdone, and Lucio—no bawds, brothels, or their clients—these are not small changes. More generally, the melancholy of Shakespeare's clowns, the broad comedy of his low-life characters, and the complexities of viewpoint axiomatic to most contemporary understandings are understated or absent. Shylock is 'much disliked by all good men'; Antonio is 'the kindest man that lived' (Lucas, 3.60). With so much that is characteristic stripped away, the comedies, whether conceived as 'happy' or 'dark', shrink back into the romance elements that Shakespeare derived from his sources.

The tragedies are treated similarly. There is no Gloucester plot in *King Lear*, which removes the violence of the assault on Gloucester and the sexual triangle, Goneril–Regan–Edmund. Poor Tom is simply a beggar; Edgar is introduced only for the final duel with Edmund. As with the comedies, moral complexity is reduced. This is especially the case in presenting the relations of parents and children. Goneril and Regan are simply wicked—failing in their duty to Lear, and cruel. *Othello* requires a tour de force of delicacy in dealing with Desdemona's choice so as neither to blame her for error nor imply that her behaviour could be taken as a model. Moralizing inserted into the narrative of *Hamlet* on the proper behaviour of children in reproving parents (Hamlet to Gertrude) has little to do with how characters and events are presented in the play. Altogether the tale presents a clearer, more rational, and more sympathetic account of Hamlet's character and motives—his suspicions about Claudius and Gertrude, his love for Ophelia, his delay in taking revenge. The most striking changes are those to the plot of *Macbeth*. Lady Macbeth is involved in planning the murders of Banquo and Fleance, and she shows no remorse. As Lamb told the diarist Henry Crabb Robinson, she is 'one of Shakespeare's worst characters': 'her sleep-walking does not suit so hardened a being'—and so in the *Tales* it is omitted.[70]

In what they omit, as in the varied reframings of what they include, the Lambs' plot outlines are a form of creative criticism, interpretive interactions with their subjects, sometimes revealing aspects of the plays less visible to modern views as well as cultural anxieties of Romantic readers, particularly in relation to children. Shakespeare is thus drawn into a debate about educating the imagination. Few would now claim that the plays are 'strengtheners of virtue' teaching 'courtesy, benignity, generosity, humanity' (Lucas, 3.2). How far silently adapting the plots to make them appear this is different from the kind of arrangement by selection, foregrounding, and recontextualizing evident in the history of criticism, or the cutting and reordering with which Shakespeare has regularly been presented in the theatre, is debatable. The anxieties about age and gender which prompt the Lambs' shapings, and which are displayed in their preface, are at least explicit.

The publication history of the *Tales* indicates that it must often have been through Charles and Mary Lamb that Shakespeare became known in English culture over the following hundred years, probably to adults as much as to children. In its many translations, including at least two African languages and Chinese, the *Tales* is one of the most important Shakespearean legacies of the whole Romantic period, a major conduit of Shakespeare's work in many areas of world culture.

Germany

'Our Shakespeare'

'One may boldly assert that there is no nation beside the English to whom [Shakespeare] belongs so particularly as to the Germans, because nowhere else ... is he so much read, so deeply studied, so warmly loved, and with so might insight admired.' So wrote August Wilhelm Schlegel in 1796.[1] 'The Germans only, of foreign nations, are approaching towards a knowledge and feeling of what [Shakespeare] is. In some respects they have acquired a superiority over the fellow-countrymen of the Poet.' So wrote Wordsworth in 1815—certainly not knowing that he was echoing Schlegel. Wordsworth went on to deplore the cliché of Shakespeare's supposedly 'wild irregular genius', whose faults of artistry were compensated for by great but irregular beauties, and to state the ground of the superior conceptions he praises as discovered by German criticism. German criticism had been the first to understand 'that the judgement of Shakespeare in the selection of his materials, and in the manner in which he has made them, heterogeneous as they often are, constitute a unity of their own, and contribute all to one great end, is not less admirable than his imagination, his invention, and his intuitive knowledge of human Nature'.[2] That this attribution of priority to German criticism—in effect to August Wilhelm Schlegel (whose *Lectures on Dramatic Art* were published in German in 1809–11 and in English translation in 1815)—immensely (and probably justly) annoyed Coleridge is not so significant as that Wordsworth does here correctly identify a leading theme of German criticism of Shakespeare.[3] In German literature and criticism the revisions that this view of Shakespeare's judgement and

Shakespeare and the Romantics. David Fuller, Oxford University Press (2021). © David Fuller.
DOI: 10.1093/oso/9780199679119.003.0003

artistry implied became the basis not only of a new understanding of Shakespeare but also a new understanding of the nature of poetry and of criticism. In Germany Shakespeare was seen in the period as the archetype of the Poet, and a proper understanding of his work became the basis of a new aesthetic.

Hence the German idea of 'unser Shakespeare': *our* [German] Shakespeare. Shakespeare was the archetypal and exemplary Germanic author—Germanic in the widest sense: characteristic of the nations of northern Europe, as distinct from the culture of southern Europe, the culture of Greece and Rome. This view of Shakespeare implied a new view of literary art. It freed German writers from the ideals of French neoclassicism, to create a modern literature that was characteristically Germanic. Shakespeare was the key figure of German literary self-discovery.[4]

This begins with Gotthold Ephraim Lessing (1729–81). Between 1759 and 1765, with his friends Friedrich Nicolai and Moses Mendelssohn, Lessing produced a series of *Letters concerning the newest Literature*. The most notable of these, Lessing's Letter of 16 February 1759, attacked Johann Christoph Gottsched (1700–66), whose *German Theatre* (6 vols., 1740–5), containing mainly translations of French neoclassical drama, was intended as a model for new writing in German. Citing *Hamlet*, *Othello*, and *King Lear*, Lessing denounced this 'Frenchified' (*französierend*) repertoire: the model suited to German culture, 'a much greater tragic poet than Corneille', is Shakespeare, whose Germanic qualities are identified as the grand, the terrible, and the melancholy. Lessing also introduced an idea much developed in the following generation, the idea of 'genius': 'a genius can only be set ablaze by a genius, and most easily by one [that is, Shakespeare] who seems to owe everything to Nature, and does not deter by displaying the laborious perfections of art.'[5]

Lessing is among the first in Germany to invoke the conception of genius, which, in various forms, became central to Romantic aesthetics—the creative personality of extraordinary endowments that are set apart from creative gifts of a more common order. In its full form the idea indicates a gamut of possibilities: genius may operate with natural unforced copiousness (Mozart) or through struggle (Beethoven); it may be shown in everything its possessor did (Leonardo) or in ways more highly focussed (Raphael); it may sum up the final phase of a culture (Bach) or bring a new phase of culture into being (Wagner); it may be manifested in a life copiously documented (Goethe) or a life of which nothing is known (Homer); and it may be manifested in life as in art (Napoleon).[6] As a power 'which enlarges the circle of human knowledge, which discovers new materials of nature' (Fuseli), it demands respect, awe, even (as Fuseli has it) reverence.[7] It signals an order of creativity not to be judged in ordinary terms—often, because of its novelty, creating the terms by which it is to be judged. This conception of genius gave rise to the idea of art as a special mode of knowledge which, while it may require education, skill, and craft, may also be compromised or stifled by education (deflected from originality by convention), and may at least appear to dispense with skill (the simplicity of the popular ballad preferred to the sophistication of the classical ode). Art therefore ceases to be imitation built from models with known criteria (Corneille, Racine). Genius, though individual, speaks not for educated elites but from and for a whole culture. Nevertheless, by a characteristic paradox—because genius speaks in advance of the culture's self-realization—its typical heroic figures are often marginalized, alienated, and at odds with their cultures; and they are often dangerous—Hamlet, Prometheus, Faust, Don Juan, Cain, Manfred, Satan. It is an idea flourishing in, though not initiated by, an age of revolution. Its reverberations lasted throughout the nineteenth century and beyond, and its aesthetic manifestations have no simple or single social implications.[8] Not university-educated, using native as well as European materials, writing for a popular theatre, and by accepted criteria of educated taste wild and unruly, for late eighteenth-century German literati Shakespeare was the incarnation of this idea.

The idea has been criticized from a variety of points of view—for implications about the relation of art to society; for implications about the relation of art to tradition; for its gender implications; and much else. It is seen as a basis of 'bardolatry'—that is, the supposedly excessive and uncritical admiration of Shakespeare, which on another view is due recognition of extraordinary creative power. In late eighteenth-century Germany advanced criticism recognized that how to judge what exceeded received standards of judgement was a genuine problem, and that the answers derived from the past needed to be profoundly refreshed, significantly modified, or perhaps overthrown. Shakespeare played a substantial role in ushering in the new. In the vanguard of this, Lessing was a conservative neologist. What he announced in the *Letter* of February 1759 he developed in the *Hamburg Dramaturgy*.[9]

The *Hamburg Dramaturgy* chronicles and discusses the brief experiment of the Hamburg National Theatre (1767–9), the first attempt to establish a 'national theatre' in Germany, for which Lessing was recruited as dramaturge, that is literary advisor, editor, adaptor, commentating on every aspect of plays, acting, production, and audience. Lessing's 104 essays, written weekly over the two years of the theatre's existence, were entirely occasional—responses to every aspect of theatre prompted by issues as they arose, its plays, its actors, its aesthetics, and the place of theatre as an educative public institution. At times in the *Dramaturgy* Lessing appears to endorse a simple opposition between genius and criticism. 'Genius laughs at all of the categorizations of the critic' (§7, here specifically those of genre). The 'wealth [of genius] does not consist in the stockpiled reserves of his memory but rather in that which he engenders from himself, out of his own feelings' (§34). 'A genius has to make something first, so that we can perceive it as possible' (§21).[10] 'Oh, you inventors of general rules, how little you understand the art, and how little you possess of the genius that produced the models on which you established those rules and can violate them at will!' (§48). But really Lessing's antithesis is only between genius and bad criticism, the mechanical application of learned practices. Genius may be in conflict with established 'rules': it is not fundamentally in conflict with principles of composition or interpretation. Genius leads, but the idea of genius is not a ground for critical anarchy (§96); the philosophical critic responds to the rule-breaking of genius with new conceptions, or with a re-examination of the old.

The *Hamburg Dramaturgy* shows how Lessing addressed this. Lessing is an anti-dogmatic thinker. Though in opposing ways of thinking he regarded as outmoded or false, fierce and even violent polemic is a characteristic mode, his aim is always positive: through refutation to affirmation.[11] He is fundamentally open-minded, perspectival, and eclectic—as is evinced by his dealings with the most advanced speculations in theology. Just how advanced his own theological views were is uncertain. He clashed with orthodox German

Protestantism (Johann Melchior Goeze, senior minister of the Hamburg Lutheran state church). He helped give currency to the writings of a radical deist (in eighteenth-century terms an atheist), Hermann Samuel Reimarus, parts of whose *Apology for Rational Worshippers of God* he helped to publish. His parable of the three rings (in his play *Nathan the Wise*) representing Christianity, Judaism, and Islam is strikingly relativistic: it implies that each religion is to be judged not by its claims to truth but by its fruits in practice. Though the posthumous report of his friend F. H. Jacobi that he had been a follower of Spinoza (again in eighteenth-century terms virtually an atheist) was contested by his equally close friend Moses Mendelssohn, he at least helped to lay the foundations for the rediscovery of Spinoza in Germany which was central to the dominant philosophy of the next generation (Schelling, Fichte, Schleiermacher). Similarly, in politics he was in tune with advanced thinking, an opponent of the absolutism of the autocratic states into which pre-French Revolution Germany was divided. The most famous of his writings on aesthetics, *Laokoon*, is congruent with this, a critique of contemporary assumptions derived from Horace about the relations between visual art and poetry. Fundamentally Lessing writes here against being so possessed by a critical doctrine—*any* doctrine—that it dictates what we think, even what we are able to perceive; criticism that, in straitjacketing art to its presuppositions, fails to think freely—though whether Lessing's ability to observe freely entirely escapes his own doctrines is open to question.

Lessing's writings in theology, philosophy, social issues, and aesthetics show a consistent positive orientation towards advanced Enlightenment attitudes. Nevertheless, in the *Hamburg Dramaturgy* he disclaimed any idea of a coherent theory of drama:

> I remind my readers here that these pages are intended to contain anything but a dramatic system. I am under no obligation to resolve all the difficulties I pose. My thoughts might seem to become more and more disconnected, they may even seem to contradict: they need only be thoughts that provide my readers material to think for themselves. Here I want nothing more than to disseminate *Fermenta cognitionis*. (§95)

'*Fermenta cognitionis*': the aim is to provoke independent thinking, to prompt an attitude of mind that questions. But while Lessing made no attempt in the *Dramaturgy* to extrapolate a summa of principles, the fundamental implications of the series were nevertheless highly influential.

In Lessing's attack on the aesthetics of French neoclassical theatre as represented by Pierre Corneille and Voltaire, Shakespeare is the great positive exemplum. Since the plays performed by the Hamburg theatre were exclusively French and German, Shakespeare figures in the *Dramaturgy* only occasionally, but the ways in which he figures are an index of Lessing's understanding of the wide cultural implications of his work.[12] Lessing argues that, while the French claim to write tragedy in the manner of classical Greece as theorized by Aristotle, 'No other nation has more misunderstood the rules of ancient drama than the French' (§101). The French misrepresent Aristotle, taking the outer garment, codified as supposed 'rules' about the unity of time, place, and action, for the inner substance, which is entirely about the emotional experience of tragedy. A proper understanding of Aristotle requires a grasp of his crucial terms, what he meant by pity or compassion (*eleos*/*Mitleid*) and fear (*phobos*/*Furcht*)—not (though this was the word often used by German critics) terror (*Schrecken*). 'Compassion ... requires someone who suffers undeservedly, and fear requires someone like ourselves' (§74). This understanding of Aristotle Lessing pursues through a series of papers (§§74–8, 81–3) in which he shows where to look—to the real emotional effect of the work, not some conventional account of what that is expected to be; and he shows how to think—with engaged attention to the meanings of critical terms and arguments that really connect aesthetic with lived experience. The essential element of tragedy is 'the fear that the misfortunes we see hanging over that person could befall us ourselves; it is the fear that we ourselves could become the pitied object. In short: this fear is compassion directed at ourselves' (§75). It is with this idea of tragedy in view that Lessing insists on the psychological penetration and truth of passion central to Shakespeare, that 'deep insight into the nature of love' found in *Romeo and Juliet*, or the nature of jealousy found in *Othello* (§15)—the passions not as they are supposed to be in literary convention, but as they are in reality. This is what generates the sympathetic identification with the protagonist essential to the tragic effect. Shakespeare is, with Sophocles and Euripides, the embodiment of this Aristotelian view of tragedy (§81).[13]

It is not only feeling for character that generates the sympathetic engagement essential to the tragic effect. Shakespeare's handling of the supernatural is also exemplary. Lessing contrasts the Ghost in *Hamlet* with the Ghost in Voltaire's *Sémiramis* (§11), considering the beliefs of the audience, the stagecraft with which these are negotiated, and the art with which Shakespeare engages the audience to suspend its unbelief: while Voltaire's Ghost is simply a disguised actor, the Ghost of Old Hamlet produces the effect of the supernatural for scepticism as for belief. Only with the mixed genre of comedy in tragedy is Lessing still restrained by neoclassical views of genre at which he recognizes genius laughs (§7). As he reports from Laurence Sterne, 'Prejudice of education... is the devil' (§101). Has not mixing modes been endorsed by the practice of Euripides? 'If a genius with higher purposes allows several [modes] to flow together in one and the same work, we should forget the textbook and simply ask whether he has achieved these higher purposes' (§48). Lessing introduces his most extended discussion of this Shakespearean subject via the mixing of tragic and comic in Spanish Golden Age drama and the doubtful endorsement of Lope de Vega. He quotes the extended but still equivocal endorsement of Wieland, the translator of Shakespeare: the mixed mode reflects the way serious and comic are mixed in life (§69). He discusses problems with this view from a variety of perspectives in an open-ended way, explaining what he sees as the difficulties, leaving their solution to the reader (§70). 'My thoughts may seem to contradict themselves'; *'fermenta cognitionis'*; philosophical criticism may lag behind the discoveries of genius. This is not the freedom that is to come: unresolved jostling of perspectives (Hamann); puzzle of the multivalent fragment and unfixed irony (Friedrich Schlegel, Novalis). But, in Lessing's Enlightenment way, open-ended questioning and the reader's freedom to decide are preferred to an inhibiting show of magisterial consistency.

German criticism of Shakespeare did not derive its methods entirely from the study of Shakespeare directly. A significant though often ignored figure in its development is the theologian, philosopher of language, and self-taught polymath, Johann Georg Hamann (1730–88). Hamann influenced views of Shakespeare directly through his friendship with Herder, who admired 'the Magus of the North' (as Hamann became known) and whose 'Shakespeare' (1771) is a

foundational text of German criticism. Through Herder, Hamann
also influenced the crucial figures of Goethe and Friedrich Schlegel.[14]

Hamann's *Aesthetica in nuce* ('Aesthetics in a nutshell', 1762) is not,
as its title might suggest, concerned with aesthetics generally but with
hermeneutics—textual interpretation, specifically interpretation of the
Bible.[15] It mentions Shakespeare only occasionally: Hamann humorously compares his methods to the 'signs and beckonings' of the Ghost
of Old Hamlet, and (again with some self-irony) the passion that gives
his utterance vividness to Lysander's 'lightning in the collied night /
That . . . unfolds both heaven and earth' (Nisbet, 143, 279). But
though the *Aesthetica* does not deal with Shakespeare directly, its
implications for reading any literary text—and particularly for reading
Shakespeare—had immense impact on leading writers of the *Sturm
und Drang* and Romantic periods.

Hamann's methods of argument and (though one may scarcely call
it this) exposition are in every way oblique. His formulation of positive
principles is largely by implication—a vigorous and often humorous
satire of Enlightenment rationalist confidence in adducing univocal
meanings. His main butt in the *Aesthetica* is a largely forgotten
though in his time prominent theologian, Johann David Michaelis,
but Hamann does not select opponents who are easy targets: Moses
Mendelssohn, Lessing, and Voltaire are almost equally prominent
focuses of his satire. Hamann was at odds with the dominant
'advanced' intellectual current of his age, represented above all by the
rationalism of Immanuel Kant. Kant's idea of reason as impersonal
and transhistorical, not based in culture and tradition, represented for
Hamann the epitome of error, but the pervasiveness of Kant's assumptions made them difficult to combat. In tackling this difficulty—
disrupting Kantian assumptions at their root in his mode of
discourse—Hamann is paradigmatic for anybody who wishes to
think for him- or herself in ways based in cultural and personal
identity, and particularly for anybody who wishes to think from the
passions, as, in Hamann's view, all worthwhile criticism of the arts (all
worthwhile thinking) must. 'Passion alone gives hands, feet, wings to
abstractions and hypotheses, and to pictures and signs gives spirit, life,
and tongue' (142). And 'passion', for Hamann, does not mean enthusiasm that is purely intellectual. Ceres and Bacchus are invoked, as
gods of the senses and the bodily passions. Hamann had unusual views

on sexuality for his period ('My coarse imagination has never been able to conceive of a creative spirit without genitalia'),[16] and was even more unusual in bringing these views into his philosophy and theology. Real thinking comes from the whole person: mind and body; thought, imagination, and the emotions—a unity that can only be fully achieved not by statement but by mode and style. As Goethe saw, praising 'the wondrous totality of [Hamann's] style and what he communicated', 'the principle underlying all of Hamann's utterances is this: "Everything a human being sets out to accomplish . . . must arise from the sum of his combined powers; anything isolated is an abomination"'.[17]

The *Aesthetica*'s subtitle indicates its unusual methods: it is 'a rhapsody in cabbalistic prose'. 'Rhapsody' associates Hamann's mode of utterance with the Homeric rhapsode, with interpretation through performance—here the performance of his extraordinary style: the obverse of a rationally organized treatise; unsystematic, even anti-systematic. System falsifies. As Princess Amalia Gallitzin, the patroness of Hamann's final year, recorded from Hamann in her diary: 'ma seule règle c'est de n'en point avoir' (my only rule is to have no rules).[18] Clarity he associated with facility, and facility with superficiality. Nothing worthwhile can be truly absorbed as real meaning by the whole person without struggle. Hamann challenges the reader: he is fragmentary, implicatory, open to interpretation, ironic, humorous, impassioned—a variety of tone that allows a greater range of point of view, and which is further destabilized by a palimpsest collage of argument veering here and there in often extensive footnotes. With text and notes, quotations in Latin, Greek, and Hebrew, and with constant allusive sub-quotation to the Lutheran Bible, some pages of Hamann more resemble the postmodern multi-text of Derrida's *Glas* than the norms of eighteenth-century philosophy. The analogy in England is not Hume but *Tristram Shandy*. 'In cabbalistic prose': Hamann speaks through a variety of personae, one of which is a cabbalist—a role in which he may be seen as an initiate of profound secret wisdom, a reader of meanings not found on the surface (for the fit reader he is largely this), or an obscurantist (largely this for the reader Hamann aims to distress and repel); and for any reader his peculiar methods make him something of both. In this he resembles Blake: 'What is grand is necessarily obscure to weak men. . . . The wisest of the Ancients considered what is not too explicit as the fittest for instruction, because it rouses the faculties to act.'[19]

Sometimes the reader may take Hamann straight. Sometimes he piles up cryptic allusions to the Bible and classical literature in a way that seems designed to produce uncertainty, especially since allusions are often open to a variety of applications and context does not provide guidance on which of a range of possible meanings is most probable. But this is in itself an expressive procedure: the method is analogous to Hamann's argument about the nature of meaning in myth, symbol, and the images, forms, and rhetoric of poetic texts, biblical and literary. Another of Hamann's personae (announced on his title page) is (from the Book of Job) the enthusiast Elihu, whose 'belly is as wine which hath no vent... is ready to burst like new bottles' (as befits the persona of the cabbalist, an epigraph quoted in Hebrew). Another, invoked throughout, is 'the wise idiot of Greece', that is, Socrates, not the Platonic character as conceived by eighteenth-century rationalism but, rather, himself a rhapsodist, a passionate speaker who leads the individual to discover his or her own wisdom—a revisionary view that Hamann expounds in *Socratic Memorabilia* (1759). What Hamann especially valued in Socrates was his profession of ignorance—its humility, its recognition that what ordinarily passes for knowledge is regularly compromised by a mixture of vanity and illusion rendered confident by conformity to the intellectual currency of its context. 'The ignorance of Socrates was feeling [*Empfindung*]. But between feeling and a doctrine [*Lehrsatz*] there is even greater difference than between a living animal and an anatomical skeleton of the same'.[20] There is a difficultly here in the interpretable implications of crucial terms, but Hamann's antithesis is well represented by Yeats: it is between thought cut off from feeling, 'in the mind alone', and thought that penetrates the whole being, thinking 'in a marrow bone' ('A Prayer for Old Age').

On the integration of mind and body, Hamann's originality is seldom more striking to a modern reader than in his defence, very unusual in his time, of Socrates's homosexuality as an extension of the normal experience of friendship: 'One cannot feel a lively friendship without sensuality, and a metaphysical love perhaps sins more coarsely against the nerves than does an animal love against flesh and blood.'[21] That is, affection entirely of the mind is a violation of natural feeling;

all real love contains some element of desire for physical expression: better a purely physical expression of desire than a narrowing of love to the purely mentalistic. It is a view that would act as a basis for reading Shakespeare's Sonnets in much more modern terms than the evasion-cum-repudiation representative of the period that is found in Coleridge.[22]

As Socrates is prompted in the *Cratylus* by Euthyphro, so Hamann is prompted by Francis Bacon, citations from whom, often idiosyncratically interpreted, appear in the cabbalist's multiple footnotes, which teasingly riot with the rationalist procedures of his opponents, invoking biblical texts, the often interpretable application of which is left to the reader. With multilingual quotation and an immense range of reference, ancient and modern, Hamann both demonstrates his own extraordinary heterodox learning and satirizes the usual procedures of the learned of his time. In an alternative epigraph to the whole work from Horace he presents himself not as Socrates, not as Elihu, but as a priest of the classical Muses addressing in a new song the young—those not yet trapped in the abstractions of rationalist education remote from real experience. 'We must become as little children if we are to receive the spirit of truth' (143)—that is, reborn free from the prejudices taught by the age of Voltaire and its eternal transmutations, rationalist abstract discourse in every age.

Central to Hamann is the issue of language: how does language represent in adequate terms? Not by dealing in abstractions, the usual language of theology (Michaelis), philosophy (Kant), and criticism (Lessing). 'Poetry is the mother-tongue of the human race' (141). Hamann's exemplars of this primal speech in image and symbol are, in the ancient world, Homer and the Holy Spirit (the Bible), in the modern world Shakespeare. The abstractions of eighteenth-century learned discourse—the norms of learned discourse in any age—give no adequate 'feeling for the presence of things'; 'the senses and passions'—vital to real thinking—'speak and understand nothing but images' (141). Here the interpretive reader may choose to hear Hamann speaking directly, in his own person. And also here: 'Do not venture into the metaphysics of the fine arts without being initiated into the orgies and Eleusinian mysteries' (143). The preconditions of learned knowledge are not as prescribed by institutions of learning, in the eighteenth century or since.

Finally, aware of the frailty of all attempts to produce real meaning through verbal signs, the rhapsodic cabbalist turns on himself: 'Everything in this aesthetic nutshell tastes of vanity, vanity!' The repetition echoes the total futility perceived by Qoheleth, the 'Preacher' of Ecclesiastes (1.2). Are Hamann's obelisks (little daggers of satire) and asterisks (little star-lights of perception), to which the rhapsodist's final gloss on his work refers, at bottom any different from the scholarly paraphernalia of the rationalists and pedants he opposes? Hamann leaves his readers with the question. His admirers thought they were profoundly different.

When Hamann entitled one of his last works *Golgotha und Scheblimini* (1784), he pointed to the need in all forms of understanding— theology, philosophy, the arts—for a comprehensive combining of extremes: the equivalent in the arts of a theology that takes full account of divine–human abasement (Golgotha) and human–divine exaltation (Scheblimini: Christ at God's right hand; Psalm 110). This is the range in unity of dramatic mode and poetic language of which, for the German Romantics, Shakespeare was the supreme exemplar: the antithesis of neoclassical aesthetic criteria of unity through limitation. The implications of Hamann's extraordinary 'nutshell'—which add to this multiple meaning; criticism and creative form; and the reader's engagement in constructing meaning—echo on through the Shakespeare criticism of those who followed Hamann throughout the period.

The argument fundamental to the view of Shakespeare of Johann Gottfried Herder (1744–1803) was new. '[A people not adopting Greek drama as a model] will *create* its drama out of its history, out of the spirit of the age, manners, opinions, language, national prejudices, traditions, and pastimes' ('Shakespeare', 1773).[23] The ramifications of this view go quite beyond its significance for Shakespeare: all art must be understood in relation to its cultural circumstances—all art, and everything else. Contrary to Enlightenment suppositions about one universal human nature, which meant that art created in and for the culture of ancient Greece had established criteria valid for other cultures in other times, Herder is among the founders of the relativistic historical outlook: understanding and judgement must relate to places and times. They must also relate to a culture as a whole, not only the culture of an educated elite but also popular culture, what Herder called *Volkspoesie*—'more alive, ... more free, ...

closer to the senses, . . . more lyrically dynamic', and, like Shakespeare, not composed for print and the eye but for voice and the ear.[24] Herder evolved his view of cultural relativism, developed in later writings about the philosophy of history, partly through his writing about Shakespeare. Quite how this new understanding should be accomplished—by what Herder called 'Einfühlung' ('feeling one's way in', empathy)—is open to interpretation, but it means attempting to understand, by knowledge and imagination interiorized so as to become intuitive, the whole context in which a work was produced and to which it was addressed. Herder may have found the idea in the great art historian (virtually the inventor of the discipline) Johann Joachim Winckelmann (1717–68), whose work he both admired and contested, but Winckelmann thought only in terms of the relation of Greek art to Greek culture. Herder saw that the idea was universally applicable, and that this undermined the assumption that standards derived from Greek art could be applied, as they were before Herder, to Germanic culture. It is the beginning of historical criticism that appears in England only later, but which, in different forms, dominated much nineteenth- and twentieth-century writing about Shakespeare and remains a central assumption of criticism.

Even more than his literary contemporaries, Herder was a polymath, with important writings on philosophy, theology, politics, and aesthetics. These writings were major influences on Goethe and on the following generations, from the literary criticism of August Wilhelm and Friedrich Schlegel to the theology of Schleiermacher, the philosophy of Hegel, and beyond. As with Lessing and others of his contemporaries, Herder's literary criticism is part of a broad programme about intellectual, spiritual, and social life; about understanding the past and creating the future.

His most important statement on Shakespeare is the essay of 1773 published in a collection brought together by Herder, *Von deutscher Art und Kunst* ('On German Character and Art'). This also contained his essay on the supposed ancient Scottish bard Ossian and folk poetry, and an essay by Goethe on German architecture.[25] The fundamental issue of the collection is clear in its title: the relation of German art (poetry, drama, and architecture) to Germanic culture, that is the culture of northern Europe as distinct from the culture of southern Europe epitomized by Greece. The collection is often seen as a manifesto of the so-called *Sturm und Drang* (Storm and Stress) movement of the 1770s and 1780s in Germany, a reaction against Enlightenment rationalism and a precursor of Romanticism. A representative work of the *Sturm und Drang*, Goethe's *Götz von Berlichingen*, recuperating national history as subject matter, written in the year of Herder's 'Shakespeare' and modelled on Shakespeare's history plays, is welcomed at the end of Herder's essay as itself a model for new writing in German. As with Lessing, Herder's interest is in critical approaches to Shakespeare as an issue central to the fundamental direction of German culture.

Unlike Lessing, Herder is not wary of the idea of genius: Shakespeare is a 'mortal... endowed with divine powers'; he is a 'son of the gods'; in his handling of people and events he is analogous to 'the Creator of the world' (*SWA*, 298, 299). Genius is a conception that recognizes this extraordinary greatness and originality. Where Lessing (more Enlightenment) is wary of a confusion of critical principles, Herder (more *Sturm und Drang*) is open to the unruliness of enthusiasm. However, though Herder disputes Lessing's account of the origins of Greek tragedy, replacing Lessing's process of simplification with a process of elaboration less congruent with the critical suppositions adduced from neoclassical drama, much of his view is otherwise similar to Lessing's. He accepts the fundamental understanding of Aristotle: the purpose of tragedy is a convulsion of the heart (*Erschütterung des Herzens*), the agitation of the soul (*Erregung der Seele*); the means by which this is accomplished are fear and pity (*Furcht und Mitleid*: *Werke*, 2.505, 508). He also accepts the application of this to Shakespearean tragedy: beneath the differences of form arising from differences of culture, 'Shakespeare is Sophocles' brother... inwardly wholly like *him*' (*SWA*, 303). Beyond this, Herder asks, what would a modern Aristotle say? He would not say as Aristotle said because he would think as Aristotle thought—in relation to the culture from which the plays developed and to which they were addressed. Greek tragedy is related to the forms of drama out of which it grew and its culture's world view. In imitating the outward forms of this French neoclassical tragedy is a statue without a daemon: the inner essence is lost because the fundamental world view in relation to which that existed has changed.

And even in its imitation of outward forms neoclassical tragedy is a distortion: it misunderstands the supposed Aristotelian unities. The significant classical unity to Herder, unity of place, means not the illusion (supposedly derived from Aristotle) that the events of the drama should take place in a timescale within which they might happen if they were not fiction: the real issue about place is the appropriateness of setting to character and incident—to illustrate which, Herder gives examples from *Macbeth*. His account of *King Lear* indicates the kind of substantial unity that underlies apparent disparity: 'the soul of the event breathes in even the most disparate scenes' (*SWA*, 300). Or, of the quite different variety of *Othello*, 'It is all a vital and profound part of... a single tragic event' (*SWA*, 303). Herder describes the diversity of elements, tones, and structure of Shakespeare's plays through compound paradox: they are 'multiformly simple and uniformly complex' (*SWA*, 297; *vielfach Einfältiger und einfach Vielfältiger*, *Werke*, 2.507). To elicit the relationships that clarify this to the understanding makes new demands of criticism, demands that are permanently new because they are at once both intellectual (can be learned) and temperamental—can be cultivated, but acquired, if at all, only within limits; and must be exercised ever anew, in the living moment.

To experience this, Herder requires a different approach to engaging with the drama, an approach that takes seriously what is really meant by convulsion of the heart and agitation of the soul. These are not just words. Underlying Herder's whole discussion is a contrast of attitudes: educated taste responding with judicious admiration to a simulacrum; passionate imagination radically engaged by creative power. This is reflected not only in what Herder says but also in how he says it. No more mouthing (French) critical platitudes, man-oeuvring signs empty of meanings—'Cacklogallinian' detachment (*SWA*, 305; *Kaklogallinier*, *Werke*, 2.518). To convey living aesthetic experience Herder models a different mode of criticism, a mode that does not merely refer to but incorporates the passion essential to real understanding. No thought without feeling. What is evident in the characteristically *Sturm und Drang* rhapsodic enthusiasm of 'Shakespeare' is explicit in Herder's *Critical Forests, or Reflections on the Art and Science of the Beautiful*: 'First Grove, Dedicated to Mr. Lessing's *Laocoön*' (1769). The clash that Herder identifies in this between Lessing and Winckelmann is a permanent clash between different ideas of criticism—as analysis and as appreciation. It is a clash between Enlightenment and *Sturm und Drang* that is taken up by German Romantic criticism of Shakespeare in Friedrich Schlegel's emphasis on the importance of creative form in criticism. It echoes on into the nineteenth and twentieth centuries, Winckelmann in Pater, and Pater in Christopher Ricks—neither lacking analysis (on the contrary, both brilliantly intellectual), but both framing analyses in terms that imply analysis is not enough.[26]

One fundamental difference between Winckelmann and Lessing is that Winckelmann is a critic of visual art and Lessing a critic of poetry. It is a difference crucial to Lessing's argument in *Laokoon*—that visual art is present to the viewer in a single moment; that poetry is present to the reader through extension in time. Winckelmann and Lessing, Herder argues, employ different modes of criticism, but while their distinct modes may be cognate with their difference of focus, neither is necessarily confined to one or the other art. Winckelmann's style 'is like an ancient work of art' (§1, *SWA*, 54); he writes 'with the same feeling as if he had fashioned the statue himself' (§2, *SWA*, 55). Lessing 'seems . . . to present us with the occasion of each reflection, to take it apart and put it back together again piece by piece' (§1, *SWA*, 54). It is purposeless, Herder argues, to judge one mode by the other: each has its own validity. But the history of criticism has judged one by the other: it has made the judgement that Herder resists—that Lessing's mode, taking apart, analysis, is superior to recreation as though from within, appreciation. Herder himself combines the two; he is both 'interpreter and rhapsodist' (*SWA*, 298): enthusiasm without analysis loses sight of one purpose of criticism—to deepen knowledge, to make it live more consciously; analysis without enthusiasm loses sight of another purpose of criticism—to intensify knowledge, to make it live more vitally.

On this basis Herder analyses, and contradicts, Lessing's account of Sophocles' *Philoctetes*, like Winckelmann, recreating from within. Proceeding from his own fundamental impression of the play, he analyses its step-by-step progress as a dramatic text, incorporating into that analysis the moment-by-moment responses of the audience. 'Let us open our Sophocles, let us read as if we were watching the drama' (§2, *SWA*, 55). What is said by the main character, what is heard (pre-articulate sounds), what is seen (including in moments without text), how the (sympathetic) response of the other onstage character guides the responses of the audience, how an alternative (antagonistic) response is undermined by context, how the end-of-scene Chorus modulates the feeling of the whole, how the audience responses are guided by their cultural presuppositions, and how all these elements interact. Herder tests feeling by analysis; in analysis he never loses sight of feeling. It is exemplary theatrical criticism: text, stage, cultural context. What 'Shakespeare' sketches in outline with different aspects of *Othello*, *King Lear*, and *Macbeth*, the account of *Philoctetes* shows how to realize.

Herder's relativistic, historicist outlook, situating art in its time and place, is one of the real advances of criticism. As an axiom of criticism it has become what axioms often are, a dead platitude when not thought afresh. As a default position and in isolation it is at odds with Herder's equally central view: no thought without feeling. Criticism has often welcomed adopting a historical perspective, the simplicities of detachment—meaning then, not (also) now—but at the expense of creative interaction signalled in style and form, the complexities of engagement—meaning then *and* now. Herder modelled and required both. The next generation in Germany followed his lead; but Herder's most direct influence was on the most important writer of his age not only in Germany but in Europe, Johann Wolfgang von Goethe (1749–1832).

'The French Revolution, Fichte's *Theory of Knowledge*, and Goethe's *Wilhelm Meister* are the three greatest tendencies of the age': revolution in society, in philosophy, and in imagination and sensibility.[27] For Friedrich Schlegel these are interconnected: there can be no real change in how society is ordered without correspondent changes in ideas and feelings. In Germany Shakespeare is central to these changes: Books 3, 4, and 5 of Goethe's *Wilhelm Meister's Apprenticeship* (1796) are concerned with the impact on Wilhelm of his reading of Shakespeare, and the understanding and performance of *Hamlet*. In this, the archetypal novel of personal development, education, and cultural formation (*Bildungsroman*), Shakespeare, and specifically *Hamlet*, are crucial to who Wilhelm becomes. The novel not only contains critical discussions of Shakespeare and of *Hamlet*: it also shows how Wilhelm and other characters interact with the play—that is, how it can relate to people's real lives: who they are, how they feel, and how they think. The kind of interaction between life and art that criticism can usually do no more than argue for, through fiction Goethe can show. Goethe presents this neither as ideal, nor as error, but as fact: this is how people read when engaged in making real meanings.

Because Wilhelm is in part an autobiographical figure, a portrait of the artist, the most straightforward encapsulation of his view of Hamlet's character is often taken as Goethe's.

> It is clear to me what Shakespeare set out to portray: a heavy deed placed on a soul which is not adequate to cope with it.... A fine, pure, noble and highly moral person, but devoid of that emotional strength that characterizes a hero, goes to pieces beneath a burden that it can neither support nor cast off.[28]

This is a view typical of the period, broadly similar to that of Coleridge (Raysor, 1.34–40; 2.223–6). But the novel is the portrait of an artist as a young man. Quite as much as Joyce with Stephen Dedalus, Goethe constantly, and to an unfixed degree, ironizes Wilhelm's feelings and ideas. He shows Wilhelm's immaturity and errors, which, even when sympathetic and noble, are often also impetuous and based in a partial view of his circumstances. And his views develop as he and the company work on the text and the production: different views are given at different points; earlier views are explicitly disavowed as Wilhelm moves towards a less character-based, prince-dominated view of the play. Even at the end of the novel, when it is evident that Wilhelm has absorbed a good deal from his experience and has in a sense served the 'apprenticeship' of the title (*Lehrjahre*, years of learning), he can hardly be taken as on his way to becoming the author. The formulation about the character of Hamlet in Book 4 is Wilhelm's, not Goethe's, and is only one element in a wider presentation of Wilhelm's and his company's interactions with the play.

Wilhelm's views of drama, which culminate in his discovery of Shakespeare, parallel those of German culture in the period. He begins under the influence of Gottsched, whose *German Theatre* (mainly translations of French neoclassical drama) was intended as a model for new writing in German. Wilhelm's first experiences of theatre are drawn from this (I.6); he studies and praises the greatest exemplar of its aesthetics, Racine; in this he is aligned with educated aristocratic taste (III.8). The Gottsched view is overthrown by Wilhelm's discovery of Shakespeare, which opens to him a new, intensely imaginative, quasi-magical world in which he becomes instantly absorbed (III.9). While Wilhelm's reactions are expressed in terms that convey his youthful impetuosity, this is genuine reading of a kind that that enables self-discovery and self-development. His enthusiasm for the ways in which his intuitions about life are given form, and for the power with which 'living nature' is realized in Shakespeare's work, are youthful versions of the characteristic *Sturm und Drang* views found in Herder's 'Shakespeare' and Goethe's birthday tribute (1771).[29] Investigating the human fullness of Shakespeare's work epitomizes for Wilhelm the fundamental aim of all his actions in the novel: the harmonious development of his whole personality.

How *Hamlet* works as part of that process is by a mixture of direct identification with the Prince and imaginative sympathy with elements of the play more obliquely present in Wilhelm's own make-up. The sudden death of his father, his feeling of disinheritance (the selling of his grandfather's art collection which indicates an alienating redirection of the family ethos), his disillusion and loss of a sense of purpose based on betrayal by a woman (his first love, Marianne): all these directly connect him with Hamlet. When Wilhelm insists that his reading of the character is drawn from attention to the whole text, with no reading in and no special emphases (IV.13), he fails, therefore, to understand what the novel shows: that the resonances of a text are shaped by what the reader brings to the reading. Then, though hopeful and optimistic himself, Wilhelm is drawn to the role of Hamlet out of a less directly experiential feeling for characters of extreme melancholy: his closest relationships in the novel are with his adopted 'family', the alienated outsiders, the apparently orphaned Mignon and the darkly enigmatic Harper. Both are figures who, like Hamlet, wish for oblivion from the pains of consciousness, which the Harper ultimately finds in suicide. For the Romantic generation these characters were two of the most resonant figures in the novel. Their mysteriously melancholy lyrics are among Goethe's most famous poems, and became well known beyond the novel in settings by his later preferred musical collaborator, Carl Friedrich Zelter, as well as by Schubert, Schumann, and Hugo Wolf. In his autobiography, *Poetry and Truth* (Parts I–III, 1811–14), Goethe recalls how in the period in which the novel is set (the 1760s and 1770s) his contemporaries were haunted by Hamlet's soliloquies, and how Hamlet-melancholy appeared to articulate the spirit of the times. The retrospective *Poetry and Truth* views this imaginative identification with sceptical humour ('they had seen no ghost, and had no royal father to avenge'),[30] but the novel combines irony with sympathy. The figures of Mignon and the Harper, and especially their melancholy and at times despairing lyrics, like Hamlet's soliloquies, transcend the contexts in which they arise and the situations to which they refer. While the novel's progress-and-resolution narrative might seem at odds with this, their profound melancholia gives the novel as a whole an affinity with *Hamlet* beyond that of character and situation.

Direct identification and oblique imaginative sympathy: Goethe shows both operative in the partial understanding of *Hamlet* which is nevertheless a real and significant aspect of Wilhelm's development. The company member who plays Ophelia, Aurelie, bears on this: she too models the strengths and problems of identification with a character, but without complementary imaginative extension beyond the self. Aurelie is keen to perform Ophelia because she feels a special affinity with the role: her life too has been crucially shaped by an experience of betrayal in love—an experience that will eventually lead to her death. The response of the audience within the novel implies that drawing on real experience makes Aurelie's performance emotionally vivid: the art–life interaction works. On the other hand, Aurelie's unwillingness to accept Ophelia's mad songs because she finds their sexual explicitness repellent implies a limitation in her insistently experiential relation to the character (IV.16). Life–art interaction works, but (Goethe implies) some complement, whether of more oblique imaginative sympathy or of greater critical distance, is also required.

Understanding character is far from Goethe's only concern. In line with Goethe's own advice to actors, the manager of Wilhelm's company insists on performance that conveys the music and structure of prose (IV.14) and the rhythms of verse (IV.19). Wilhelm's care with the portraits used in the closet scene (V.9) is a synecdoche for the importance of imagining stage effects that intensify feeling and meaning. The usual practice of contemporary German theatre in adapting Shakespeare for the stage is also elaborately presented. Defending the full text of *Hamlet* against the company manager's pragmatic desire to make cuts, Wilhelm uses the image of a tree (branches, twigs, leaves, buds) to convey an idea of organic unity distinct from the symmetries of neoclassical aesthetics. 'Everything is related to everything else'— and so the text cannot be cut (V.4). But while this may be the aesthetic ideal, Wilhelm also accepts that Shakespeare needs to be presented differently to different audiences and cultures, and eventually decides, like every German director of the period, that he can improve *Hamlet*. He works from the standard translation of the period in which the novel is set, by Christoph Martin Wieland,[31] restores Wieland's cuts, and begins his reworking on this basis. Set in immediate conflict with his declared conception of the organic unity of all the parts, Wilhelm's hubristic confidence in rewriting may be read with other ironies of his presentation, but the same fundamental approach to staging Shakespeare was endorsed by Goethe. As manager of the court theatre in Weimar from 1791 to 1817, Goethe mounted standard reworked texts of the play by Franz Heufeld and Friedrich Schröder, and in his final major statement about Shakespeare, 'Shakespeare und kein Ende' (Shakespeare once again [literally, 'without end'], 1815), he argued the validity, even necessity, of such adaptations.[32] Though the reader hears the grounds for and outline of Wilhelm's proposed rewritings (V.4), and despite a teasing offer from the narrator to provide the full adapted text (V.9), its details are never made clear— except that, unlike some adaptations of the period, and contrary to the company manager's wishes, Wilhelm refuses to keep Hamlet alive at the end (V.9). Though anathema to English literary critics, such rewritings (also normal on the English stage of the period) can have the virtue of opening up serious critical questions—as with Wilhelm's view that without giving the international context implied by the Fortinbras plot adequate onstage articulation, the play is in danger of being narrowed to a domestic tragedy (V.5). Nevertheless, there is a paradox here: boundless admiration recognizing extraordinary creative power; readiness to identify 'faults' and propose improvements. Even the extraordinary abilities of Goethe cannot save this confidence from the excoriation of Hazlitt and Lamb on rewritings that diminish and trivialize. The response of Coleridge ('self-suspicious ... when I seem to see an error of judgement in Shakespeare') is greatly to be preferred.[33] But the paradox is not purely contradiction. Even the vagaries of so great a writer as Goethe can be instructive. Wilhelm's company manager sees that the audience wishes the tragic hero to live. Wilhelm's objection is just: 'the whole play has crushed him to death' (V.9). It is the ground of Kent's acceptance of the death of Lear: 'he hates him / That would upon the wrack of this rough world / Stretch him out longer.' Nevertheless, the response that Kent rejects, the desire of Edgar in whatever context to preserve life, is a profoundly human feeling. It is the response registered in the outrage of Samuel Johnson, who was so distressed by the death of Cordelia that he avoided rereading the play. In tragedy the hero's death is a necessary outcome of the whole play, but it is also terrible. The extinguishing of an extraordinary consciousness that has registered profound and sympathetic responses to the pressures of agonizing events: however proper to the ethos of the play as a whole, in *Hamlet* this also properly remains painful. Pity and terror, the hero as surrogate sacrifice, or whatever other theory of tragedy is supposed is not accomplished by unresisting acquiescence. The need that the hero should die; the wish that the hero should live: both are present. The paradox that registers that— the rewritings Wilhelm rejects but Goethe endorsed—is much less an evasion than is equanimity bred of comfortable familiarity.

There are in *Wilhelm Meister* many dialogues about character, performance, and text—all suited to the character and situation of the speaker; many treated with indeterminate irony; none finally placed as valid or invalid either by contextual implication or by narrative commentary. Many perspectives are entertained: no single perspective is endorsed. Evaluation is left to the reader. In a discussion of the critique of *Hamlet* in *Wilhelm Meisters Lehrjahre*, Friedrich Schlegel distinguishes between normal activities of criticism and criticism as it is found in Goethe's novel, which he calls 'poetic': poetic criticism 'will add to the work, restore it, shape it afresh'. Goethe's fictional dialogues about *Hamlet* and its stage presentation are a special kind of critical work; but insofar as Schlegel is right that 'every great work . . . knows more than it says, and aspires to more than it knows',[34] their implications about the open, personal, and situated nature of interpretation are not only valid for 'poetic' criticism.

At the opposite pole from Goethe's open and indeterminate exploratory criticism in fiction are the magisterial *Lectures on Dramatic Art and Literature* (*Vorlesungen über dramatische Kunst und Literatur*) of August Wilhelm Schlegel (1767–1845). Delivered in Vienna in 1808 and published in 1809–11, these are the single most important work of Shakespeare reception in Romantic German culture.[35] While Coleridge's lectures of the same period remained in manuscript for a generation, and were not printed in full until the twentieth century, Schlegel's lectures were read throughout Europe. It is partly through Schlegel that Shakespeare came to occupy the towering position in European literature and the arts that he has ever since enjoyed. The lectures were immediately translated into French (1813), into English (1815), and thereafter into other European languages, with a pirated edition following in America. Their influence was extended by the advocacy of Germaine de Staël (*De l'Allemagne*, 1813; published in English in the same year). Coleridge read them (in German) and developed (or, on another view, plagiarized) their opposition between mechanical and organic form in his lectures of 1811–12. The English translation was reviewed by Hazlitt in one of the longest of his magazine articles (Howe, 16.57–99). 'The work is German', he began, indicting it of supposedly characteristic cultural failings, especially that it is 'mystical' (on Hazlitt's view the same objection would apply to Coleridge), and that it sacrificed flexibility and shades of opinion to a desire for system. Hazlitt's critique—in relation to Schlegel disputable—in relation to the subsequent history of Shakespeare criticism is prophetic: critics of a certain kind 'write, not because they are full of a subject, but because they think it is a subject upon which, with due pains and labour, something striking may be written'. Nevertheless he judged Schlegel's account 'by far the best . . . which has been given of the plays of that great genius by any writer, either among ourselves, or abroad' (Howe, 16.57, 59); and he incorporated extensive quotation from the lectures into the Preface to his *Characters of Shakespeare's Plays* (1817).[36] Shakespeare (with the Golden Age Spanish playwright Pedro Calderón de la Barca) is the climax of Schlegel's lectures, and the central exemplar of their fundamental purpose, requiring a new criticism and new models for Romantic drama— that is, drama reflecting and responsive to a contemporary world view. To demonstrate his supremacy, Shakespeare is set, as never before, in the context of European drama from its beginnings in Greece to its present in Germany. For Schlegel literary history, literary theory, and the detailed discussion of individual works are inseparable, and in this his comprehensiveness is new. While much of what he writes is applied Lessing, Herder, and Goethe, with Shakespeare they had written from intuitions derived from a limited number of works. With the multilingualism typical of German literati in his time (reading in Greek, Latin, French, Italian, English, and Spanish), Schlegel tests and develops these views over the widest possible range.

Schlegel's Shakespeare criticism did not begin with the Lectures of 1808. On the contrary, his work on what was to become the standard translation of Shakespeare into German (completed by Tieck and others) was largely carried out between 1797 and 1801.[37] Earlier criticism of Shakespeare had appeared in two extended essays over a decade before the Vienna lectures: 'Some Remarks on William Shakespeare occasioned by *Wilhelm Meister*' (1796; 'Etwas über William Shakespeare bei Gelegenheit *Wilhelm Meisters*') and 'On Shakespeare's *Romeo and Juliet*' (1797; 'Über Shakespeares *Romeo und Julia*') were both published in Friedrich Schiller's journal, *Die Horen* ('The Horae', goddesses of the seasons, beauty, and order)—a journal, like Schlegel's 1808 lectures, designed to convey advanced thinking about the arts to a wide educated public.[38] These essays were written when Schlegel was living in Jena, at first working in association with Schiller and soon thereafter with a group of writers and philosophers identified with the founding of the Romantic movement in Germany—Johann Gottlieb Fichte, Friedrich Schelling, Ludwig Tieck, Novalis (Friedrich von Hardenberg), and August Wilhelm's brother, Friedrich. Both essays raise central issues of Schlegel's Shakespeare criticism.

The essay prompted by *Wilhelm Meister* includes the claim that because in Germany Shakespeare is read so frequently, studied so deeply, loved so passionately, and admired with so much insight he is 'ganz unser', totally ours (*KS*, 1.99). The essay also discusses the need for a new translation of Shakespeare that would better embody all the qualities of his language: in pressing against the limits of current German such a translation (on which Schlegel was then beginning to work) would both extend the potential of German as a literary language and naturalize Shakespeare yet further as a German author. Schlegel argues that to convey Shakespeare's full meaning translation must render not just sense but form, rhythm, tone, and music; all that stems from Shakespeare's 'Mannigfaltigkeit', his diversity of styles—rhymed verse, blank verse, rhymed stanzas (songs), colloquial and high rhetorical prose, the multifarious kinds of language which are as much part of what the plays mean as narrative, character, and dramatic structure. For Schlegel Shakespeare is specifically a *poetic* dramatist. Translation that attempts to replicate 'expression and versification' is a form of critical exploration.[39] It must take account of the importance to expressivity of the 'music' of verse, including the freedom with which Shakespeare treats the rhythms of verse structure, his fluidity of syntax, and the interplay of structure and syntax, verse form and grammatical shapes. It is Schlegel's ability to balance all these often conflicting demands that made his translation (completed in the 1820s and 1830s by Ludwig Tieck and others) the classic translation in German.[40] Writing with the experience of one who had extensively practised the arts of translation, Schlegel's stress in the Vienna lectures on the importance of the acoustic qualities of poetry and prose to meaning is an authoritative critical guide for any reader, actor, or director, German or English, about how these are realized, whether in performance or in imagination.

The starting point of Schlegel's *Romeo and Juliet* essay is the idea, also fundamental to the 1808 Lectures, that Shakespeare has 'finer, more spiritual conceptions of dramatic art than we are accustomed to ascribe to him' (*KS*, 1.123)—in the Lectures, that he is 'not a blind and wildly luxuriant genius' but 'a profound artist' (358). Schlegel therefore repudiated the method endorsed by Goethe of staging Shakespeare in texts cut and adapted on the assumption that he compromised artistically to accommodate the lack of sophistication of his audience: 'Let no man venture to lay hand on Shakespeare's works thinking to improve anything essential: he will be certain to punish himself' (407).[41] Understanding the effects of *Romeo and Juliet*'s stylistic variety is essential: the 'harmonious miracle' of the work as a whole is founded on its central antithesis of love and hate, an antithesis echoed not only throughout the characters and narrative but also in the language, the high-flown poetic romance of the lovers contextualized and complemented by the bawdy comic prose of Mercutio and the Nurse. In its fullness and variety the play is 'at one and the same time enchantingly sweet and full of pain, pure and passionate, tender and impetuous, full of elegiac softness and shattering tragic power' (*KS*, 1.140). Elements that offended Goethe are for Schlegel supreme evidence of

Shakespeare as a conscious artist. Nothing of significance comes from the narrative source: everything of importance is Shakespeare's invention. Like God, the Romantic artist 'creates out of nothingness [*ex nihilo*]' ('aus Nichts', *KS*, 1.125).

Schlegel's Lectures are predicated on the historicism of Herder: judgement is contextual; the drama of the modern world is not to be understood in relation to criteria derived from ancient Greece. But Schlegel develops this to a more extended contrast between classical and what he calls 'Romantic' art and the world views they embody. World views, and a world-minded approach to them, are fundamental: the perspectives of criticism must be comprehensive. 'The true genius of criticism' requires not only (as with Winckelmann and Herder) an ability to adapt the mind to 'the peculiarities of other ages and nations': it requires 'universality of mind' (18). While the perspectives of the *Lectures* are purely European, in his eagerness to take large views Schlegel's future as the founder of Sanskrit studies in Europe and translator of the *Bhagavad Gita* is present in embryo. In Schlegel's large context Shakespeare appears as 'the origin and spirit of the romantic' (24), fundamental to which is Christianity, not in its beliefs and doctrines but its influence on sensibility: even among those who reject it, it is 'interwoven with all human feelings' (25). Schlegel propounds a fundamental ancient–modern distinction based on a contrast between Greek religion and Christianity, between poetry of enjoyment (this world as all sufficient) and poetry of desire (projection forward to a world beyond this). While each culture can engage with the whole gamut of human feelings—the ancient with tragedy, the modern with 'the liveliest joy' (27)—their characteristic underlying tones are antithetical; and that of the modern is melancholy, yearning which can never fully be satisfied. Schlegel's view of tragedy is based on this.

Rejecting classical tragedy as a model for contemporary writers, unlike Lessing and Herder, he also rejects classical criticism (Aristotle) as a model for contemporary readers. The aim of tragedy is not, as Aristotle had said, 'to purify the passions by pity and terror' (68—a discussion in which he specifically rejects the account of Aristotle given by Lessing in the *Hamburg Dramaturgy*). The aim of tragedy is much more general: it is to elevate us 'to the most dignified view of humanity' (152). Schlegel surveys a range of ways in which human beings are potentially subject to sufferings caused by fate or by chance, aware of which 'every heart which is not dead to feeling must be overpowered by an inexpressible melancholy.... This is the tragic tone of mind' (45). Tragedy is the representation of these materials in drama in such a way as to show 'violent revolutions in fortunes, either prostrating mental energies or calling forth the most heroic endurance' (45), that is, either Hamlet or Lear. It is a view that does not exclude the account of Aristotle as understood by Lessing, but it does not require it: it allows for a wider range of responses to a wider range of situations.

Schlegel develops these ideas in relation to Shakespeare and Romantic drama, beginning from an elaborated restatement of his fundamental contrast between classical (ancient) and Romantic (modern) art.

The ancient art and poetry rigorously separate things which are dissimilar; the romantic delights in indissoluble mixtures: all contrarieties; nature and art, poetry and prose, seriousness and mirth, recollection and anticipation, spirituality and sensuality, terrestrial and celestial, life and death, are by it blended together in the most intimate combination. [Classical art is] an harmonious promulgation...of a world submitted to a beautiful order....Romantic poetry...is the expression of the secret attraction to a chaos which lies concealed in the very bosom of the ordered universe, and is perpetually striving after new and marvellous births; the life-giving spirit of primal love broods here anew on the face of the waters. The former is more simple, clear, and like to nature in the self-existent perfection of her individual works; the latter, notwithstanding its fragmentary appearance, approaches more to the secret of the universe. For Conception can only comprise each object separately, but nothing in truth can ever exist separately and by itself; Feeling perceives all in all at one and the same time.   (342–3)

This is a magnificent statement of a Romantic view of the world—in which the Romantic artist (brooding on the face of the waters: Genesis 1:2) is the God of his creation. The individual accounts of Shakespeare plays that Schlegel elicits from this, however, are only in muted ways commensurate with its daring and complexity. While multiple perspectives can be seen as potentially brought into relation with one another from some fixed point which grounds them all, for Schlegel's associates—his brother Friedrich, Novalis, Karl Solger—the attraction to the secret central chaos that they called 'Romantic irony' was more fundamental than this. On the understanding that life and art are inherently incomplete, finite, fragmentary, perspectival, Romantic irony posits as a supremely valid aesthetic stance the ability to engage at one and the same time apparently opposite polarities: engagement at once subjective and objective; the disruptiveness of feeling and the stasis of contemplation; the commitment of love with the detachment of scepticism. Criticism can investigate this, but the rationalist conventions and totalitarian aspirations of normal critical discourse are at odds with its adequate embodiment, which is necessarily, like art, suggestive, open-ended, mythological, metaphorical—availing itself of all the modes of discourse of art. Literary criticism is (in its ideal forms, must be) a mode of writing creative like any other artistic discourse. This is all very well for writers for an esoteric journal (such as the Schlegels' *Athenaeum*, 1798–1800) with a readership willing to be puzzled. It is a possible condition for a creative lecturer (such as Coleridge) with an audience willing to accept 'immethodical rhapsodies' (Crabb Robinson) as a precondition of profound, albeit fragmentary, insight. It is scarcely a possible condition for a lecturer offering expository discourses to an immediate audience of broadly educated auditors and to a readership of a European literary public. This is not a context in which discourses opposed in their very manner to Enlightenment reason can operate. The lecturer speaks as it were *ex cathedra*. As August Wilhelm puts it himself in the *Athenäums-Fragmente*, 'No matter how good a lecture delivered from the height of the podium might be, the best of it is dissipated because one can't interrupt the speaker'—hence the fragment and the dialogue as typical forms of German Romantic criticism.[42] In his choice of platform August Wilhelm was committed to modes of critical discourse that, from a Romantic viewpoint, carried with them some simplifications. Complexities might appear, but in stabilized forms.

In *Henry V* the king is 'endowed with every chivalrous and kingly virtue' (428), and Schlegel also presents the alternative view: the war with France is designed to divert attention from his usurped title; his acceptance of ecclesiastical endorsement can be construed as self-interested; his supposedly romantic marriage has a political imperative; his grand military success is a prelude to national disaster. While all of this is 'intended for irony' (432), this irony is a straightforward opposition of alternative meanings. The account of *Henry VIII* spells this out. There is a respectful presentation which can be taken as favourable, supposedly contrived for Elizabeth I; and a contrary reading for 'the intelligent observer'—the king is a tyrant, haughty, revengeful, and voluptuous; his 'scruples of conscience [about his marriage to Katherine of Aragon] are no other than the beauty of Anne Boleyn' (439).[43] While Schlegel's conclusion about offering readers 'the right point of view' may mean only 'not the wrong point of view'—that is, not the standards of classical drama—nevertheless his specific readings, even when they admit the existence of alternative viewpoints, regularly stabilize the options.

While Schlegel devotes a separate lecture to each major grouping of Shakespeare's plays—comedies, tragedies, and histories—his most intense and imaginative engagement is with the history plays. They (not *The Faerie Queene*, not *Paradise Lost*) are the English national epic. The series of dramas 'furnishes examples of the political course of the world, applicable to all time' (420)—and specifically to his own. It is often said that Schlegel's lectures on the histories, given in Vienna in 1808, reflect the context of the Napoleonic Wars—the defeat of Austria at Austerlitz in 1806, and the evident danger that became the occupation of Vienna by Napoleon in May 1809 and the second defeat of Austria at Wagram in July of that year.[44] It is probable that for Schlegel's auditors references in his discussion of the history plays to 'tyranny', 'despotism', and 'usurpation' would have suggested this context; but the immediate situation was quite different from that of the plays, which are about not international but internecine conflicts. There is, however, an undoubted application to contemporary politics, and Schlegel points to it clearly: the mob in the French Revolution. Jack Cade's Rebellion shows 'the anarchical tumult of the people, [delineated] with such convincing truth, that one would believe [Shakespeare] was an eye-witness of many of the events of our age' (434). His account of 'fury giving birth to fury, vengeance to vengeance . . . when all the bonds of human society are violently torn asunder' (434) shows imaginative engagement intensified by a vivid sense of living relevance.

Schlegel's most interesting and unconventional reading, however—particularly given his understanding of modern European culture in terms of a fundamental melancholy—is of *Hamlet*. Where what might have been expected is a version of Hazlitt ('It is we who are Hamlet'),

or of Coleridge ('I have a smack of Hamlet myself, if I may say so')—
identification with a hero seen as epitomizing the spirit of the age—
Schlegel takes a surprisingly hostile view of the Prince. He begins from
a standard (moralizing) view of period: 'The whole is intended to show
that a calculating consideration, which exhausts all the relations and
possible consequences of a deed, must cripple the power of acting'
(404). The striking aspect of his account is his explicit dissent from
Goethe—by which he means from Goethe's persona, Wilhelm. While
admitting virtues in Hamlet, Schlegel largely stresses negative qualities: weakness of resolution (with no complementary view of this
'weakness' as the obverse of a profound copiousness), 'a natural inclin-
ation for crooked ways' ('er hat einen natürlichen Hang dazu, krumme
Wege zu gehen', *KS*, 6.170), harshness and insensibility towards
Ophelia, malicious joy in destroying enemies (who might be seen as
a fratricidal adulterer and a group of sycophants to power), and above
all 'no firm belief either in himself or in anything else' (405). All of
these views of Hamlet are arguable, and all in some sense part of the
character; but all can also be modified by contextualization, and it
would be more consistent with Schlegel's theoretical view of Romantic
art as multi-perspectival if he assumed less straightforward contexts of
judgement. His final judgement that the action of *Hamlet* is not
conducted in 'the solemn way requisite to convey to the world a
warning example of justice' (406) indicates some unreconstructed
residue from the nominally repudiated critical world of Samuel
Johnson.

'Man can give nothing to his fellow men but himself' (21); poetry is
'the fervid expression of our whole being' (50); poetry is 'the expression
of the secret attraction to a chaos which lies concealed in the very
bosom of the ordered universe' (342). Despite Hazlitt's view of a drive
towards the sclerosis of system, or the Romantic ironists' critique of a
loss of subtlety in crucial areas of Romantic theory,[45] there is underlying Schlegel's magisterial comprehensiveness a passionate Romantic
individualism. His willingness to think afresh on the basis of real
experience the relation between 'human nature and the essence of
tragic poetry' (235); his novel vision of the expressive powers of
Shakespeare's language, derived in part from his work as a translator;
the view of Shakespeare's artistry which enabled him to see beyond
clichés old and new; his vision of Shakespeare, especially in the

histories, as both for all time and his contemporary: all this is combined with literary history, critical theory, and specific judgements
derived from wide reading in ancient and modern languages. It is
evident why Schlegel's magisterial comprehensiveness was inter-
nationally persuasive. If the price of comprehensiveness was some
loss of shading, Schlegel recognized that true fullness was unspeak-
able: 'Ich weiß nicht, wo ich anfangen soll, weil ich gar nicht würde
aufhören können, wenn ich alles sagen wollte, was ich bei seinen
Werken empfunden und über sie gedacht habe' (*KS*, 6.114; I know
not where to begin, for I should never be able to end, were I to say all
that I have felt and thought about his works).

Friedrich Schlegel (1772–1829) wrote much less on Shakespeare
than his elder brother, and his impact on criticism in the Romantic
period was confined to an advanced-thinking intellectual coterie. But
Shakespeare was central to the formulation of Schlegel's ideas about
writing and their consequences for interpretation, and his ideas, particularly on multiple and unfixed meaning, have been more congenial
to modern and postmodern criticism than those of almost any other
writer of the Romantic period. So that, though Friedrich's ideas and
their presentation are considerably different from those of August
Wilhelm, Shakespeare again is crucial.

Schlegel began as a classicist. His aim was to do for Greek poetry
what Winckelmann had done for Greek art: establish the criteria for
its understanding on the basis of immersion in the whole culture from
which it sprang. This is the primary aim of *On the Study of Greek Poetry*
(completed in 1795; published in 1797).[46] The essay makes a distinction between classical poetry, which is 'beautiful' (perfection of form is
primary), and modern poetry, which is 'interesting' (subject matter
predominates over form); a difference also expressed as between the
'objective' (impersonal) and the 'characteristic' or 'mannered' (individual). Schlegel develops this opposition by a contrast of Sophocles and
Shakespeare as representative figures, associating their formal difference with a distinction of world view. Sophocles is 'aesthetic tragedy':
though the individual may be destroyed, the conflict of humankind
and Fate is resolved. Shakespeare is 'philosophic tragedy': the conflict
of humankind and Fate is unresolved. Contrary to the bias of his
polemic about the superiority of classical poetry, however, Schlegel
expresses unreserved admiration for Shakespeare. He is 'the pinnacle

of modern poetry'; 'of all artists...the one who most completely and accurately characterizes the spirit of modern poetry in general' (33). It is characteristic of Schlegel that he should allow this friction between argument and intuition. Despite the (temporary) bias of his aesthetic, Schlegel's intuitive sense of Shakespeare's greatness led him to a new understanding of the validity of the modern. Ultimately Shakespeare prompted a reshaping of his theory of literature which had a profound effect on subsequent German criticism, not only in the nineteenth century but also through Schlegel's late twentieth-century rediscovery as a precursor of postmodern criticism.[47]

On the Study of Greek Poetry develops Schlegel's account of Shakespeare through a view of *Hamlet*, 'one of the most important documents for the characterization of modern poetry' (32). The play exemplifies 'philosophic tragedy': it shows a discordant universe mirrored in the individual who is destroyed by it. While Schlegel praises the account of *Hamlet* in *Wilhelm Meister*, he also sees Goethe as failing to articulate the work's fundamental issue, the 'tragic world view, which rests upon the soul-piercing, meditative feeling about the eternally unresolvable dissonance of a human existence that has been utterly ruined' (115; 1822 revised text). There can be no resolution, no Aristotelian 'catharsis': like August Wilhelm, and contrary to Lessing and Herder, Schlegel rejects Aristotle's view of tragedy. Hamlet's alienation, personal in its specific causes, reveals a fundamental truth about the human situation—the indissoluble disharmony between the thinking and active forces. It has been suggested that, like Coleridge and Hazlitt, Schlegel felt a degree of identification with Hamlet, and did not like the self-dissonance this revealed.[48] However this may be, he came to see this condition as authentically modern rather than disabling, and the harmony revealed by Greek art and poetry, though admirable as an ideal, as not possible in contemporary circumstances—an understanding which led not only to a new theory of literature but to a new sense of the relation of an authentic self to modern life. Even in the essay the disharmony revealed in *Hamlet* is not understood as implying the kind of critique of Hamlet's character suggested by Goethe and Coleridge. Rather, it implies a different view of tragedy: 'the eternal *colossal dissonance* that ceaselessly separates humanity and fate' (33).

Schlegel soon saw that, while he continued to accept the essay's descriptions of classical and modern tragedy, those descriptions could be valued quite differently—as between a harmony (perfection) that is static and a disharmony (imperfection) that is nevertheless dynamic. Only a year after the essay's publication he described it as 'a mannered prose hymn to the objective quality in poetry'.[49] 'Mannered': its perspective is in part Romantic, albeit unconsciously so; its criteria situational, not fully sharing the perspectives it is designed to exalt; and 'the worst thing about it . . . is the complete lack of necessary irony'—it needed more overt flexibility of perspective. The issue of variety of perspectives, often identified as forms of irony, now became central to Schlegel's criticism, and in this too his view of Shakespeare played a major part.

After this attempt at coherence of overall argument which both simplified and fell apart, out of the epigrams and aphorisms of the French Revolution republican aristocrat Nicolas Chamfort Schlegel developed the form of the fragment, several hundred of which he published in three collections over the following three years (*Kritische [Lyceums-]Fragmente*, 1797; *Athenäums-Fragmente*, 1798; *Ideen*, 1800). These fragments stress paradox, multiple meaning, irony, and creative-expressive form in criticism, in their manner as in their substance, and are expressly paradoxical in their attitude to system: 'It's equally fatal for the mind to have a system and to have none. It will simply have to decide to combine the two' (*AF*, 53). Fullness of being is chaotic: logic and system are impositions. Criticism should present perception, not process. 'The main point is to know something and say something. To want to prove or even explain it is in most cases wholly unnecessary' (*AF*, 82). Supposed demonstrations by argument are evidence of intellectual timidity: they evade articulating perception in its bracing or perplexing nakedness. Perplexity being a form of wisdom, the mode of the fragments is often riddling. Schlegel takes over an indicative phrase from Lessing: they are *'fermenta cognitionis'* (*AF* 259); their aim is to provoke. While there are connections for the reader to discover or create, juxtapositions are also often chaotic. Even the implication of a unitary speaker is an illusion: the *Athenäums-Fragmente* include items by August Wilhelm Schlegel, the philosopher Friedrich Schleiermacher, and the poet-philosopher Novalis, but with no separate authorship assigned. It is also fundamental to the fragments' mode that 'a critical judgement of an artistic production has no civil rights in the realm of art if it isn't itself a work of art' (*LF*, 117). Being a critical work of art, a fragment is, like any other art work, open to multiple interpretations, and often requires the reader's active engagement for its elucidation—as in this conjunction of Spinoza and Shakespeare: 'Philosophers still admire Spinoza's consistency, just as the English only praise Shakespeare's truth' (*AF*, 301). Consistency, in Schlegel's view, is at best the least of Spinoza's virtues; but is perhaps not a virtue at all. Since for Schlegel all profound perception involves paradox and multiplicity, consistency is perhaps an index of small-mindedness, a 'virtue' admired by simpletons. As for praise of Shakespeare's 'truth', the value of this depends on the association with English criticism, which elsewhere Schlegel excoriates ('that harmoniously shaped artistic banality of which the greatest English critics are such classics', *LF*, 69; English criticism shows 'common sense... [in which] there isn't even the faintest trace of a feeling for poetry', *AF*, 389). When Schlegel himself praises Shakespeare's 'truth', it is with an opposite meaning: the truth of his tendency to chaos, and the subterfuges of art by which this is embodied—precisely the reverse of Johnsonian common sense. On this reading, the partial praise of *Athenäums-Fragment* 301 ('still admire... only praise') is ironic indictment. The true critic recognizes the reader as an active participant: 'he doesn't imagine [the reader] calm and dead, but alive and critical. . . . [He] enters with him into the sacred relationship of deepest symphilosophy or sympoetry' (*LF*, 112); 'sympoetry' (Schlegel's invented term)—the work, the critic, the reader together create meanings. There are valid forms of commentary 'where the text is only the point of departure or the non-self' (*LF*, 75), interacting with the selves (critic, reader) by whom living meaning is constructed. 'The finished view of a work of art is always a critical fact': that is, it records the best articulation the writer could achieve of a real meaning; but equally it is also an 'invitation to everybody to attempt to seize his own impression just as purely and to articulate it just as forcefully'.[50] As Schlegel puts it elsewhere, 'We cannot prove [aesthetic judgements], but we must legitimate ourselves with respect to them'.[51] Critical judgements can be demonstrated as they appear present in the work to a given reader, but this demonstrates only how they come into being for that reader, not their necessary presence for others. Every reader potentially sees afresh and constructs a work in his or her own terms. Ever paradoxical, however, Schlegel also espoused a more impersonal view, that the task of the critic is to present 'not just the impression a work has made yesterday or makes today on this or that person, but that it should always make on all educated people'.[52] Can this paradox be resolved? Schlegel would argue that, while the critic should aim for and even believe in the possibility of meanings inherent in the work, finally it must be recognized that all that the critic can articulate is meanings perceived by a particular reader. Shakespeare's peculiar openness to variety of interpretation epitomizes this fundamentally paradoxical condition of criticism.

The fragments which specifically comment on Shakespeare have two themes: Shakespeare's profound artfulness, and exemplification of the many forms of this by which meaning is left open to readerly creation and multiple construction. 'Should we criticize Shakespeare's works as art or as nature? . . . [a question] that can't be answered without the deepest consideration and the most erudite history of art' (*LF*, 121). Shakespeare's artistry is so concealed as to appear natural, and so in tune with the deepest conceptions of existence as to be drawn from nature, though all this nature can only be fully understood by knowledge working with 'the deepest consideration'. But erudition should not be overvalued: working alone, it is likely to degenerate into the trivialities of scholarship ('The origin of the Greek elegy, it is said, lies in the Lydian double flute. Won't it be looked for soon in the human spirit as well?', *AF*, 315). *Athenäums-Fragment* 253 sets out most fully Schlegel's view of Shakespeare's artistry:

In the nobler and more original sense of the word correct (Ger., *korrekt*) – meaning a conscious main and subordinate development of the inmost and most minute aspects of a work in line with the spirit of the whole – there probably is no modern poet more correct than Shakespeare. Similarly, he is also systematic as no other poet is: sometimes because of those antitheses which bring into picturesque contrast individuals, masses, even worlds; sometimes through musical symmetry on the same grand scale, through gigantic repetitions and refrains; often by a parody of the letter and an irony on the spirit of romantic drama; and always through the most sublime and complete individuality and the most variegated portrayal of the individuality, uniting all the degrees of poetry, from the most carnal imitation to the most spiritual characterization.

Shakespeare is 'correct', not in the trivial (French neoclassical) sense of conforming to supposed 'rules', but in the profound sense of enacting a design in which each part is related to the whole. Similarly, aesthetic relationships on every scale can be seen as 'systematic', but again not in any ordinary sense—relationships of similarity or contrast, of opposition direct (parody) or oblique (irony), echoes, but in another key or with different orchestration; the kind of Gothically symmetrical repetition that Schlegel elsewhere refers to as structural 'rhyme' (*LF*, 124: 'Shakespeare is a master of it'). And while, with the gamut of characterization, the extremes may be located in opposite types—the carnal Falstaff, the spiritual Hamlet—each also partakes profoundly of the other, as most obviously in the carnal-spiritual Othello or Cleopatra. This is the Coleridge and August Wilhelm Schlegel view of Shakespeare as a conscious artist, but with the variety of ways in which conscious art can be present made more explicit.

Of the fragments in which Shakespeare, though unnamed, is a major implied presence, the most important are among the most extended and the most discussed: *Lyceums-Fragment* 108, and *Athenäums-Fragmente* 116 and 121. *Athenäums-Fragment* 116, on the nature of Romantic poetry, of which elsewhere Shakespeare is named as the supreme exemplar, is a collection of paradoxes attempting to define the romantic by simultaneously pointing to, dissolving, and reaching beyond defining qualities. *Lyceums-Fragment* 108 and *Athenäums-Fragment* 121 are on irony, also for Schlegel a central Shakespearean quality, understood at its most extreme as 'an absolute synthesis of absolute antitheses', a crucial example of the paradoxes that suggest though they can never define Romanticism. The final sentences of *Athenäums-Fragment* 121 are positively a description of Schlegel's idea of Shakespeare: 'a mind ... that contains within itself simultaneously a plurality of minds and a whole system of persons, ... in whose inner being the universe which ... should germinate in every monad, has grown to fullness and maturity.'[53] Variety, multiplicity, universality: a proper sense of the scale and scope of great art is fundamental to appropriately capacious and adventurous thinking about meanings.

It is characteristic of Schlegel's approach to criticism that he should set out a view of Shakespearean fundamentals in terms of concepts to be applied by the reader in his or her own way, rather than the detailed working out of their application to particular examples. This is consistent with Schlegel's views that 'the primary condition of all understanding . . . is an intuition of the whole', and that the exploration of particular examples may too readily proceed 'to that degree of detail where all feeling ceases'.[54] These comments come in a history of criticism which concludes that, when the natural sensibility to art fostered by Greek culture disappeared, the methods used in criticism to revive this, or to substitute for its absence, were excessively conceptualized. Both issues—the fundamental role of intuition, and modes of criticism that recognize art's address to the whole person, emotional as well as intellectual—reflect the love and wonder that breathes through the tonal range of Schlegel's prose, his inventiveness with form, and his attitude to ideas.

In what amounts to a farewell to the fragments, the ultra-teasing 'On Incomprehensibility' ('Über die Unverständlichkeit', 1800), as part of an exposition of gradations of irony drawn from *Lyceums-Fragment* 108, Shakespeare appears as the master ironist: his 'infinitely many depths, subterfuges, and intentions . . . [are] in this respect [of containing multiple semi-concealed perspectives] as in so many others much more full of intentions than people usually think'.[55] Shakespeare magnificently exhibits the quality of great work, that it 'must never be entirely comprehensible' (*LF*, 20). It must, as Wallace Stevens puts it, 'resist the intelligence almost successfully'.[56] But Schlegel goes further than Stevens. A great work will resist the critical intelligence *finally*. For all that critics ever have written or will write, there will always be, beyond the articulation of emotional, imaginative, and intellectual subtlety, beauties and conceptions that cannot be represented in terms other than those of the work itself. For Schlegel, criticism as exemplified by his riddling and paradoxical fragments properly imitates this incommensurateness of art and intellect of which Shakespeare is a supreme exemplar.

Schlegel's last work concerned with Shakespeare, the *Dialogue on Poetry* (*Gespräch über die Poesie*, 1800), embodies in a new way his view of the properly creative form of criticism, and begins from a reaffirmation of the necessarily personal nature of criticism: '[Everyone] bears within him his own poetry which must and should remain his own as surely as he is himself, as surely as there is anything original in him. And he must not allow himself to be robbed of his own being, his innermost strength, by a criticism that wishes to purge and purify him into a stereotype' (53). This is basic to the whole work, enacted in its form as in its content. The diverse views expressed are valid for those who hold them: all arise from a feeling for the poetry of existence. Different views are juxtaposed, 'each of them capable of shedding new light upon the infinite spirit of poetry from an individual standpoint' (55). While it is open to interpretation whether the work's multiple voices are finally hierarchized, the form is undoubtedly perspectival. Each of the elaborated views is delivered in a different mode (lecture, speech, letter, essay), each is criticized by the group, and none elicits more than partial agreement, so that even the more apparently univocal aspects of the work, each illustrating a different model of critical discourse, are fragmented and destabilized by multi-voiced critique. The characters of the *Dialogue* are based loosely on members of the Schlegel circle, including the women whose significant roles are an index of the group's forward-looking culture. Dorothea Schlegel (wife of Friedrich, and daughter of Lessing's associate Moses Mendelssohn), in the *Dialogue* 'Camilla', was a novelist, essayist, anthologist, and translator, including of Germaine de Staël's *Corinne*. Caroline Schlegel (from 1796 to 1801 wife of August Wilhelm, and ironically the daughter of Hamann's butt in the *Aesthetica*, Johann David Michaelis), in the *Dialogue* 'Amalia', contributed to August Wilhelm's essay on *Romeo and Juliet* and worked with him on his translation of Shakespeare.[57]

Shakespeare is the climax of each of the *Dialogue*'s set discourses. 'Epochs of Literature' (mode of A. W. Schlegel) illustrates the contention that 'the discipline of art is its history' (60): as with Winckelmann and Herder, art is related to its cultural circumstances. With the exemplary ironist, Cervantes, Shakespeare is the apex of this historical survey, 'a romantic basis for the modern drama which is durable enough for ages to come' (72). The 'Talk on Mythology' (mode of the idealist philosopher Friedrich Schelling) counterpoints 'Epochs': modern literature requires an underlying world view (a mythology) giving coherence to the mutations of history and cultural change and relating these to contemporary realities. Here Shakespeare is admired for his 'artfully ordered confusion . . . symmetry of contradictions . . . perennial alternation of enthusiasm and irony', which are 'an indirect mythology'; the play of his art is a form of modern mythology, an 'imitation of the infinite play of the universe' (86, 89). The 'Letter about the Novel' (mode of Friedrich Schlegel himself) contrasts classical and romantic. The novel is considered not as it became in later nineteenth-century norms but as it was becoming in *Wilhelm Meister*—a mixture of epic (portrait of a whole society), dramatic (dialogues without authorial intervention), lyric (the poems of Mignon and the Harper), literary criticism (the discussion of the text, performance and meaning of *Hamlet*), and social philosophy (the society of the Tower). Etymologically Schlegel connected the novel (German, *der Roman*) with romance and the Romantic, and saw it as ultimately descended from the drama of Shakespeare ('the true foundation of the novel', 102).[58] The central issue, however, is not genre but ethos: 'that is romantic which presents a sentimental theme in a fantastic form' (98). The definition sacrifices fullness to the epigrammatic, but Schlegel expands: the sentimental is that in which feeling prevails, love as *eros* and *agape*, human and divine; a fantastic form encodes the mysterious (human) and the supernatural (numinous, quasi-divine). Again the presentation situates Shakespeare at its climax: drawing together the qualities that here define the Romantic, his work is 'the actual centre, the core of the Romantic imagination' (101). The 'Essay about different styles in Goethe's early and late works' (mode of Ludwig Tieck) again counterpoints 'Epochs': understanding the past is the basis for creating the future. Here too Shakespeare is central. With its hero explored and contextualized so as to draw out the essence of a fundamental human situation, *Wilhelm Meister* is Shakespearean, comparable to *Hamlet* in its 'conspicuous duplicity' (112). 'The critic is a reader who ruminates. Therefore he ought to have more than one stomach' (*LF*, 27). In the *Dialogue*, wherever the multiple perspectives alternating irony with enthusiasm turn, Shakespeare provides a model.

Schlegel's last fragment of his final collection, *Ideas*, is a tribute to Novalis, whom he saw as 'closest to me in these images of uncomprehended truth' (*Ideas*, 156). Central to that closeness was Novalis's idea of what it means to understand art: 'Only then do I show that I've understood an author: when I can act in his sense, when I can translate him and transform in diverse ways, without diminishing his individuality' (*AF*, 287). Written by Novalis, this is entirely characteristic of Schlegel. Understanding of art is active. It is not of the mind alone: it permeates the whole being. It is an ideal that criticism has rarely carried out so thoroughly as did Schlegel. His penultimate fragment conveys his hope of this modestly, and with an injunction to the reader:

Ich habe einige Ideen ausgesprochen, die aufs Zentrum deuten, ich habe die Morgenröte begrüsst nach meiner Ansicht, aus meinem Standpunkt. Wer den Weg kennt, tue desgleichen nach seiner Ansicht, aus seinem Standpunkt.

I have expressed a few ideas pointing towards the heart of things, and have greeted the dawn in my own way, from my own point of view. Let anyone who knows the road do likewise in his own way, from his own point of view.

(*Ideas*, 155)

The dawn Schlegel greeted was that of a characteristic modern German literature—the rising sun of which was Goethe; and, to support that literature, a characteristically German criticism—fundamental to which were the ideas he derived from Shakespeare.

Of the Schlegel circle, Ludwig Tieck (1773–1853) was the most successful as an imaginative writer. His tale of the supernatural *Der blonde Eckbert* (*Fair-haired Eckbert*, 1797) and his satire *Der gestiefelte Kater* (*Puss-in-Boots*, 1797) are classics of their kinds. Thomas Carlyle included two of Tieck's novellas in his representative collection of translations *German Romance* (1827), and a selection of Tieck's works have maintained a place in any survey of German Romantic prose ever since. His *Phantasus* (1812) suggested aspects of Wagner's *Tannhäuser* (1845), and Wagner discussed with him the libretto of *Lohengrin* (1850); his dramatic poem *Leben und Tod der heiligen Genoveva* (*Life and Death of Saint Genoveva*, 1800) was the basis of the libretto for Schumann's only opera (*Genoveva*, 1850); and the lyrics of his verse-and-prose romance *Liebesgeschichte der schönen Magelone und des Grafen Peter von Provence* (*Love Story of the beautiful Magelone and Count Peter of Provence*, 1797) provided the texts for Brahms's song cycle *Die schöne Magelone* (1869)—all of which indicates Tieck's currency among the following generation in Germany.

Shakespeare was the central preoccupation of his life. As he put it himself,

The centre of my love and understanding (*Erkenntnis*) is Shakespeare's spirit, to which, involuntarily, and often without knowing it, I refer everything. Everything, whatever I experience and learn, is bound up with him (*hat*

Zusammenhang mit ihm), my ideas as well as my nature. Everything explains him and he explains the other beings (*die anderen Wesen*), and so I study him continually.[59]

Tieck enacts the principle of Novalis: the real study of Shakespeare interacts with his whole being, is a crucial form of experience, central to how he feels (*meine Liebe*), how he thinks, to his whole nature. There is a modern point of view, characteristic of professionalized study, from which this kind of love and enthusiasm, the way in which Tieck sees Shakespeare as interpenetrating his whole existence, is regarded as 'bardolatry'. But Tieck was no sentimental enthusiast. He was a successful novelist and poet who combined imaginative freedom with attitudes to disciplined critical thinking of a scholar (with only the bizarre weakness of a will to believe in the authenticity of large parts of the Shakespeare apocrypha—plays which no scholar then or now accepts as by Shakespeare). Tieck did all he could to find out about Shakespeare's predecessors and contemporaries in the drama, about construction and staging in the Elizabethan theatre, and about Shakespeare's text, for which he studied the major English editors and commentators. He read the English critics of Shakespeare from Pope to Elizabeth Montagu: his disdain was therefore at least informed ('no English critic in print has yet understood him').[60] He came to England to read Shakespeareana not available in Germany and to see Shakespeare performed on the English stage—but thought no better of English theatre, encumbered by scenic realism, than of English criticism. As a dramaturge he engaged in a variety of theatrical experiments to test his critical views in performance. For Tieck the love and enthusiasm that emotionally disengaged professionalism attacks as 'bardolatry' was a necessary qualification for writing criticism at all: 'soll nur der Begeisterte, der ganz den Dichter in sich aufnehmen kann, als Kritiker sprechen' (only the enthusiastically inspired person, who can entirely take the poet into himself, should pronounce as a critic).[61]

Tieck's enthusiastic openness to Shakespeare was lifelong, and was intended to culminate in a study reflecting all its aspects, which he was never able to complete. The proposed book went through at least five draft plans between 1794 and 1815, and Tieck continued to make notes for it well beyond this. Its ambition, indicative of his view of

Shakespeare's supreme status, required setting its subject in large contexts—the contexts of his medieval predecessors, his playwright contemporaries, and European culture more widely. Though the book was not written, its main ideas appear scattered through Tieck's completed writings on Shakespeare—essays on Shakespeare and the supernatural ('Über Shakespeares Behandlung des Wunderbaren', 1793; published as a preface to his prose translation of *The Tempest*, 1795), and on the Boydell Gallery engravings ('Über die Kupferstiche nach der Shakespearschen Galerie in London, Briefe an einen Freund', 1794); published 'Letters on Shakespeare' (*Briefe über Shakespeare*, 1800); prefaces to translations of Shakespeare-related plays (*Das Alt-Englisches Theater*, two volumes, 1811, 1816; *Shakespeares Vorschule*, two volumes, 1823, 1829); essays on *Romeo and Juliet*, *Hamlet*, and other plays (collected in *Dramaturgische Blätter*, 1824–6); and annotations to the completion of A. W. Schlegel's translation, which he oversaw from 1825 to 1831.[62]

In his uncompleted projects, partly the effect of diverse and copious interests, Tieck is similar to Coleridge, whom he knew personally (they met twice, in 1806 and 1817), with whom he corresponded enthusiastically, and who judged his knowledge of Shakespeare and his contemporaries 'astonishing'.[63] He is unlike Coleridge, however, in that nobody in the following generation edited his uncompleted manuscripts. *Das Buch über Shakespeare* appeared only in 1920, a century after Tieck had in effect abandoned it, and in a culture that had so changed that, again unlike Coleridge, the time for absorbing and building from his criticism directly had passed.[64] Seen from the perspective of a further century, central elements of Tieck's ideas can be seen as both in advance of his contemporaries and of more than historical validity.

In 'Shakespeare's handling of the marvellous', like his German contemporaries Tieck stresses Shakespeare's artistic judgement, but unlike them his focus is the theatre, not the study. Shakespeare's judgement is theatrical as well as literary. Tieck draws an analogy between the illusion created by stage presentation, as sustained and modulated by Shakespeare, and the state of dreaming, in which waking ideas of truth and fiction are non-operative and the marvellous seems 'ordinary (*gewöhnlich*) and natural' (*KS*, 1.44). Each element of the play is understood in relation to this quasi-dreaming illusion. Ariel and Caliban are complementary non-human figures of air and earth; Ferdinand and Miranda more mimetic of human passions, but not with power or complexity that disrupt the magic of spirit and grotesque. As with the artfully judged transitions between mimesis and magic in *A Midsummer Night's Dream* (the integration of fairies and lovers, mythic figures and mechanicals), delicately judged modulations between different areas sustain the illusion of the whole. Everything is understood relationally, as it functions within the quasi-dream state created by performance.

In Tieck's review of the Boydell Gallery engravings staging is again a primary issue. The engravings, which he thought poor, reflect performance conventions inimical to the plays' properly imaginative theatrical realization—a view he would later develop in practical terms in his work as a theatre director and dramaturge. Properly imaginative illustration (whether drawn from the text or from a different kind of theatrical realization) raises the possibility that the artist might 'become as it were a commentator on the poet' (gleichsam der Kommentator des Dichters wird; *KS*, 1.16): creative interaction is seen as potentially a form of exploratory criticism.

In the *Letters about Shakespeare* the fiction of addressing a correspondent (first used in the essay on the Boydell engravings) allows Tieck to pose and answer his own questions, advise, cajole, address misunderstandings in a familiar style that draws the reader in through a dialogic approach. With *Romeo and Juliet* he argues an anti-Romantic view of the lovers, and especially of Romeo, of the kind implied (and most readers have thought discredited) in the play by Friar Lawrence. But, as elsewhere, Tieck's focus is not primarily character but the whole, the play's combination of youthful passion and tenderness with mortality, despair, and death, in which (contra Goethe) Mercutio's bawdy wit and extravagant fantasy and the Nurse's pragmatism are important counter-tones, ballast to the exaltation of the lovers, however that is viewed.

Tieck's opinion was always his own, as in his sympathetic and feminist-inclined interpretation of Lady Macbeth—the opposite of Samuel Johnson's 'merely detestable', and beyond even the more humanized portrayal by Sarah Siddons: the 'compunctious visitings of nature' to which she refers, and which surface in her sleepwalking, should be ever present and barely suppressed.[65] As often with Tieck, it is a view directed to the theatre—performable rather than strictly text-based. Similarly with Ophelia, he proposes a reading the words may bear but do not of themselves dictate. Assuming the then unusual view that (as he takes her mad songs to imply) Ophelia and Hamlet were lovers, he argues that much in the role usually acted innocently or coolly should be played with suppressed passion.[66] Like Lessing with his *fermenta cognitionis*, Tieck's aim in clarifying his own readings is 'to stimulate the reader to reflect'.[67] He practises what—though named by Coleridge ('practical criticism')—was rarely carried out so scrupulously before the twentieth century, for example, in his extended discussion of 'To be or not to be'. Another reader may not agree with how he construes individual words, fundamental drifts, or dramatic contexts; but more than with any other writer of the period Tieck shows how he reads in detail, and with an imaginative sense of interpretive possibilities that can be acted. The *Hamlet* essay's subtitle, 'on the way [the play] can be performed on stage', points his focus: meaning as realized in the theatre.

These writings are congruent with Tieck's most distinctive contribution to Shakespeare studies, practical work which emerges from his scholarship on the history of the theatre. Contrary to Goethe, Tieck argued that Shakespeare only appeared untheatrical in the conditions of early nineteenth-century theatre, which were wholly unlike those for which he wrote: elaborate scenery worked against the free function of imagination in realizing the poetry and contrary to the plays' dramatic movement; changes of setting slowed transitions, prevented fluid juxtapositions, and created a need for cuts. Tieck was cited as a predecessor by Rudolf Genée (1824–1914), the theorist of the late nineteenth-century experimental Munich court theatre, which stripped away spectacular effects and stressed the expressivity of the language, supported by the actor's body—movement, gesture, ensemble.[68] He was thus a leader, alone among his contemporaries in Germany (and largely elsewhere), in realizing that an understanding of Shakespeare's theatricality depended on a proper conception of the kind of theatre for which he wrote—a Romantic period predecessor of the bare-stage ideas of Peter Brook, on which much later twentieth-century and contemporary Shakespeare production is based.[69]

With Wagnerian ambition, and with the help of the theatrical architect Gottfried Semper, as dramaturge at the Hoftheater in

Dresden (1825–41) Tieck built a reconstruction of the Elizabethan Fortune Theatre in which he presented Shakespeare. While Tieck's precise understanding of the Fortune's structure was erroneous, his bare stage, focus on language, and fluid movement of dramatic sequence were accurate and revolutionary. This stage enabled the controlled prompting of the audience's imagination that he imagined in his criticism. It is an example, unique in the period, of the interaction of historical scholarship, critical ideas, and theatrical presentation.

Tieck's most famous production (not at the Dresden 'Fortune' but in Potsdam) was his 1843 staging of *A Midsummer Night's Dream*, for which he commissioned the best known of all Shakespearean scores.[70] While Mendelssohn's extensive incidental music can scarcely have facilitated the replication of Shakespeare's dramatic movement, its characterization of fairies, lovers, and mechanicals by melody, harmony, and orchestration does assist with another of Tieck's desiderata, bringing out and integrating the different levels of reality evoked. Mendelssohn's music helped Tieck to achieve what he saw as a Shakespearean effect, albeit by non-Shakespearean means. With costume designs drawn from different historical periods—classical (Theseus and Hippolyta), early modern (mechanicals), German folkish (the lovers), and fantastic (the fairies)—the production was a radical combination of the historically informed, critically sophisticated, and experimentally prescient. After he had abandoned the plan for a comprehensive critical book on Shakespeare, Tieck developed the principles he had begun to evolve fifty years earlier as a student through the unusual route of theatrical practice: imaginative reading, understanding the elements of a play relationally, as experienced in the kind of theatre for which the plays were written.

Coda: Hegel and Heine

Neither Georg Wilhelm Friedrich Hegel (1770–1831) nor Heinrich Heine (1797–1856) was a 'Romantic'; but both were of the Romantic Age, responsive to its pressures and its central concerns, even when they repudiated these. Both wrote notably on Shakespeare. Hegel's ideas on tragedy, in which Shakespeare is the central exemplar of the modern, are scattered through four books published between 1807 and

1837, two of them made up from lecture materials (notes and transcripts) edited by Hegel's students after his death. They have been widely regarded as some of the most notable writings on tragedy since Aristotle.[71] Heine's book on Shakespeare's heroines (*Shakespeares Mädchen und Frauen*, 1838; literally *Shakespeare's Maidens and Women*) was, with Anna Jameson's, among the first to discuss Shakespeare's presentation of women as a separate subject.[72] It was written two years after his *Die Romantische Schule* (1836, *The Romantic School*), which makes clear Heine's distance from the Schlegel group. *Die Romantische Schule* was one half of a two-part book, published first in French (Heine was living in Paris) with the overall title (from Germaine de Staël) *De l'Allemagne*. Though Heine described this as a continuation of de Staël, it was in part a repudiation of what he regarded as the politically reactionary (anti-Napoleonic, anti-liberal) and Christian-ascetic attitudes of the Schlegel group. Heine knew both Schlegel and Hegel through direct contact: he attended lectures by August Wilhelm while nominally studying Law at the University of Bonn in 1819/20, and lectures by Hegel at the University of Berlin in the early 1820s. Hegel was associated with the Schlegel group through Schelling, but his originality means that Hegel is more readily connected with what flowed from him—though how far this is of the left (in its contribution to Marxism) or (more obviously) conservative is debated: different elements of his wide-ranging ideas can be and have been adopted by philosophies with opposite tendencies. Hegel was a philosopher of aesthetics in part because his comprehensive metaphysics aimed to survey every major area of human activity with a world-minded perspective. But he also loved the arts, and his ideas on poetry and drama arise from his enthusiasms as well as a search for truth.

With tragedy Hegel implicitly rejected both Lessing's and Herder's endorsement of Aristotle and the alternatives adumbrated by August Wilhelm and Friedrich Schlegel, which were more intimations of an outlook than a developed theory. Hegel's theory is his own, and fundamental to it is a contrast between ancient and modern tragedy, in effect between Aeschylus and Sophocles (like the Schlegels, Hegel regards Euripides as already exhibiting features of decadence) and, 'above ... all [the moderns] ... at an almost unapproachable height', Shakespeare (*Aesthetics*, 1227).

Though Hegel's views on tragedy mark a new beginning, the first modern theory of tragedy, they were largely ignored by his contemporaries. They entered British and American criticism only in the twentieth century through the conduit of the great Shakespearean critic, A. C. Bradley.[73] They were developed in European criticism first by their transformations in Nietzsche (*The Birth of Tragedy*, 1872), but this too was largely ignored until the twentieth century. Nevertheless, Hegel was responding to his contemporaries, especially Schelling, who (with the poet Friedrich Hölderlin) was Hegel's roommate when they were students at the University of Tübingen; and he exemplified his views both from classical tragedy and from Shakespeare. Hegel's argument is that in classical tragedy the characters act out a clash of socially acknowledged ethical powers, whereas in modern (Renaissance) tragedy the characters act from 'the *subjectivity* of their heart and mind and the privacy of their own character' (*Aesthetics*, 1225): this distinction gives rise to a different kind of experience of tragedy in which conflict is interiorized, what is at stake is individual integrity, and the waste of the good is as a result more various, not moral good but any quality of serious human value. In the problematic case of Macbeth, for example, Bradley argues that this includes courage, conscience, and imagination.

The pattern of classical tragedy is clear, Hegel argues, in the *Antigone* of Sophocles: the claims of family (represented by Antigone) are opposed to the claims of the state (represented by Creon). Both are forms of the good, but in their conflict one must destroy the other. While Hegel admits that the great range of Shakespearean characters and situations makes generalization problematic, he argues nevertheless that, however much Shakespeare's characters present a predominant typical passion—jealousy in Othello, ambition in Macbeth—they always also remain individual: 'such an abstraction does not devour their more far-reaching individuality at all' (*Aesthetics*, 1227). The characters of classical tragedy are representative; the characters of Shakespearean tragedy are individual. Hegel enforces his ancient–modern contrast through an argument about the differences and similarities of the *Coephorae* of Aeschylus and *Hamlet*, both plays about a son's revenge for a murdered father. In the *Coephorae*, as in *Antigone*, there is a conflict between forms of the good: the son's duty to each parent in a situation where both have incurred some guilt

(Clytemnestra for her husband's murder; Agamemnon for their daughter's sacrifice). It may be argued that Hegel simplifies to produce a clear contrast with *Hamlet*—that the Christian context may be understood as giving Hamlet's ethical imperatives a complexity absent from those of Orestes; and that Gertrude is not, as Hegel claims, simply innocent: there is, as in Aeschylus, an issue of ethical violation (of the bonds of marriage).[74] While it is arguable, however, how far particular issues of interpretation might modify Hegel's perceived fundamental patterns of difference between ancient and modern tragedy, underlying this contrast is a greater emphasis on conflict than on suffering.

Hegel's concentration on what is new in his argument—his greater emphasis on conflict than on suffering—should not distract from other significant elements: though the part played by accident may be great (and Hegel stresses this), the agency of the one who suffers and the audience's sympathetic response to the sufferer remain important, as does the hero's response to suffering, whether that is a response of utter desolation or of endurance, or a response that leads to some greater understanding of the causes, including the sufferer's responsibility.

The final major element in Hegel's account of tragedy is a movement through conflict to reconciliation: 'finality lie[s] not in misfortune and suffering but in the satisfaction of the spirit.... [The audience can be] morally at peace: shattered by the fate of the heroes but reconciled fundamentally' (*Aesthetics*, 1215). What reconciliation may mean has been the subject of debate.[75] On some views of tragedy a sense of reconciliation is not present at all: as Friedrich Schlegel argues of *Hamlet*, the final perception is of a conflict that cannot be resolved, that is inherent in the nature of things. But for Hegel, however terrible death may be in relation to the central figure, there is another element: 'the woe that we feel is only a grievous reconciliation, an unhappy bliss in misfortune' (*Aesthetics*, 1232). The examples Hegel cites in relation to this evidently paradoxical formulation are *Hamlet* and *Romeo and Juliet*. With *Hamlet*, in Hegel's view, Hamlet wishes for death from the beginning of the play, before he knows about his father's murder; his melancholia is a 'disgust at all the affairs of life' (*Aesthetics*, 1231), and so death is for him (as he describes it to Horatio) a kind of 'felicity' (5.2.352). With *Romeo and Juliet* the issue is different: death for the lovers is unmitigated agony; but for the audience, in Hegel's view, the noble experience they exemplify, forced to its quintessence by the conditions that overwhelm it, is destroyed by malign chance, not (or at least not entirely) by its essential nature. Destroyed by conditions in part peculiar to their circumstances, the lovers exemplify a supreme beauty in the nature of things. Whether each of Shakespeare's tragedies can be construed in terms comparable to these is open to question, a question that arises in its most problematic form with *King Lear*. Could it be that, however crushing the catastrophe may be—Lear's death in utter misery at the death of the loved child whom his greatest wish was to save—for the audience, this is combined with a sense of the greatness of spirit of the love evinced by that misery? However it is construed precisely, Hegel proposes an experience of tragedy in which reconciliation as well as conflict is an essential element. It may be that Hegel's attempt to see tragedy in this new way suggests that in the major works of Shakespeare, at least in Hegel's terms, there is finally no common pattern.[76]

Heine's *Shakespeare's Maidens and Women* was written as text for a series of steel-plate engravings. Heine began with no great investment in the project: it was largely a commercial writing task for which he was amply paid. He wrote only about the tragedies—in which he included the histories and (because of Shylock) *The Merchant of Venice*; commentary on the comedies is confined to a selection of illustrative texts. Nevertheless, this allowed him to articulate a fundamental view of Shakespeare as well as a summary account of English, German, and French Shakespeare criticism, and to range freely beyond the nominal subject of the presentation of women on favourite topics, political and social, including Germany and the Jews.

If the Boydell illustrations show (as Heine puts it) 'the vapid weakness of English painters' (36), it would be difficult to find adjectives for the engravings from which Heine's text nominally begins. They are conceived within simpering conventions of the feminine as far removed from Shakespeare's range and vigour as it is possible to imagine. Even Queen Margaret is simpering. Heine laments the absence of Tamora's 'magnificent wickedness' (71). Goneril and Regan are not illustrated (and not discussed). Only Lady Macbeth stands out, conceived within the same conventions but their antithesis, a grotesque virago. Heine briefly praises but largely ignores the engravings his text is designed to sell and confines himself to comment on their subjects.

In Heine's account Shakespeare is heir to the profound and sophisticated imagination of Roman Catholic religion, to customs and beliefs inherited from pre-Reformation England. He lived, however, in the context of freedom of thought encouraged by Protestantism, but before Puritan antagonism to the old religion, and therefore to the spirit of poetry, had taken its iconoclastic grip. All of this Heine sees as one form of the larger historical antagonism between Athens and Jerusalem, the classical and the Hebraic, love of this life and ascetic hatred of that love. For Heine, Shakespeare lived in a culture in which the life-loving impulses of paganism, preserved within Roman Catholic eclecticism, were acted upon creatively by Protestant freedom of thought not yet hardened into intolerance. Shakespeare's 'every word breathes forth the happiest paganism': he is 'a believer in the creed of life' (32). Insofar as Shakespeare is made to sound like an ideal form of Heine himself, this is consistent with Heine's view of criticism. He mocks the view of historical writing that Leopold von Ranke (1795–1886) was beginning to establish, with its criteria of objectivity encapsulated in the slogan 'wie es eigentlich gewesen' (how it actually was): objectivity in history, and in literary criticism, is 'nothing but a tiresome lie' (19; *nichts als eine trockene* [arid] *Lüge*, 14): the historian 'writes unconsciously in the spirit of his own times' (19), and so does the literary critic—in the spirit of his times and of his personal predilections, witness (Heine argues) the Christian baptism conferred on Shakespeare by the pietistic criticism of Franz Horn. It may be, as has been argued, that Heine's apparently relaxed eclecticism of method is in reality the vehicle of a disciplined critical theory, according to which the critic's cultural position presents opportunities for seeing what the presuppositions of earlier readers have obscured; the history of how a work has been understood is part of its meaning; and understanding involves passional and imaginative engagement— which is why any claim to disinterested judgement is false.[77] But if such an underlying discipline of criticism is present, Heine's overt mode belies it—as when a diatribe against England, mercantilism, and the Industrial Revolution, with an extended quotation from the anti-clerical and republican historian Jules Michelet (1798–1874) on the supposed industrial imperatives underlying the Hundred Years

War (90–3), concludes by linking medieval battles to Waterloo ('the triumphs of Englishmen have always been a disgrace to humanity', 95). Similarly, when Heine recalls the wish of his friend Ludwig Börne that Shakespeare were alive to explain the nineteenth century to itself: Heine finds Shakespeare is alive in the nineteenth century, commenting implicitly on contemporary issues—aristocracy and republicanism, the oppressed and their oppressors, the interpretation of history, even, *avant la lettre*, on King Louis Philippe of France. The book's method is, to say the least, personal and eclectic. One bias of its perspectives is indicated only half-humorously by Heine's opening fiction of a Christian friend who was unable to reconcile himself to the Saviour being a Jew: Heine professes a similar problem with accepting that Shakespeare was English.

By way of preface and epilogue to his commentary on the engravings Heine surveys the recent European history of Shakespeare criticism. In England Samuel Johnson is a 'John Bull of erudition' (34), mocked not only for pedantry but also for his Ciceronian inflexibility of expression. Hazlitt is praised as the only English Shakespearean critic of any importance, 'pre-eminent in every way' (26). Anna Jameson is quoted at length and approvingly, but only on Portia (141–3); her larger claims about Shakespeare's presentation of women are not discussed. Garrick is regarded as a better commentator than the English critics, praised also because he taught Germans a more natural style of acting. In general (Heine follows Hazlitt) actors are the best commentators, though their perspective is limited: they see only the characters and their truth to nature, not the poetry and dramatic art of the plays. However, like August Wilhelm Schlegel and Wordsworth, Heine finds that 'Germans have entered into the mind of Shakespeare better than Englishmen' (26). He praises Lessing, Herder, and Goethe, but A. W. Schlegel and Tieck only with reservation: the prose of Eschenburg's translations is preferred to Schlegel for its exactness, vigour, and accurate reflection of Shakespeare's tonal variety. In following Shakespeare's metres, Schlegel produces 'colourless cleverness' (29). Tieck, once admirable, in his later writings shows only 'pedagogic gravity' (31); he is mocked particularly for his views of the 'good Lady Macbeth' (108). Heine's account of French criticism is even more equivocal: French admiration of Shakespeare is at bottom vitiated by the artificiality of French taste. The precise terms of failure in Hugo, Vigny, and Musset, different in tragedy and comedy, prompt some characteristic anti-Romantic mockery—but there is an exception: the statesman-historian François Guizot (1787–1874) is admired unreservedly for his understanding of the fundamental mode of Shakespearean comedy—not the realism of either Aristophanes or Molière, but romance. What Guizot analyses, Heine evokes: a dream of intermingled merriment and melancholy from which he awakes to sounds of universal laughter may be understood as both mocking the efforts of criticism and celebrating the joyous mystery of Shakespeare's comic vision.

Though Shakespeare's women are Heine's nominal subject, his comments on them are largely conventional. The most striking section of the book is, like much else in it, not about women at all: Jessica and Portia provide Heine with an opportunity to discuss Shylock. Heine was born to Jewish parents, had some experience of anti-Semitism as a student, and converted, perhaps reluctantly, to Lutheran Protestantism in his twenties, partly from a sense that discrimination against Jews would limit his access to European culture. The whole opposition of Christians and Jew in *The Merchant of Venice* prompts an extended and impassioned diatribe on popular hatred of the Jews in Germany, its historic causes, and their modern transformations. To an imaginative rhapsody about encountering in Venice the ghost of Shylock Heine attaches forebodings which with hindsight appear a foreshadowing of Nazism: 'What greater martyrdom may there not yet be in store for [the Jews]?... If ever Satan gain the upper hand, then the poor Jews will have to suffer a persecution which will outweigh any of their previous sufferings' (147–8).[78] This fiction about Shylock, recognized by the agonized voice expressing suffering for the loss of his daughter, is designed to induce an attitude to the character consistent with the arguments Heine presents about the play. He emphasizes the mercantile interest of Bassanio's and of Lorenzo's 'love', treats Jessica's elopement as a betrayal of her Jewish culture, and presents the play as fundamentally not only about Christians and Jews but about all oppressors and oppressed peoples. It is a reading prescient of post-Holocaust perspectives.

Shakespeare's presence in Heine's work is by no means confined to *Shakespeares Mädchen und Frauen*. In the mock epic *Atta Troll: ein Sommernachtstraum* (1841, its subtitle from Shakespeare) Shakespeare rides in the 'Wild Hunt' of German legend with other characters of myth, legend, and history damned by Puritans. In the French version of *Die Romantische Schule* Heine identifies three 'Ages of Man' which in Germany have characteristic literary models. For old age, Don Quixote: everything is illusory. For middle age, Faust: everything is worth trying. For youth, Hamlet: everything needs putting right—but why by me?[79] 'Germany is Hamlet' is Ferdinand Freiligrath's epigram (1844), meaning that pre-unification Germany was indecisive and politically paralysed. For Heine, this is German youth at least. But in *Die romantische Schule* Heine observes Hamlet not only in German culture. As with Hazlitt ('it is *we* who are Hamlet'), as with Coleridge ('I have a smack of Hamlet myself'), for Heine personally Hamlet is a model: not Hamlet the epitome of Romantic *Weltschmerz*, disabled by melancholia, but Hamlet the sardonic ironist hemmed in by surveillance and censorship, an active Hamlet who must confront power obliquely and with stratagems, but who is 'honest through and through'.[80] This Hamlet has more than a smack of Heine.

In Heine's memorial to the writer and political activist Ludwig Börne (1840) Shakespeare appears as the greatest writer after God— or, at least, after the writers of the Old Testament, who present 'the absolute spirit'. By comparison even Homer seems a product of art. Shakespeare lies between Homer and the Holy Spirit: 'With him, too, the word sometimes appears with that imposing nakedness which awes and moves us.... [He] is at once Jew and Greek; or rather, both elements, spiritualism and art, prevail and are reconciled in him, and unfold in higher unity.'[81] Where in the modern period the default position and readiest cliché is scepticism, in the Romantic period in Germany even Heine, the greatest of sceptical ironists, treats Shakespeare with admiration that borders on reverence.

4

France

Revolution and After

In France Shakespeare was not only not (as in Germany) 'our Shakespeare': he was distinctly not 'ours'. He was alien. He may have been a genius. He was also a barbarian, uneducated and wild. He was ignorant of the canons of art as these had been deduced from the drama of classical Greece and recreated in France, the leading civilization of modern Europe. This, at least, was the view of Voltaire, who introduced Shakespeare into French culture in these terms. In France, therefore, Romantic Shakespeare comes later: after Voltaire; after the Revolution; even, in its fullness, after the Restoration.

Unlike Germany, at the beginning of the Romantic period France had its own theatrical tradition, the most prestigious in Europe, national institutions supported by the court and regulated by the Académie française. And not only the verbal theatre of Corneille, Racine, and Molière, but also ballet and opera—Lully, Charpentier, Rameau; a sophisticated culture that made France the heir of the classical world and the apex of European civilization. As with Samuel Johnson in England, the often explicit background to discussion of Shakespeare in late eighteenth-century France is Voltaire (François-Marie Arouet, 1694–1778), above all his forcefully expressed critique of Shakespeare in the *Lettre à l'Académie française* (1776), its judgements based on principles adduced from Sophocles by Aristotle as these were understood in France, and on the practice of the great French classical dramatists, Pierre Corneille (1606–84) and Jean Racine (1639–99). As in Germany, and with some prompting from German criticism, from around 1800 the Romantic generation in France began to work out new aesthetics precisely by looking beyond this. Unlike in Germany, however, with its mixture of creative writers

Shakespeare and the Romantics. David Fuller, Oxford University Press (2021). © David Fuller.
DOI: 10.1093/oso/9780199679119.003.0004

and philosophical critics and historians, in France the main impetus for a new view of Shakespeare came primarily from creative artists—dramatists, novelists, and poets; but also the composer Hector Berlioz and the painters Eugène Delacroix and Théodore Chassériau, who were equally prominent in the Romantic 'Shakespearizing' of French culture.

Voltaire's immense prestige as a social and political commentator, historian, philosopher, dramatist, and above all forward-thinking advocate of intellectual freedom and religious toleration gave his view of Shakespeare an authority that commanded serious attention. His views were discussed—and combatted—by Lessing and Herder in Germany and by Elizabeth Montagu in England.[1] Even in France Voltaire was not without forceful opponents: in his *Du Théâtre* (1773) the playwright Louis-Sébastien Mercier (author of a celebrated utopian novel, *The Year 2440*) adumbrated many of the arguments of the Romantic generation: that real unity is unity of interest, which may be independent of the classical formula of time, place, and action; that comedy and tragedy can coexist because humour (laughing with), as distinct from wit (laughing at), can be allied to pathos; that it was a strength of Shakespeare's drama that it grew out of national traditions with an appeal to all classes and was not, like French classical drama, addressed only to an elite. But Voltaire's authority swept aside even the most articulate opposition.[2]

The background to Voltaire's emphatic denigration of Shakespeare in the *Lettre à l'Académie française* was—as he points out—the consequence of his own (as it had turned out, dangerous) release of Shakespeare's 'untutored' power into French culture by more positive comments in the 1720s and 1730s. By the 1770s Shakespeare was beginning to be taken into French culture beyond Voltaire's expectations—through the free 'translations' of Pierre-Antoine de la Place (1707–93), the adaptations of Jean-François Ducis (1733–1816), and the more exact translations of Pierre Le Tourneur (1737–88). La Place began his multivolume *Le Théâtre anglais* (1745–8) with four volumes including ten plays of Shakespeare rendered in a mixture of translation and summary, summaries of the rest of his oeuvre, and a preface setting out what became the central issues of debate in terms sympathetic to Shakespeare. The volumes were published in the same decade as Gottsched's *German Theatre*, arguing (against Shakespeare) for French aesthetics in German drama: though the national perspectives were different, the substance of debate about Shakespeare was European.

Ducis—an adaptor who could not read English and worked at first from the translations of La Place, later from those of Le Tourneur—produced acting versions of plays including *Hamlet*, *Romeo and Juliet*, and *King Lear* first staged between 1769 and 1792 and performed throughout the Romantic period. Le Tourneur published a twenty-volume prose translation of Shakespeare's works between 1776 and 1782, which remained the standard translation in French until it was displaced by that of Victor Hugo's son, François-Victor (18 volumes, 1859–66). If Le Tourneur tended, as Victor Hugo later complained, 'd'émousser' Shakespeare (to smooth him down), Ducis transformed him into a classical dramatist: his *Hamlet* (1769) is rewritten for a small cast, with onstage violence reduced (Hamlet does not die), and the unities observed (the action in one place, extended over a single day, and with no comic gravediggers).[3] Little of their originals was left in each of his Corneillian transformations, which diverged further from Shakespeare than the Dryden and Tate versions that Coleridge, Hazlitt, and Lamb deplored on the English stage. They were so remote from the spirit and letter of Shakespeare as to be Shakespeare in name only. Nevertheless, Voltaire saw Ducis not as mangling English drama but as corrupting French taste, and the success of his *Hamlet* adaptation, and more immediately of Le Tourneur's first volume with its bold and unequivocally laudatory preface, prompted his attack on Shakespeare in *Lettre à l'Académie*, read in 1776 and published in French and English the following year.

From his earliest comments Voltaire showed a divided attitude of admiration for Shakespeare's genius and power and (to put mildly what Voltaire often expressed extremely) depreciation of his supposed lack of art. His first published view sets the pattern: '*Shakespear* boasted a strong, fruitful Genius: He was natural and sublime, but had not so much as a single Spark of good Taste, or knew one Rule of the Drama'.[4] This supposed dichotomy, between gifts bestowed by Nature and taste acquired by education, is a division typical not only of Voltaire but also of the culture which his long life straddles, from the Ancien Régime to the eve of the Revolution. From the 1760s, moreover, as England began to supersede France as the major

European world power of the age, criticism of Shakespeare became for Voltaire a patriotic duty. The consistent elements of his critique are Shakespeare's supposed lack of dramatic economy (contrasted with the concentration of Racine), his incoherent melange of tone and genre (comedy in tragedy), and (the kind of criticism also made by Samuel Johnson and other neoclassical critics in England) the often supposedly 'low' colloquialism of his language, whether judged 'obscene' or just mundane—all aspects of Shakespeare's work that came to be quite differently valued by Romantic criticism: as breadth of vision, variety of perspective, and language more vigorous and socially inclusive than the constriction-supposed-refinement of art.

In the *Lettre à l'Académie* Voltaire is seldom less than an effective polemicist: if Shakespeare is the genius Le Tourneur claims, he argues, why does his translation bowdlerize? Iago's obscenities, the lewd jokes of the Porter in *Macbeth*, the mixture of cobblers and Senators in *Julius Caesar*: why is all this, Voltaire asks, softened or omitted in the translation? When Le Tourneur defends the gravediggers in *Hamlet* (omitted, as Voltaire observes, by Garrick) on the same grounds as the cobblers in *Julius Caesar*, Voltaire invokes the unities, those 'judicious rules laid down by the Greeks'. He cites the opening scene of *Romeo and Juliet* for its indecent wordplay; the opening of *King Lear* with its frank discussion of the conception of the bastard Edmund; or, more simply (a Voltaire favourite, from *Hamlet*), 'not a mouse stirring'. Voltaire sees his case as proven when he invokes this and similar examples of ordinary language inappropriate to tragedy. He makes a straightforward separation between the language of life and the language of art: the language spoken in the streets cannot be spoken, even by characters from the streets, on the stage. He assumes an elite theatre of educated taste separated by canons of art from the world in which it is based, and criteria of aesthetic judgement that are permanent. The relativist in religion and advanced thinker in so many other areas is a non-relativist conservative in art. As Herder in Germany was arguing that cultural products and cultural values are dependent on their time and place, Voltaire argued that the criteria of educated taste are universal, the same in all nations and ages. In drama they are exemplified by Racine. That Shakespeare's breadth of human sympathy relates to his writing for a popular theatre nowhere enters his view— rather the reverse: for Voltaire, what he presents as Shakespeare's gross artistic faults result from his need to appeal to an uneducated audience. Voltaire epitomizes the view the Romantic generation overthrew and reversed.

But overthrow and reversal were far from immediate. The dominant view in the next generation remained Voltaire's, albeit with a more positive bias. This is the view from which Germaine de Staël (1766–1817) and François-René de Chateaubriand (1768–1848) at least begin. Anne Louise Germaine Necker—by her marriage to a Swedish diplomat Baroness de Staël-Holstein, and commonly known to her contemporaries as Madame de Staël—was the daughter of the finance minister of Louis XVI, Jacques Necker. A novelist (*Delphine*, 1802; *Corinne, ou l'Italie*, 1807), commentator on politics and society (*Considerations on the Principal Events of the French Revolution*, 1817), and champion of the rights of women, she lived at dangerously close quarters to the Revolution and engaged in prominent conflicts with Napoleon. Noted for her brilliant conversation, she hosted an intellectual salon and mixed with major literary and cultural figures of the period in France, Germany, and England. She is a central figure of European Romanticism. She wrote two encyclopaedic works of cultural commentary, *De la littérature* (1800; English translation, 1803) and *De l'Allemagne* (completed in 1810, but first published in English in 1813). In both books Shakespeare is an important presence.

De la littérature was written in the aftermath of the Revolution, the horrors of the Terror, and the Revolution's disappointment of the ideals that were its hope. Though the title is usually abbreviated, this gives a misleading impression.[5] The full title is indicative—*De la littérature considérée dans ses rapports avec les institutions sociales*: social institutions and cultural assumptions are consistently central to the discussion. The book's subject is 'the influence of religion, manners and laws on literature, and . . . the influence of literature on religion, manners, and laws' (13)—a programme derived in part from Herder, as was a distinction between southern and northern European cultures. In de Staël's account the Germanic north is melancholy, introspective, independent, values liberty, shows a greater respect for women, and, Protestant in religion since the Reformation, is philosophical, not superstitious. It is not to be judged by criteria derived from cultures of the south.

On this basis de Staël aimed to look beyond the wreck of ideals and the turmoil of immediate post-revolutionary circumstances to see how all forms of writing interact with and contribute to society, to take large but also carefully grounded views of 'the power of literature over . . . the primary motives of mankind' (14). The Revolution was 'a new era for the intellectual world' (205), the era of liberty and political equality. The possible forms of this new world were her subject—including its new literary forms. 'Political equality will give a new character to our tragedies' (251): Racine wrote for an aristocratic elite, Shakespeare for all classes. His work, with its wide social appeal, is a model for the new age.[6] Tragedy must portray not heroic exceptions but emotions 'which touch our entire being by their analogy with human nature' (251). In this Shakespeare is uniquely gifted: he can elicit pity for unheroic suffering, for mental agonies, and even for madness caused by the passions of love and death common to all (141, 147–8). But these views are not worked through in detail. A distinction between the 'rules' of art, conventions with which genius can dispense, and 'taste', which, derived from Nature, has a permanent validity beyond convention, is ground for a moderate apologia, but Shakespeare can still be indicted by a range of mutedly neoclassical criteria (144–7). His appeal to all classes can also be seen as submission to gross judgements; his presentation of violence on stage as destructive of theatrical illusion; his mixture of modes and tones are deplored by the standards if not in the manner of Voltaire. Though de Staël offers some bases for new understandings of Shakespeare, her comments on particular plays—drawing together the 'weak minds' of Henry VI and King Lear (140); judging that *Macbeth* would have been 'more admirable if its grand effects were produced without the aid of the marvellous' (142); seeing Falstaff as a popular caricature without truth to life (152)—indicate that even the more forward-looking of her general principles are not absorbed into her particular judgements. Nevertheless, *De la littérature* adumbrates a more full-blooded Romanticism.

Il serait impossible de créer comme eux [les anciens] dans leur genre. Pour les égaler, il ne faut point s'attacher à suivre leurs traces; ils ont moisonné dans leur champ; il vaut mieux défricher le nôtre.   (255)

It would be impossible to create like the ancients in their mode. To equal them it is not necessary to stick to following in their tracks; they have harvested in their field; it is better to break new ground in our own.

'Il vaut mieux défricher le nôtre': it is a slogan for the future.

The future—with its new view of Shakespeare—is more obviously present in *De l'Allemagne*, the preface to which makes clear that culture wars are real conflicts.[7] The book was printed and ready for publication in 1810 when Napoleon's Minister of Police, Jean-Marie Savary, ordered that the copies be pulped, the plates destroyed, the manuscript confiscated, and de Staël exiled. France was at war with Germany and Germanic (including English) culture: the book was (in Savary's words) 'not French'. Never shy of controversy, and seeing it as a mark of honour to be subject to Napoleonic censorship, when the book was published (1813 in English; 1814 in French) de Staël printed Savary's letter in her preface. The accusation that her work was 'not French' she refuted: her (qualified) praise of Germany was to help France join the modern intellectual and artistic world, to suggest directions that would preserve what was valuable in French culture and traditions in ways corresponding to the new world ushered in by the Revolution.

Shakespeare appears as, in the widest sense, a 'Germanic' writer, and a major figure of that new world. His work had been discussed as a model for modern writing from Lessing, Herder, and Goethe to the brothers Schlegel, all of whom de Staël considers. From 1804 August Wilhelm Schlegel had become a close personal associate. Though his antagonism to French neoclassicism is tempered in de Staël's presentation by her love of Racine, his Vienna lectures of 1809–11, to which Shakespeare is central, are praised as 'seeking to bring creative genius alive again', a kind of appreciative criticism that she sees as scarcely less than a mode of genius in itself (2.71, 72).[8] Nevertheless, how much his or any other German Shakespeare criticism really affected de Staël's views is open to question. Many of her judgements remain quasi-Voltairean ('Shakespeare is sometimes less than art, sometimes beyond all art', 1.257). *De l'Allemagne* does, however, reverse the judgement of *De la littérature* on the mixed mode of Shakespearean tragedy intolerable to neoclassicism: the interaction of pathos and comedy is now seen as able to heighten the power of the whole.[9] But finally de Staël's view is congruent with the latter-day classicism of Goethe. Shakespeare did not write for the theatre. His drama is too philosophical, his understanding of human nature too complex and subtle for the medium: he demands to be read and studied.[10]

As in *De la littérature*, de Staël is divided. The total effect of her sometimes equivocal views is, however, to signal possibilities beyond her residual neoclassicism.

La littérature romantique est la seule qui soit susceptible encore d'être perfectionnée, parce qu'ayant ses racines dans notre proper sol, elle est la seule qui puisse croître et se vivifier de nouveau; elle exprime notre religion; elle rappelle notre histoire.   (1.214)

Romantic literature is the only kind that is capable of being brought to perfection, because having its roots in our own soil, it is the only kind that can grow and bring new life; it expresses our religion; it recalls our history.

This might seem a Schlegelian aphorism comparable to *Athenäums-Fragment* 116 ('Romantic poetry is a universal progressive poetry'), but de Staël's meaning is more general. 'La littérature romantique' (it is clear in context) means writing drawing on ethics and sensibility that stem from Christianity, not (as did neoclassicism) from paganism. Nevertheless, it is an affirmation that the future must be different from the past, and different in a specific way: not transplanted from the south but indigenous to the north. The next generation decided more unequivocally that this meant, in place of Racine, Shakespeare.

François-René de Chateaubriand was, like de Staël, a well-known public figure—a novelist, and social and political commentator. He was also an active politician, employed both by Napoleon and in Restoration administrations, though with no simple doctrinaire allegiance but, rather, attempting to draw together opposed royalist and liberal factions. His most famous fiction, the novella of sensibility *René* (1802), like Goethe's *Werther* and Byron's *Childe Harold's Pilgrimage*, enjoyed a great vogue among Romantic-period readers and made isolation, melancholy, and *mal du siècle* fashionable. *Génie du christianisme* (1802), a defence of Catholicism against Enlightenment and Revolutionary atheism, was widely influential in its views of the power of religious art, the beauty of nature as a source of religious feeling, and the poetry and drama of Catholic liturgy. Though the book discusses dogma and belief, its stress on the arts, nature, and feeling made it a central text for early French Romanticism. Years spent in England as an aristocratic émigré from the Revolution meant that Chateaubriand read English fluently and had a good understanding of English history and culture. As a commentator on Shakespeare he seems, therefore, well qualified by knowledge and imaginative predisposition, but his views belong largely to the eighteenth century.

In 'Shakespere ou Shakespeare' (1801; the spellings imply 'the French view or the English?') Samuel Johnson's answer to Voltaire ('the petty cavils of petty minds') is rejected, and Shakespeare is criticized for failures of art in throwing together unrelated materials, not observing the unities, and mixing polished and colloquial language.[11] In the much later book *Essai sur la littérature anglaise* (1836), a history of English literature in its cultural contexts from the earliest records to Byron and Scott, in an extended discussion of Shakespeare Chateaubriand admits some inadequacies of his former view ('I judged Shakespeare through classical spectacles . . . but a microscope is not capable of seeing a work as a whole'). Nevertheless, the central arguments of the *Essai* are reprinted from 1801 with only minor changes.[12] Fundamentally his view remains the same: Shakespeare was a natural genius, but subject to the gross faults of his age. The Romantic views prevailing by 1836 are, he argues, an exchange of errors, excessive admiration of what was formerly excessively deplored. Comment on isolated passages from a range of plays shows him responsive to Shakespeare's poetry and powers of portraying intense and profound feeling, but he deduces from this no critical principles beyond a positive-slanted inflection of the beauties-and-faults, genius-without-taste arguments of neoclassicism. The book shows the degree to which, in tune with conservative educated taste in France, the views of Voltaire continued to influence the perception of Shakespeare way beyond the cultural moment of their origin.

The final preparation for the triumph of Romantic views of Shakespeare in France was a revision of Le Tourneur's translation in 1821 by the politician and historian François Guizot (1787–1874). While Guizot's position as a major political figure lay in the future—in opposition to Charles X, and in government, eventually as First Minister, under Louis Philippe—he was already a significant figure in French politics, held a chair of History at the Sorbonne, and had translated Gibbon's *Decline and Fall*. The grandly published multi-volume revision of Le Tourneur, with introductions and annotation, that appeared under his name was a major literary event and a clear sign of Shakespeare's new status in French culture. Guizot was responsible for six tragedies (but not *Hamlet*), all ten histories, and three comedies. Most of the rest of the translation was revised by Amédée Pichot, already well known as the translator of Byron. The revision was serious and thorough, and included translating where, out of deference to neoclassical proprieties, Le Tourneur had paraphrased. Guizot wrote an extensive overall introduction and prefaces to individual plays.

Guizot's introduction and prefaces offer some of the best French criticism of Shakespeare before the successes in drama of the Romantic Movement. Following Herder, and like de Staël, Guizot assumes that literary forms are related to their social context, that 'dramatic art has relative rules which flow from the changeful nature of society'.[13] His is a more thoroughly historicized attempt than de Staël's to understand the forms of Shakespeare's plays in relation to their social context in the history of English society and institutions, and their literary backgrounds in medieval and Tudor drama. He prefigures Stendhal in seeing French society of the post-Revolution and post-Restoration period as an accelerated analogy to English society of the Elizabethan age, with its bases in the civil wars of the fifteenth century which brought the Tudor dynasty to power, and in the religious upheavals of the sixteenth century which the Elizabethan Settlement brought to a close. For Guizot, 'the principle of common deliberation upon matters of common interest, which is the foundation of all liberty, prevailed in all the institutions of England, and presided over all the customs of the country' (44). While this view can be criticized as a partly mythic idea of Elizabethan society as a whole, its implications for Elizabethan theatre are less questionable, and as a historical view it also had a contemporary political purpose. Guizot is writing in 1821 with an eye to the cohesion he saw as lacking in French society, disrupted in opposite directions by the Revolution and the Restoration, and with a view of theatre, the most popular of literary forms, as potentially a social force—as was acknowledged by the French state in its policing of what could be presented.[14] Romanticism in France was a political as well as an aesthetic movement, the Académie française a conservative instrument, designed to keep things as they had been culturally in the context of the Bourbon Restoration returning things to as they had been politically. For Guizot, Shakespeare's theatre comes from a particular state of society. It also feeds into a particular state of society. The liberal political agenda of Victor Hugo and his translator son François-Victor is already embryonically present in Guizot's Shakespeare, albeit in a more moderate form. For Guizot Shakespeare offered a model of drama appropriate to contemporary France—socially comprehensive, with bases in popular feeling and taste, modelling liberties which are complex but not chaotic, freedoms which are consistent with order.

In overturning the view of Voltaire, Guizot goes further than de Staël. He begins even-handedly, arguing that Voltaire and Shakespeare represent rival dramatic systems between which he will not attempt to judge, but the introduction is eventually more committed: 'the classical system had its origins in the life of its time; that time has passed' (181); 'Shakespeare offers to us a more fruitful [*plus féconde*] and a vaster system' (177). Unlike de Staël, but like the English and German Romantics, Guizot presents Shakespeare as a conscious artist, but working on principles wholly different from those of neoclassicism. The fundamental issue is unity of impression, 'that prime secret of dramatic art, [which] was the soul of Shakespeare's conceptions' (135). Unity of impression may arise from diversity of materials—even must arise from diversity if the drama is to be an adequate picture of great actions. Guizot often selects his exemplifications of this principle from the materials that for Voltaire showed Shakespeare's supposed lack of art. His discussions are brilliantly suggestive, as with his accounts of the gravediggers in *Hamlet* and the Porter in *Macbeth*—both occasions where he presents low comedy precisely as intensifying tragedy; or his account of the opening of *Julius Caesar*, with its plebeian characters prefiguring so much that bears on both parties of the main political action.[15] In each case fundamental coherence is shown to be given a more profound inflection by superficial heterogeneity.

Advanced-thinking as he was, however, Guizot retains elements of Voltaire. Shakespeare's greatest tragedies are, for him, those nearest to the neoclassical—*Othello*, in which the main action takes place (at least in the short version of its double time scheme) within a day; *Macbeth*, in which, though the action may be calculated as encompassing an extended period, Shakespeare artfully creates an impression of each stage following immediately from its predecessor. The entirely un-neoclassical *Hamlet*, however, 'perhaps contains the most remarkable examples of its author's . . . most glaring defects' (200), foremost among them 'a fantastic mixture of coarseness and refinement of language' (212). 'En fait de génie', he concludes, 'Shakespeare n'a peut-être point de rivaux; dans les hautes et pures régions de l'art, il ne saurait être modèle' (211: In point of genius Shakespeare has perhaps no rivals; in the high and pure regions of art, he cannot be taken as a model). In spite of Guizot's often brilliant perception of Shakespeare's art that, even as it apparently defies the canons of art, focuses a protean variety of materials and modes to create the all-important unity of impression, with the most testing case, the diversity of *Hamlet*, he falls back on the Voltairean view, albeit with the positive inflection of de Staël. Thinking beyond the neoclassical taste within which they were educated, and even as they felt the power of Shakespeare in the theatre and in reading, de Staël and Guizot could not entirely escape the narrow aesthetic principles of the culture within which they were brought up. What was required was the deep scepticism, learned conterminously with his education, of the great novelist Stendhal: from early youth his passionately rebellious nature identified the literary-critical principles taught by his education as instruction in falsehood.

Stendhal (Marie-Henri Beyle, 1783–1842) sets the keynote for a new beginning: 'I adored Shakespeare and felt an insurmountable repugnance for Voltaire and Mme de Staël'.[16] Adoration of Shakespeare and rejection of what he despised as the 'puerile' views of Voltaire (21.143) are a constant subject in his writing. Stendhal began reading Shakespeare with love and wonder as an adolescent. His account of his childhood and youth, *The Life of Henry Brulard*, records reading the complete Le Tourneur translation volume by volume when he was twelve or thirteen. He read Le Tourneur repeatedly in his late teens ('I know not how many times', 21.132). He also read Shakespeare in English, and probably knew the full range of Shakespeare's work better than most of his European contemporaries, whether in France or in Germany. His admiration of Shakespeare he described as 'heartfelt, passionate' (*sentie, passionnée*, 21.295). In *Souvenirs d'Égotisme* he recorded considering for his tombstone the inscription, 'This soul loved Cimarosa, Mozart, and Shakespeare'—a crescendo of which Shakespeare is the climax (36.72). It was, he believed, this love of Shakespeare—'that inner doctrine founded on the true pleasure, the deep, considered pleasure amounting to happiness' (21.295)—that saved him from the neoclassical taste offered by his education. Shakespeare appears in the autobiography as a salvific figure, fundamental not only to Stendhal's aesthetic but to his whole being: 'Je crus renaître en le lisant' (As I read him I felt reborn).[17]

The stimulus that prompted his *Racine et Shakespeare* (1823) was a cultural clash both aesthetic and political. In 1822—a year after the death of Napoleon—a company of English actors attempted to perform Shakespeare in English in Paris. They were driven from the stage. Stendhal saw an opportunity to attack what he regarded as the out-of-date conservative aesthetics of the post-1815 Restoration establishment that controlled the press, the theatres, and the Académie française. He followed up the first short epitome of his argument with a second pamphlet (1825), in which he developed the underlying issue of classicism versus Romanticism.[18]

Stendhal began, as others had, with an attack on the idea of the classical unities as integral to theatrical illusion, but the novel ground of Stendhal's attack immediately indicates his originality, based in his intellectually clear-sighted and emotionally vivid engagement with theatre. Emotional engagement, he argues, is essential to theatrical effect, but this depends not on supposing events that might in reality take thirty-six hours can be represented in two (if illusion is elastic, why should that elasticity have limits?), but on split-second moments of complete emotional and imaginative involvement in the drama—in effect, split-second illusions of reality. There are (Stendhal claims) more of these in Shakespeare than in Racine. Much of Stendhal's larger argument follows from this. Any aspect of performance that compromises the possibility of these crucial moments of full passional-imaginative engagement is deplored: breaking the 'fourth wall' to acknowledge the presence of the audience (37.270); declamation encouraged by the formality of the alexandrine that places poetic beauty above dramatic force.[19] Plays have their full meaning not in reading but in performance, through the emotions excited by drama: theatre is (in the Wagnerian formulation) a *Gesamtkunstwerk* (total art work) in which all the elements of performance combine with text to produce meaning. Criticism cannot offer conclusive demonstrations of the crucial moments of feeling: the audience (reader) must consult experience, and everyone's experience will be different. In a radical extension of this, Stendhal argues that all ideas of beauty are relative; taste (he quotes Goethe) is 'local and momentary' (37.279), from which it follows that modes of critical utterance too are situated and personal, albeit also related to broad shifts in cultural assumptions: the courtly audience of Racine is separated by a great gulf from the post-Revolutionary audience of the 1820s. Criticism must recognize and address this: criticism too is both personal and relative to its age. Stendhal accordingly writes himself into his text, frequently with humorous self-deprecation as a complement to his bold and equally humorous polemical élan, and with a flexibility of persona character-istic of all his work. Individual idiosyncrasy can be moulded for cultural typicality. He becomes voices of his age: a soldier who fought with Napoleon (Henri Beyle); a little-known author struggling to publish his pamphlet (Stendhal); and 'The Romantic', albeit as scep-tical dissident rather than devout believer.

Like contemporary German critics, but unlike de Staël, Stendhal presents Shakespeare not as the Voltairean wild (barbarous) genius but as an artist. His idea of emotional unity, independent of the classical unities, accepts the mixed mode of tragedy and comedy: the issue is not simple rule-bound criteria of means but a more sophisticated critical conception which no rules can help perceive, coherence of effect. He is also aware that, like any really new idea, this is genuinely difficult to see, that it takes an immense effort of clear-sightedness not to mistake perceptions rooted in habit for what habit makes them appear—perceptions rooted in nature. While the outward forms of Shakespeare's plays are important in offering alternatives to the inflex-ibilities of neoclassical dramatic structure and verse form, even more important is what Stendhal sees as their inner essence—their relation to the audience of the 1590s. Like Guizot he argues that this is similar to that of contemporary France, an audience recovering from profound and extended social upheaval. (Stendhal apparently thought of the fifteenth-century civil wars that are the subject of Shakespeare's history plays as part of a historical movement continuous with the sixteenth-century disruption in religion that led to the Elizabethan Anglican Settlement.) Stendhal recognizes that Shakespeare's language, like his dramatic structures, is much more flexible than Racine's—the rhythms of his poetry more free, his vocabulary not limited by ideas of poetic diction. Nevertheless, to break down the dominance of the alexandrine, the new drama modelled on the essence not the forms of Shakespeare must be in prose: prose is the true vehicle of characteristic French expressivity. Underlying all this is Stendhal's account of the Romantic, by which he paradoxically associates Shakespeare with the great classical dramatists, Sophocles and Euripides: all wrote in terms that reflected their contemporary reality. This is, in Stendhal's sense, Romantic: to be, in one's own age—as even Racine was in his—modern.

Much of Stendhal's writing about Shakespeare is focussed on his work as a model for new writing in the 1820s. Critical principles and practices are usually no more than implicit, or at least not developed. 'In drama it is the *preceding scenes* that make us *feel* the word we hear spoken in the immediate scene': it is an excellent perception (37.270 [1823]), so good that Stendhal repeats it (37.147 [1824]); but to explore and exemplify is not his mode. 'Intelligenti pauca' is the epigraph of *Racine et Shakespeare* Part 1 (37.1): for those capable of understanding a few words will suffice. The epigraph to Part 2 is an indicative few words: 'The old man: "Let us continue". The young man: "Let us examine". There is the nineteenth century' (37.51). His great novel *The Charterhouse of Parma* ends with a dedication 'To the happy few': that is, those who read, and think, for themselves.

Some of Stendhal's writing is more straightforwardly literary-critical. Unlike many of his contemporaries, he was interested in comedy—in the nature and value of laughter, moral comedy versus comedy as pleasure and celebration of life. In France this meant Molière versus his successor, Jean-François Regnard, where, though Molière is admitted to be the greater genius, Regnard is the Stendhalian model. For Stendhal the real moral of Molière lies not in his overt subjects (the greed of Harpagon, the hypocrisy of Tartuffe) but in his comic mode, which depends (in Stendhal's view) on the fear of being different, of not seeing as others see. Its principle is '*être comme tout le monde*' (37.224): be like everybody else. But the courage not to conform, not to be like everybody else, is for Stendhal a primary virtue, a basis of everything in life that is worthwhile. For Stendhal, therefore, comedy is not to make us laugh 'at the expense of sad humanity' (37.247). The noble purpose of comedy is not to prompt the laughter of malice and fear but to elicit the laughter of pleasure, laughter that celebrates life. This—Regnard with genius and a profound understanding of humane feeling—is the Shakespearean mode. Its great example is Falstaff. With Falstaff, as elsewhere, Stendhal is a relativist. To the moralist all things can be moralized. Falstaff too can be understood in the mode of Molière. Beyond a certain point there is no reasoning on such things; but one can ask which interpretations stem from attitudes of greater value. Stendhal is, as always, present in his own perspectives, and on Falstaff his stance is paradoxical. Stendhal is a republican, but 'a *republic* is the contrary of *laughter*'. Republicanism is exaggeratedly serious: it tends to the moralistic; Stendhalian laughter is outside its scope. What does the moralist see in Falstaff's account of eleven buckram men grown out of two (*1HIV*, 2.4)? 'A flat lie told for a base pecuniary interest.' Of what use is such an interpreter? 'To adorn the warden's pew in a Puritan church.' Stendhal is the critic as Falstaff. He comically accepts the diversity of his own real preferences: 'What can I do? I was born French.'[20] This is not, however, to read only what one brings to reading. Art shows us nature, but it shows us nature more fully and more resonantly than we would see it without the aid of art (37.279–81). The severe moralist may eagerly read into Falstaff an un-Shakespearean moralism. With whatever ambiguity, the non-moralist who has ears to hear is led to hear more deeply, to interpret more profoundly, the laughter of humane pleasure.

In his *History of Painting in Italy* (1817), after a diatribe against the critical orthodoxies digested from Voltaire that were promulgated through the French education system by *Lycée, ou cours de littérature ancienne et moderne* of Jean-François de la Harpe (1739–1803), Stendhal formulates a view of the purpose of criticism.

Les bons livres sur les arts ne sont pas les recueils d'arrêts à la La Harpe; mais ceux qui, jetant la lumière sur les profondeurs du coeur humain, mettent à ma portée des beautés que mon âme est faite pour sentir, mais qui, faute d'instruction, ne pouvaient traverser mon esprit. (26.264–5.)

Good books about the arts are not collections of judgements in the manner of La Harpe; but those which, throwing light on the depths of the human heart, put within my reach beauties that my soul is created with a predisposition to feel, but which, as the result of a lack of education, were not able to able to reach my spirit.

Critical toolkits and ready-made judgements have no relation to real experience of art. But neither can we understand complex and sophisticated creations by immediate and naked intuition. Education is necessary. Education is also a great danger. La Harpe is not, for Stendhal, just a historical figure: he is a permanent tendency of the Teacher—the codified, the impersonal; everything that the chaotic manner and vividly personal mode of Henri Brulard and other Stendhal personae denied. Education, like art, must be addressed to the whole person: 'coeur . . . âme . . . esprit'—heart, soul, spirit. For Stendhal, Shakespeare kept alive this sense of art, and a resultant sense of the difficulties of criticism. If there is a recipe, it is the paradox of nakedness with sophistication.

'Coeur, âme, esprit' are only more extravagantly present in Stendhal's successor in this cultural battle, Victor Hugo (1802–85). Hugo's decisive intervention in the culture wars of Romanticism was, like Stendhal's, in part prompted by performance. A company of English actors, including Edmund Kean, Charles Kemble, and William Charles Macready, performed Shakespeare in English in Paris in 1827, but this time to great acclaim.[21] Their season opened at the beginning of September. Hugo's contribution to the Shakespeare debate of the 1820s, the preface to his play-for-reading *Cromwell*, was written in the following month.[22]

The method of *Cromwell*'s preface is part argument, part accretive assertion. Hugo postulates three ages of world history—broad periods, rhapsodically constructed, as much mythic as historical. Their purpose is polemical: to establish the idea that forms of civilization change, and with them forms of poetry. It is the argument of Stendhal, and ultimately of Herder—that a new age requires new literary forms—but on the vaster scale of a mythological world history. Its terms are not the court of Louis XIV versus the post-Revolutionary demos, but the primitive, the ancient, and the modern. Each of these broad periods has its literary exemplar, though the dominant form is never regarded as exclusive: each contains the others. The characteristic poetry of the primitive is lyric (the Bible: Hugo is flexible in his categories). The characteristic poetry of the ancient is epic (Homer—of which classical drama is merely a mutation). The modern age, the age of Christianity, contains new elements: meditation, analysis, and controversy. This requires a new literary form, the drama, which recognizes that the way to be harmonious in art is no longer to be selective but to be dialogic, multiple, comprehensive: to include tragedy and comedy, the terrible and the absurd, epic (history) and lyric (song), and above all, most characteristic of the modern, the sublime with what Hugo calls the grotesque. Its great exemplar is Shakespeare. It is a view of world literature and the modern that exalts Shakespeare precisely for that combination of opposites that Voltaire and neoclassicism deplored.

For Hugo, the major new element is the grotesque: 'la plus riche source que la nature puisse ouvrir à l'art' (the richest source that nature can open to art),[23] a principle of contrast that makes beauty more beautiful, sublimity more sublime. It constitutes a fundamental difference separating ancient from modern art. Hugo's extended discussions (159–67, 195–6) illustrate the multifarious qualities of the grotesque, the comprehensiveness that makes it so important. It is seen in Shakespeare through multiple imbricated relationships, each defined in part by the co-presence of others: the sublime of Lear by the grotesque of Poor Tom; the grotesque of Falstaff by the pragmatism of Prince John, the idealism of Hotspur, the respectability of the Lord Chief Justice, and the calculating Machiavellism of the Lancastrians. Hamlet's meditations on death take in Alexander the Great and Yorick. Ophelia is buried with the jokes and songs of her gravedigger and the agonized mourning of her brother. The imbricated elements imply a critical principle: the kind of interaction of the heterogeneous— present in life as in art—observed in particular instances by Guizot; an aesthetic not of selection, as in classicism, but of fullness, which Hugo identified as Romantic. Oppositions may be separated: the devilish Iago, the angelic Desdemona. More commonly they are mixed: man as beauty of the world and quintessence of dust.

This exaltation of the heterogeneous 'grotesque', and its aesthetic of fullness and depth through contrast, prompts a discussion of what Hugo calls the 'pseudo-Aristotelian' unities. This is conducted in terms established by others: what in Greek drama was artistic and flexible in neoclassical drama is artificial. The unities are 'wretched quibbles posed to genius . . . by mediocrity, envy and routine' (170), rules designed to evade problems that genius, remaining faithful to the nature of its material, can overcome. Of the great writers who have produced works according to the rules, 'like the Hebrew giant [Samson] they carried the doors of their prison with them to the mountains' (172). Of the rules and rule-givers, 'the drama has but to take a step to free itself from all the webs which the troops of Lilliput placed around it as it slept' (166). Of the unities themselves, 'the cage . . . contains nothing but a skeleton' (170). Hugo's energetic satire is a magnificent example of his criteria: sublime in energy, grotesque in imagery. But while art is a mirror of life's diversity, art must not simply reflect: art must concentrate. Unlike Stendhal, Hugo does not propose that the new drama should be in prose. It should be in verse, for which not the refinement of Racine but the comprehensiveness of Molière is the nearest approach in French to Shakespeare.

Hugo's term for this new mode is significant: 'le drame' implies an inclusive form, in English 'melodrama', but without negative connotations of excess, exaggeration, and sensationalism. Discussions of French acting and 'declamation'[24] suggest that the issue was partly a matter of the relation of poetic styles to modes of acting—the quasi-operatic stylization and decorum of French classical actors in declaiming the alexandrine versus the more naturalistic heightening of English actors in speaking Shakespeare's variety of styles in poetry and prose, and its nearer relation to the style of the melodrama of French popular (boulevard) theatres. In dramatic mode and in manner of performance 'le drame' returns theatre from an elite to the demos.

Not all of this has precise implications for how Shakespeare should be read, but, if he is the equivalent for modern culture of the Bible and Homer, that suggests at least that he should be approached with large views, no diminishing reference to modes of thought bound by adherence to limiting formulae in life or in art, and with a sense of greatness amounting to reverence. As Hugo has it in his much later book on Shakespeare (presenting Shakespeare through the words of Pontius Pilate as the man-god of literary art), 'L'art, comme la réligion, a ses *Ecce Homo*'.[25]

Hugo's *Cromwell* was followed up with a different kind of Shakespearean intervention, a translation by Alfred de Vigny (1797–1863) of *Othello*. Like Hugo, and like many French contributors to Romantic criticism of Shakespeare, Vigny was a major writer, recognized as a poet and novelist before he collaborated with Émile Deschamps (1791–1871) on a translation of *Romeo and Juliet* (1828; not performed), and translated *Othello* as *Le More de Venise* for the Comédie-Française (1829).[26] This was the first Romantic-generation translation of Shakespeare to be performed in what was then a bastion of cultural conservatism. It was distinct from the standard reading version of Le Tourneur–Guizot in being in verse. Vigny used a flexible but still rhymed alexandrine, the form of French neoclassical tragedy, because (he argued) French audiences would not accept Shakespeare's mixed style: its juxtapositions of verse and prose could not be made to sound natural in French. Though Vigny retains the 'handkerchief' (*mouchoir*) which epitomized neoclassical difficulty with Shakespeare's 'ordinary' diction supposed inappropriate to tragedy, his use of rhymed verse throughout means the translation is often un-Shakespearean in tone. His bowdlerization of Shakespeare's sexual language—another concession to the norms of French taste—means that Othello's jealousy is not coloured by the physicality that the terms of Iago's insinuations give it in Shakespeare: it is less visceral—both less repulsive (a repulsiveness of which Iago is the source, Othello the victim) and less sympathetic (more cerebral, more potentially subject to control).[27] Vigny also changed aspects of plot and characterization, amongst much else reducing the role of Bianca (who appears in only one scene, not performed in 1829), and substantially reworking the final scene: there is no stabbing of Emilia by Iago, and the play ends abruptly with the death of Othello—'le frappant – ainsi' (and smote him thus). This too Vigny described as a concession to French taste, 'that the final emotion should be the most vivid and profound'.[28] Shakespeare's characteristic modulation to a reflective close in which the tragedy begins to be absorbed by the characters and the audience is seen, like his mixture of prose and poetry, the commonplace and the sublime, as un-French.

The play is most famous in the history of French theatre for its preface, 'A Letter to Lord ***', occasioned by demonstrations from an anti-Romantic faction in the audience on the first night. This outlines a theory of drama,[29] and discusses what Vigny found in Shakespeare (the implicit contrasts are with French neoclassical drama): a portrait of life as it is outside of fiction, rather than dramatic conventions of a plot with a catastrophe; fullness of character rather than roles limited to actions required by the plot; and a prompting to explore stylistic variety ranging from what he calls (implying an analogy between verse drama and opera) recitative to song, quasi-colloquial speech to the elevated styles usual in French tragedy.

That *Le More de Venise* was premiered between Dumas's *Henri III* (February 1829; French national history, based on Shakespearean models) and the most notable of all French Romantic dramas, Hugo's *Hernani* (February 1830), indicates how crucial Shakespeare was to the development of Romantic aesthetics in France, as he already had been in Germany. *Hernani*, with its polemical preface defining Romanticism as 'liberalism in literature', offered slogans: 'Liberty in art; liberty in society'; and (the voice of the people resembling the voice of God) 'TOLERANCE AND LIBERTY'.[30] Vigny's *à la française* adaptation of *Othello* recruited Shakespeare as an icon in this culture war. Where Hugo had cited Shakespeare as a model in an aesthetic-political context in his preface to *Cromwell*, Vigny presented Shakespeare directly, albeit French-inflected, and with a preface implying similar challenges.

The present-day reader, especially a reader trained in sophisticated modern disciplines of literary criticism, is likely to find Hugo's later return to Shakespeare criticism trying. Hugo himself admits in the preface that his *Shakespeare* (1864) should have been called *À propos de Shakespeare*, but even on the widest view of what bears on understanding a great writer, Hugo's *à propos* is likely to seem generously extensive. Though not world-minded in the way desiderated by Yeats, who would like to think how an idea would seem on Mount Meru (Hindu, Buddhist, Jainist) as much as on Mount Sinai (Jewish, Christian) and Mount Olympus (pagan), Hugo is Western-world-minded. He aims to set Shakespeare in the context of ancient Israel (its prophets, chroniclers, and lawgivers) and ancient Greece (its epic and dramatic poets and its philosophers); and Shakespeare is set not only in this vast literary context but also in a context of the arts and the sciences. The French Revolution is understood to have initiated a new phase of world history which requires for its articulation a new genius (unnamed but scarcely un-implied: Victor Hugo). Much of the result is obviously unsatisfactory. Hugo's biography of Shakespeare could scarcely be more inaccurate; he is given to presenting platitudes as discoveries; he presents himself as a prophet of the new phase of history with predictions that the most doctrinaire liberal would be unlikely to defend. Shakespeare is created in Hugo's own image, including politically. As well as being one of the most famous writers of the age, Hugo was by the 1860s a figure of international political consequence, not only (though notably) on the issue of capital punishment, on which his pronouncements were widely recognized and effective, but more generally as a socialist opponent of the Second Empire in France, to which his opposition was also effective beyond Europe. Hugo's Shakespeare is accordingly politicized: he is a socialist.[31]

Nevertheless, despite evident weaknesses, the book deserves to be considered in terms of Hugo's aims: to write for a wide audience, not (however well intentioned) an intellectual and artistic coterie, and to return works written for a whole culture as far as possible to a mass readership, when, for the first time in history, education in literacy was producing such a readership. Hence his impassioned polemic about art for all and poets as 'instructors of the people' in the context of the new age of post-revolutionary construction—the need for widely available texts, translations, performances, even commentaries.[32] Hugo's expectations about the effects of mass literacy may now seem unrealistically utopian, but they were widely shared by nineteenth-century liberal intellectuals, who could hardly be expected to foresee all the malign social and intellectual influences by which the effects of mass literacy would be qualified and corrupted.

Hugo explained another fundamental aim of the book as to exemplify a stance towards art and criticism: 'Admirer. Être enthousiaste. Il m'a paru que dans notre siècle cet example de bêtise était bon à donner' (To admire. To be an enthusiast. It seemed to me that in our century it was good to give this example of foolishness)—'example de bêtise', that is, his book.[33] Of course, Hugo regarded his 'bêtise' as St Paul regards the 'foolishness' which is contrary to the 'wisdom' of this world (1 Corinthians 3:19): what seems foolishness to the academician is wisdom to the artist. Hugo searches for ways in which criticism can recognize this wise 'folly', and for him these are not found by focussing on what the rational intellect can demonstrate but by encouraging freewheeling, imaginative participation. In the very mode of his pronouncements Hugo is opposed to criticism that is (as he sees it) the literary arm of the temperance society. On this he is both funny and passionate, because 'the beautiful intoxicates (*grise*), what is great goes to one's head (*porte à la tête*), the ideal causes giddiness (*donne des éblouissements*)'.[34] How to write criticism that does not implicitly exclude beauty that intoxicates was a problem that other Romantic-period critics may have addressed with more sophistication. None addressed it with less inhibition. The virtue of Hugo's book is as provocation to large-minded views and engaged reading; but as specific criticism—as in the discussions of *Hamlet*, *Othello*, *King Lear* and *Macbeth* (II. ii.3–6)—it is poor stuff compared with the interpretive introductions of the edition by his son, François-Victor Hugo.

Hugo's book was at first conceived as an introduction for the complete translation of Shakespeare by François-Victor, published in fifteen volumes between 1859 and 1865.[35] This included the first complete French translation of the Sonnets (originally published separately, 1857), and three additional volumes of apocrypha (1866–7), including several works now generally accepted as by (or in part by) Shakespeare—*Titus Andronicus*, *Pericles*, *The Two Noble Kinsmen*, and *Edward III*. The translation is a late fruit of the Romantic Movement, as François-Victor explains in his introduction:

> In order for a literal translation of Shakespeare to become possible the literary movement of 1830 had to be victorious. It was necessary that the liberty that had triumphed in politics should triumph in literature, the new language, the revolutionary language, the right word and the right image, had to be definitively created. (I.34)

Only now can the full range of Shakespeare's language—including colloquial and (still more) indecent expressions previously prohibited by the decorum of theatrical tradition and a rigorous state censorship—be admitted into French art-theatre. The translation is in prose but marks the original lines of verse with dashes so that it can be used both as a reading translation and as a crib, and it always reminds the reader where the original is in verse. Hugo worked partly in the library of the British Museum, where he made full use of his access to early texts and contemporary scholarship, and he is strikingly innovative editorially in ways that anticipate modern views. He removed the folio division into acts, which he regarded as inauthentic, arguing that Shakespeare constructed in terms of scenes, and he gathered the plays in volumes in thematic groups so as to emphasize connections obscured by the usual (supposed) chronology, or by grouping according to genre, which has always been problematic with at least some of plays. The thematic organization of the volumes draws out what Hugo regarded as Shakespearean preoccupations, as with the volume 'Les Jaloux' (the jealous), which brings together Claudio (*Much Ado*), Othello, Troilus, Posthumus (*Cymbeline*) and Leontes (*The Winter's Tale*)—plays from the late 1590s to *c*.1610, characters from comedy, tragedy, 'problem play', and romance. Each volume contains an extended introduction, commentary, and annotation, and a selection of sources. The grandeur of textual scholarship, apparatus, and overall presentation is in itself a cultural statement: Shakespeare is a European classic. The translation—often silently adapted—became standard in French for reading and as the basis of theatrical performances, corresponding therefore in status to the Schlegel–Tieck translation in Germany. Hugo's most striking innovation, announced in his first volume, which prints separately the First Quarto and Folio texts of *Hamlet*, is to propose understanding quarto and folio texts not (in the manner usual until the late twentieth century) as corrupt variants of a supposed single original but as separate versions, each with its own integrity—that is, the modern view of Shakespeare's texts, a view not prevailing elsewhere until over a century later.[36]

Hugo's critical introductions are as striking as his textual scholarship. Writing from political exile in Guernsey arising from his and his father's opposition to the Second Empire of Napoleon III, the passionately situated and personal nature of his readings is both a strength and a weakness. Hugo reads for his preferences, especially in politics, in which he shared his father's liberalism, and in religion, in which he shared his father's anti-clerical scepticism. Literary criticism is for him a form of social activism—political work for an exile, changing hearts and minds. The results can be revealing when Hugo's preferences highlight real elements of a play, distorting—though never less than interesting—when a play and his preferences interact problematically. Political engagement is most evident in the volume 'The Tyrants'— Macbeth, King John, Richard III—in which he distinguishes between medieval tyrants (Macbeth, John), who deal in straightforward oppression and murder, and modern tyrants (Richard III, but vide Napoleon III), who corrupt the church and the legal system and work to deceive the new power of public opinion (III.67–8). His readings of *A Midsummer Night's Dream* and *The Tempest* (Volume II, 'The Fairies') draw on his knowledge of Elizabethan and Jacobean culture to produce similarly 'strong' readings based in his anti-clericalism. He contrasts Shakespeare's acceptance of the supernatural with Reginald Scot's denial of supernatural presences on earth (*The Discovery of Witchcraft*, 1584), and with James VI and I's belief in witchcraft (*Demonology*, 1597, 1603), and praises Shakespeare for his enlightened acceptance of neutral spiritual presences in nature that the King's rigid Christianity caused him to denounce. 'Jacques VI avait dit: Anathème aux esprits! Shakespeare dit: Gloire aux esprits!' (II.87; James VI had said, Anathema to the spirits! Shakespeare said, Glory to the spirits!). In a situation of sectarian contest Shakespeare daffed aside debate and, in keeping with the eclectic pantheism of advanced-thinking early modern mythography, rehabilitated popular tradition. Shakespeare is both of the people and wise beyond the sectarian learned.

Hugo is a similarly engaged reader in presenting the struggle of Hamlet against the murderous tyranny of Claudius as the archetypal struggle of every free spirit—the struggle between will and fate, in art, in science, in politics, and in life more generally.

> Cette lutte entre la volonté et la fatalité n'est pas seulement l'histoire d'Hamlet, c'est l'histoire de tous. C'est votre vie, c'est la mienne. C'était celle de nos pères, ce sera celle de nos neveux. Et voilà pourquoi l'œuvre de Shakespeare est éternelle. (I.98)

> This struggle between will and fate is not only the story of Hamlet: it is the story of everyone. It is your life; it is mine. It was the life of our ancestors; it will be the life of our descendants. And that is why Shakespeare's work is eternal.

With his passionate French rhetoric Hugo spells out each area of Hamlet's universal and eternal application (I.98–9). Though as an editor and translator Hugo is fully conscious of detail, and though he often reads from a markedly individual viewpoint, he never loses a sense of the fundamental grandeur of Shakespeare's conceptions.

Hugo's 'strong' readings are not, however, unproblematic. His account of Othello as an innocent victim whose only crime is to have been 'begotten on this earth', born into an evil world, is illustrative of engagement so strong as to be blind to its own constructions. Iago is evil, clever, and lucky, and Othello believes him for complex reasons, some of which are innocent (naivety based in unsuspecting nobility), and some an understandable vulnerability based in cultural insecurity (ultra-sensitive to Iago's 'I know our country disposition well'; 3.3.201). But some are surely based in violent egotism ('I will chop her into messes. Cuckold me!'; 4.1.200). The sense of radical betrayal that Iago engineers in Othello agonizingly dissolves his sense of identity ('But there, where I have garner'd up my heart, / Where I must either live or bear no life; / . . . to be discarded thence!'; 4.2.57–60): it may be that no readers should think of themselves as, in similar circumstances, likely to be free from comparable weaknesses; but that they should think of themselves as companions with Othello in innocence is an Hugoesque distortion. Hugo's assertion of Othello's innocence is the basis for a diatribe against the Christian world view (V.82–4) foisted onto Shakespeare by impassioned but perverse misreading.

France offers a form of criticism through recreation different from anything in England in this period, and more radically recreative than Goethe's setting of critical and performance issues in a fictional context, where meaning is governed by character and situation. In France Shakespeare is explored through new creative work, in music and in visual art. In this kind of work recreation is a form of criticism presenting a work in different terms, as much a form of critical practice as recreation of the original text by performance—which often means adaptation, with shaping cuts and interpretive additions, the creative work of actors, directors, and designers. Hazlitt's view that 'actors are the best commentators on the poets' can be variously reapplied: artists in other media—music, opera, dance, visual art, film—can also be excellent commentators on Shakespeare. In the Romantic period it is in France that commentary of this kind, exploring the original by recreating it in another medium, was most often attempted—by the composer Hector Berlioz (1803–69), whose work drew more from Shakespeare than that of any other composer of comparable stature; by the painters Eugène Delacroix (1798–1863), and Théodore Chassériau (1819–56), each of whom created one major series of works based on Shakespeare.

Berlioz described his first encounter with Shakespeare in his *Memoirs*. Like Hugo and other leaders of the Romantic Movement, he attended the English Stage Company performances of 1827. There,

Shakespeare, coming upon me unawares, struck me like a thunderbolt. The lightning flash of that discovery revealed to me at a stroke the whole heaven of art, illuminating it to its remotest corners. I recognized the meaning of grandeur, beauty, dramatic truth, . . . I saw, I understood, I felt . . . that I was alive and that I must arise and walk.[37]

That is, through Shakespeare Berlioz felt a new sense of his own powers (echoing Julius Caesar: '*veni, vidi, vici*': I came, I saw, I conquered); Shakespeare performed on him a Christlike miracle (echoing John 5:5–15), which he saw as determining the rest of his creative life. Shakespeare did not work unaided. As the *Memoirs* make clear, the effects of poetry and drama were intensified by the effect of the Irish actress Harriet Smithson, whose performance in *Hamlet* gave rise to 'Ophelia mania' in Paris, and whom Berlioz later married. The marriage proved unhappy and ended in separation. The effect of Shakespeare was lifelong. Berlioz composed numerous works based on the plays: the fantasia *The Tempest* (1830); the overture *King Lear* (1831); *Lélio, ou le retour à la vie* (1831, 1855), describing Shakespeare's impact on the composer's creativity; the dramatic symphony *Roméo et Juliette* (1839); *Tristia* (1852), including a ballad on the death of Ophelia and a funeral march for Hamlet; and the opera *Béatrice et Bénédict* (1862). His greatest work, *The Trojans* (1856–8), he described as 'Virgil Shakespeareanised'—that is, in its structure (historical epic with varied materials and contrasting tones), and in its transformation of the teasing love dialogue of Jessica and Lorenzo (*The Merchant of Venice*, 5.1: 'In such a night as this') into the sublime love duet of Dido and Aeneas ('Par une telle nuit'). Of the fully Shakespearean compositions the most important are *Lélio*, *Roméo et Juliette*, and *Béatrice et Bénédict*.

Le retour à la vie (*Lélio* only after the revision of 1855) is a sequel to Berlioz's most famous work, the *Symphonie fantastique*. Desolated by unrequited love, the artist still hears the symphony's 'idée fixe', the motif symbolizing the unattainable beloved. Shakespeare has acted on the narrator 'like a revolution which has overturned [his] whole being' (§1), but, unlike his love, his obsession with Shakespeare leads him from Hamlet-like despair back to life and creativity: he writes the *Tempest* fantasia, with a performance of which *Lélio* ends. As distant as possible from an anti-Romantic aesthetic of disinterested beauty, the work presents art as therapy: through Shakespeare to integrated emotional equilibrium.

With *Béatrice et Bénédict*, that Berlioz should set a comedy at all indicates the breadth of his engagement with Shakespeare, whose presence in French culture in the nineteenth century remained almost entirely through the tragedies, above all those introduced through the adaptations of Ducis: *Hamlet*, in numerous versions, including one by Dumas *père* (1848), the basis of the opera by Ambroise Thomas (1868); *Othello*, similarly in several versions, most notably those of Vigny and the opera of Rossini (performed in Paris from 1821); and *Romeo and Juliet*, most prominently in the opera by Gounod (1867). The libretto of *Béatrice et Bénédict* is by Berlioz directly from Shakespeare, without Don John (Claudio and Hero's progress to marriage is straightforward), and with Shakespeare's comic constables (no longer needed to detect Don John's villainies) replaced by a comic composer, Somarone ('great ass', but charming as well as foolish). Berlioz concentrates on the women. Hero is a typically adoring romantic heroine, her sweetness presented seriously but also in mild parody, as in the coloratura of 'Je vais le voir!' (I.3), its stylized conventions alien to Berlioz's advanced musical language. His primary focus, emphasizing Shakespeare's contrast with heroines conforming to gender conventions, is a proto-feminist presentation of the unconventionally assertive Beatrice: love inseparable from the witty sparing that asserts her independence. The extraordinary energy conveyed by Berlioz's compositional originality makes her 'Dieu! Que viens-je d'entendre?' (II.10) the opera's centrepiece.

But of all Berlioz's Shakespearean works the most significant and original is *Roméo et Juliette*.[38] Neither an opera nor a normal symphonic work, this is a Shakespearean mixture of genres—part symphony, with movements corresponding to the usual symphonic slow movement, scherzo, and finale; part oratorio, contextualizing the symphonic with dramatic narrative involving solo voices and chorus. With a text by the poet Emile Deschamps, it is based on the adaptation by David Garrick (1748), the version acted by the English Stage Company in 1827. An Introduction establishes the context of the lovers' nemesis, the Montague–Capulet feud. A Prologue summarizes the narrative in choral recitative, with fragmentary foretastes of the central movements. It also incorporates a song on the delights of first love, praising Shakespeare's unique penetration of its depths. The movements presenting Romeo's love-melancholy, the Capulet ball, the balcony scene, and the Queen Mab scherzo are largely orchestral. As Berlioz explains in a preface, melody, harmony, and instrumental colour, free of the specificity of words, gave greater scope for conveying fundamental feelings: the transient pleasures of youth (the ball); the romantic-erotic intensity of which the lovers have become the most famous archetype; and, complementary to youthful passion, the whirling fantasy and dynamic wit of Mercutio. The work's centrepiece is the balcony 'scène d'amour': tender and visionary melody, harmonized and orchestrated with implications of more disturbed passions, it epitomizes the romantic-erotic for nineteenth-century art. (Wagner later inscribed a copy of the age's most famous portrayal of Romantic Eros, his *Tristan und Isolde*, 'to the composer of *Roméo et Juliette*'.) After these largely orchestral central movements Berlioz turns to tragedy: a funeral procession, with chorus, for the supposed-dead Juliet (a scene from Garrick) is followed by the actual deaths and their aftermath. Programme music with specific narrative elements conveys Romeo's killing of Paris, his awe as he enters Juliet's tomb, and his agonized contemplation of her beauty that has apparently survived 'death'; then Romeo's taking the poison, Juliet's awakening, the joy of their reunion (from Garrick, a change Berlioz admired),[39] and their deaths. The final movement, in a more operatic mode, incorporating material cut by Garrick (5.3), returns to the context by which the lovers are destroyed: Capulets and Montagues continue the feud. A retribution-with-reconciliation monologue from Friar Laurence provides a moralizing conclusion in the French grand-opera manner of Meyerbeer. If this sits uneasily with the experimentation of the rest, its un-Shakespearean simplicity should not obscure the brilliance of the whole. The work's creative-critical exploration embodies the play's central effects on a sensibility suited to receive them with peculiar intensity.

Visual art too can be a mode of critical exploration of Shakespeare, as in the lithograph series of *Hamlet* (1843) by Eugène Delacroix and the etching series of *Othello* (1844) by Théodore Chassériau. Late in life Delacroix recalled a youthful attitude to Shakespeare which he described unequivocally as a 'passion'.[40] Taught English by a son of émigrés who had grown up in London, he visited London himself in 1825, where he saw Shakespeare performed by Edmund Kean in some of his most admired roles—Richard III, Shylock, Othello, and perhaps Macbeth. This experience of Shakespeare in the theatre was seminal for a lifelong creative engagement, which included paintings of subjects from *Romeo and Juliet, Othello, Macbeth,* and *Antony and Cleopatra.* It is especially striking that the play to which Delacroix was most drawn, *Hamlet,* with (apart from the lithograph series) fifteen paintings executed over more than thirty years (*c.*1825 to 1859), was the play most offensive to French neoclassical aesthetics.[41] An early self-portrait of Delacroix probably in costume as the Prince (1828) suggests that, like many of his contemporaries, he too felt in himself 'a smack of Hamlet'.[42]

All this might seem to signal unequivocal engagement, but in fact Delacroix's youthful 'passion' later veered back and forth between highly engaged admiration and more qualified judgements. In an extended entry about Shakespeare in his journal for 1855 he records and endorses the views of a friend on the profound human reality of Shakespeare's characterization and the artistic unity that emerges from the plays' irregularities, the 'imperceptible order' that runs through the whole, including the diversity of tones so shocking to French taste (25.3.1855). Elsewhere in the journal he comments similarly. On character, Shakespeare is a 'specially gifted genius [who] carried his torch into the dark corners of the soul', articulating emotions common to every age but new to art (16.4.1856). On unity, his works 'resemble the unity of external nature'; each makes 'a single, unified impression on the mind' (25.9.1855). More generally, his works are a 'starting point and standard of criticism' (10.6.1856). Discussions of Shakespeare throughout the journal also, however, express reservations which are both characteristically French and indications of Delacroix's ambivalent attitude to Romanticism. A Romantic in his artistic practice, in his aesthetic ideals he was more qualified. While he felt all the power of irregularity in Homer, the Bible, Michelangelo, and Beethoven, he admired even more the mastery of nature by art, convention, and control in Virgil, Raphael, Mozart, and Racine. The journal identifies what Delacroix saw as eternal different modes of art: the sublime but unpolished, the supreme modern exemplar of which is Shakespeare; and the perfect and polished, which finally he loved more and thought greater, though perfection and polish in themselves are, he acknowledged, worthless—they must contain 'the secret force that is the whole essence of Shakespeare' (16.7.1855).

The *Hamlet* lithographs are the most extended fruit of this lifelong engagement.[43] Composed between 1834 and 1843 (largely in two groups, early and late), the series as first published was made up of thirteen subjects, but is best considered as incorporating three additional subjects included in the posthumous publication of 1864. The illustrations do not present a narrative sequence, or even offer a consistent depiction of Hamlet. Though Delacroix was primarily giving pictorial form to reading that excited his imagination, the interpretive nature of the sequence was recognized by early reviewers.[44] As with all criticism there is a paradox: apparently idiosyncratic personal response—with Delacroix, alienation from his own culture, a sense of personality as fragmented—can be profoundly in tune with the deepest substance of a text. Delacroix presents Hamlet as a character of multiple personae, in some scenes a delicate, epicene youth and in others a virile young man, whose costume varies from image to image even in sequences which are dramatically adjacent. The series as a whole suggests a quality Delacroix found in Shakespeare that he felt lacking in the polarized culture of post-Restoration French Romanticism: 'an impartial capacity for holding contrary aspects of life in mind simultaneously'.[45]

Though some illustrations suggest a theatrical set rather than an imagined 'real' setting, Delacroix illustrates primarily from the text, not the stage. The individual lithographs epitomize crucial elements of the play and of Hamlet's character, but with each aspect treated separately: Hamlet's closeness to Gertrude, his suspicion of Claudius, and his isolation in mourning (1); his passion and horror with the Ghost (2–3); his repudiation of Polonius (4); his reproaches to Ophelia (5); his embittered and satirical wit (7: with Rosencrantz and Guildenstern); his desire for revenge and the failed penitence of Claudius (8); and his violence in arraigning Gertrude (10) and in killing Polonius (9, 11). This last sequence (9–11) sets in motion the later part of the play—Gertrude's withdrawing from Claudius, the revenge of Laertes, and (in Delacroix's illustrations) the madness and death of Ophelia (12–13), Hamlet and Horatio with the gravediggers (14), Hamlet and Laertes in Ophelia's grave (15), and the deaths of Gertrude, Laertes, and Hamlet (16). Only the lithograph of the play within the play (6) brings together all the main characters, and this is also unusual in showing the Player Queen as present at the murder (Figure 4.1). If the Player Queen's presence is taken as meaningful (in the play she leaves the stage before the murderer enters), this would be

Figure 4.1. Eugène Delacroix, *Hamlet*, 'Hamlet has the actors play the scene of his father's poisoning'. Lithograph (1843). The British Museum, London, Department of Prints and Drawings.

the most distinctly interpretive illustration—confirmation of Hamlet's suspicions about Gertrude's complicity in the murder ('as kill a king and marry with his brother'). Among the most striking individual images is the subject to which Delacroix as a painter most often returned, Hamlet and Horatio in the graveyard (Figure 4.2; the lithograph, dated 1843, is closely related to the painting of 1839). In a Shakespearean combination of the ordinary and the exalted, the first gravedigger, accustomed to the physical realities of death and decay, cheerfully presents to Hamlet a skull (in the play, Yorick's). Perturbed and thoughtful, as throughout the play, Hamlet meditates on all that the gravedigger's accustomedness obscures. The image is the thematic centre of a series that variously depicts the isolation and alienation of a person of acute sensibility, questioning intellect, and sometimes violent energy, the ways in which Hamlet is—as Coleridge, Hazlitt, Goethe, and Emerson variously identified—an archetypal figure for the period.

Figure 4.2. Eugène Delacroix, *Hamlet*, 'Hamlet and Horatio with the gravedig-gers'. Lithograph (1843). The British Museum, London, Department of Prints and Drawings.

Théodore Chassériau's series of fifteen etchings based on *Othello* was published the year after Delacroix's *Hamlet*.[46] Chassériau had been the favourite student of the great French neoclassical painter Jean-Auguste-Dominique Ingres (1780–1867), but they quarrelled as

Chassériau became more influenced by Romanticism. Since by the 1840s he was seen as a follower of Delacroix, his *Othello* was immediately, and unfavourably, compared with the more established painter's Shakespeare series.[47] Except in being more interpretive than illustrative, however, the two are quite different, most obviously in technique—the clear incised lines of Delacroix's lithography; the shaded drawing of Chassériau's etching. That Chassériau's series was published the year after Delacroix's suggested to contemporaries direct emulation, and the Delacroix lithographs may well have prompted the commission. It is evident, however, from Chassériau's sketchbooks that he had worked on preliminary drawings for the series from 1836–7, and that, like Delacroix, he had a wider interest in Shakespeare, which also issued in paintings—scenes from *Romeo and Juliet*, *King Lear*, and *Macbeth*, and several paintings from *Othello*, including oils based on subjects from the etchings.[48] The large number of extant preliminary drawings (over seventy) and the many different states of most of the plates, several of which incorporate substantial reworkings, are all evidence of Chassériau's intense engagement with the project.

Like *Hamlet*, *Othello* was among the best known of Shakespeare's works in France. It was regularly acted in the adaptation of Ducis (1792; revived at the Comédie-Française, 1835–49), had been central to the ill-fated attempt to present Shakespeare by English actors in Paris in 1822, was performed as part of the successful return of English actors to Paris in 1827/28,[49] and had been translated by Vigny for the Comédie-Française in 1829. Rossini's opera had also been performed in Paris since 1821 (in French from 1844), and, with its marginalized Iago, reduced Othello, and central Desdemona, it too may have influenced Chassériau's presentation.[50] In various forms, therefore, the broad outlines of Shakespeare were well known, and, particularly in Ducis's adaptation, it has been argued that, with its hero valued for ability not birth and sympathetic presentation of interracial marriage, it was a play for the age of Liberty, Equality, and Fraternity, 'a dramatization of the . . . principles embodied in the Declaration of the Rights of Man'.[51] Chassériau's interpretive emphases are consistent with this view. In diminishing the role of Iago, the designs cut out the racial animus he so forcefully expresses, give a sympathetic view of Othello, but concentrate above all on Desdemona as an archetype of doomed innocence in an environment hostile to her egalitarian choice.

Desdemona is a problematic character, particularly for modern audiences: her religious view of love, devoid of assertive egotism, can make her independence and energy, in modern ethics more commonly associated with secular rights than religious duties, difficult to understand. Brabantio is indicative in mistaking her confident self-possession for submissiveness ('A maiden, never bold'; 1.3.94), though she herself gives a more accurate picture: 'That I did love the Moor to live with him, / My downright violence, and storm of fortunes, / May trumpet to the world' (1.3.248–50). Emilia's more readily sympathetic, but also more ego-driven version of female independence, shaped by male betrayal (4.3.86–103), is contrasted with Desdemona's more thoroughly self-determining view, not predicated on a simple obverse of how others behave towards her: 'God me such uses send, / Not to pick bad from bad, but by bad mend' (4.3.104–5). This love understands accurately what is deepest in Othello, and despite the success of Iago's distortions, and through every provocation of superficial change, Desdemona sticks to that deeper understanding: 'his unkindness may defeat my life, / But never taint my love' (4.2.160–1). It is the tragedy of this fundamentally forceful, self-determining, independent but unassertive goodness that Chassériau makes central to his designs.

Of the individual plates that render aspects of the play with particular intensity not all are concerned with Desdemona. 'Honest Iago, / My Desdemona must I leave to thee' (pl. 4), the main image of Othello and Iago together, shows a strikingly inscrutable Iago backed by a sinister shadow double: the slightly bent posture of his body suggests due subordination; his facial expression (achieved only in the final, fifth state of the plate) suggests boldly detached, even confrontational, observation. This is the Iago of 'I am not what I am' (1.1.65). In 'Yet she must die' (pl. 11), Othello contemplates Desdemona asleep: despite the gloomy premonitions shown in preceding images, she lies vulnerable but apparently untroubled; the focus is the profound sadness of Othello's gaze. In 'He smothers her' (pl. 13) Othello is again central, the violent struggle of Desdemona's suffocation expressed in every detail of his posture. But Desdemona, who appears in twelve of the fifteen plates, is the main subject of the series as a whole. In the play the love of Othello and Desdemona, on the destruction of which the sense of tragedy depends, is shown largely obliquely (much less than in the other tragedies of love)—though Shakespeare exerts all his poetic art to give powerful impressions in limited compass. Chassériau shows the love more directly, in a scene of courtship narrated in the play, but not staged (pl. 2). For all the tenderness of this illustration, the posture of Desdemona (both giving and drawing back) suggests that the attractive charisma of the exotic warrior, with his intense gaze, is not without an element of fear. 'Be merry, Cassio' (pl. 6) brings the central figures together in characteristic postures: Desdemona, advocate for the rejected Cassio, untroubled, Emilia impassive, Othello (prompted by Iago) suspicious. Desdemona is here the only figure not presented in shadow: the subject is her innocence. 'Away' (pl. 7) juxtaposes a contrasting but more intense epitomizing tableau: Othello's violent rejection, Emilia's horror, Desdemona's pleading incomprehension. From this point Desdemona's suffering is central. 'If I do die before thee' (pl. 8; Figure 4.3) became one of Chassériau's greatest transformations from the series into oils: intimately supported by Emilia, Desdemona contemplates her wedding sheets as her shroud.[52] In 'The Romance of the Willow' (pl. 9), in a posture of tearful exhaustion she cradles a harp with which she has accompanied herself in her song of rejection in love and the rejected woman's forgiveness ('his scorn I approve')—an image which also became the subject of later paintings.[53] 'Have you prayed tonight, Desdemona?' (pl. 12), in which she is terrified by the implication of Othello's question, is the final illustration showing Desdemona living, though the pathos of her body stretched out in death is central to the last two images—the guilt of Iago (pl. 15), and the penitence of Othello (pl. 14; Figure 4.4).

While Chassériau's rebalancing of the drama may have been influenced by the adaptation of Ducis and the opera of Rossini, his concentration on the heroine also shows a personal engagement with the play: the transformations of Othello worked by the machinations of Iago were for him secondary to the tragedy of Desdemona. This may be a slanted reading, but, unlike the anti-Christian polemic *Othello* elicited from François-Victor Hugo, it is congruent with the drama—a recreation in visual art that shows its source from an unfamiliar perspective that is nevertheless engaged with real aspects of the play.

Figure 4.3. Théodore Chassériau, *Othello*, 'If I do die before thee' (Desdemona and Emilia). Etching (1844). The British Museum, London, Department of Prints and Drawings.

Figure 4.4. Théodore Chassériau, *Othello*, 'Oh! Oh! Oh!' (Othello with the body of Desdemona). Etching (1844). Metropolitan Museum of Art, New York. (© Photo SCALA, Florence).

The views of Voltaire, powerful for half a century after his death, had been in eclipse for more than a decade. A countermovement, beginning the greater naturalization of Shakespeare into French culture through the translation of Francois-Victor Hugo, was more than a decade in the future—alongside which Shakespeare was still made acceptable in French culture by the sentimental distortions of Gounod (*Roméo et Juliette*, 1867) and Ambroise Thomas (*Hamlet*, 1868). Another century was to pass before the great actor-director Jean-Louis Barrault could claim that 'Shakespeare is performed in France as often as Molière, more often than Racine. . . . For the French Shakespeare is a necessity.'[54]

Editors and Scholars

Inheritances and Legacies

Just as Shakespeare prompted the beginnings of English literary criticism in its modern form, so he also prompted the birth of English literary editing. The central figure of Shakespearean editing and scholarship in the Romantic period is Edmond Malone (1741–1812). Malone's contribution to editing and annotating the text of Shakespeare, and to scholarship on theatrical, literary, and cultural history bearing on understanding Shakespeare, is second to none in the period. He has a good claim to be one of the most important figures in the whole history of Shakespearean scholarship and editing.

Malone trained as a lawyer, training evident in his search for documentary evidence. He discovered important new sources related to Shakespeare's biography and Elizabethan theatre. He assembled one of the great collections of Shakespeareana, which he bequeathed to the Bodleian Library, Oxford. While his work had only a limited effect on Romantic criticism, it had major and long-lasting effects on nine-teenth- and twentieth-century theatrical and editorial practices. His work on Shakespeare's theatre had an impact on how Shakespeare is staged, beginning with William Poel (1852–1934) and The Eliza-bethan Stage Society (founded 1895), and passing, partly through the playwright, director, critic, and dramatic theorist Harley Granville-Barker (1877–1946), into the mainstream of modern Shakespeare production. His work is at least congruent with the bare-stage expres-sivity of voice and body theories of one of the most famous of twentieth-century directors, Peter Brook (b.1925). Malone's editorial

Shakespeare and the Romantics. David Fuller, Oxford University Press (2021). © David Fuller.
DOI: 10.1093/oso/9780199679119.003.0005

practices underlie the more precise formulations of the so-called 'New Bibliography' of Arthur Pollard, R. B. McKerrow, and W. W. Greg, which dominated Shakespearean editing into the 1970s and beyond. His documentary researches provide early examples of how knowledge of the social and economic circumstances of Shakespeare's time can be used in scholarship and criticism.

Malone was not alone. He began work with George Steevens (1736–1800), who had helped Samuel Johnson complete his edition of Shakespeare (begun 1756, published 1765), and who thereafter worked independently on Shakespeare's text (with major publications in 1766 and 1793), as well as on two revisions of Johnson's edition (1773, 1778). Malone fell out with Steevens, who came to regard him as a rival, but he later worked with James Boswell Jr (1778–1822), son of the associate of Samuel Johnson, whose *Life of Johnson* (1791) he had assisted and encouraged. Malone published his own edition of Shakespeare in ten volumes in 1790. Boswell Jr inherited Malone's papers and organized and edited them into a greatly expanded version of 1790 in twenty-one volumes published in 1821. A distinct contribution, separate from the partly intertwined work of Malone and Steevens, is that of Edward Capell (1713–81), who (like Steevens) emphasized the value of the early quarto texts (the versions of individual works published in Shakespeare's lifetime), and (like Steevens and Malone) annotated Shakespeare from wide reading in his contemporaries. Isaac Reed (1742–1807), a self-effacing and pacific scholar, antithetical to the self-promoting and pugnacious Steevens, both assisted Steevens with his revisions of Johnson and with his edition (1793), and also produced his own revision of Johnson–Steevens (1785) and an enlarged edition of plays by Shakespeare's predecessors and contemporaries, *Dodsley's Select Collection of Old Plays* (twelve volumes, 1780; originally published 1744). These are the editor-scholars whose work provided the best texts and the textual and contextual scholarship in the Romantic period: Steevens, Capell, Reed, and—above all—Malone.[1]

Much of the work between the summation of distinctively eighteenth-century writing in Johnson's edition in 1765 and the summation of all that was new from the late 1760s onward in Boswell's expansion of Malone's edition in 1821 implies major changes of direction—though just how major is disputed.[2] The new work was in some ways embedded in eighteenth-century writing about Shakespeare, in part because the later editors took over practices evolved by their predecessors, in part because, from Johnson onwards, new multivolume editions reprinted annotations and, in the most ambitious cases, introductions from the main eighteenth-century editors. Some of the eighteenth-century editions also remained in print well into the Romantic period. While Lewis Theobald's edition (1733) was reprinted for the last time in 1773, Steevens (1793) was revised by Reed (1803) and reprinted with the Romantic colouration of engravings of designs by Fuseli in 1805 and 1812. Johnson–Steevens–Reed (1785) was reprinted as late as 1817. Selecting from Reed (1785), Malone (1790), and his own edition of 1793, Steevens also oversaw the text printed with the engravings from the Boydell Gallery (nine volumes, 1791–1802). The practice of so-called 'variorum' editing, initiated by Johnson and continued up to Boswell–Malone and beyond, meant that annotation often incorporated the history of disputed meanings reaching back to Pope. Augustan and later practices and views of Shakespeare editing, scholarship, and criticism thus continued to circulate, in full or in part, alongside and jostling with the latest ideas. Knowledge of the editorial tradition underlying Johnson is therefore necessary to understanding the range of views that Romantic-period readers seeking scholarly help might encounter.

Most obviously those readers encountered Shakespeare presented as a classic, in multivolume reference editions, with all the paraphernalia of a tradition of scholarship and criticism, disputed readings and interpretations, including pages in which the volume of interpretation often exceeded the space given to text. Though most of the editions appeared in various formats, they were often beautifully printed on fine paper and sent for expensive binding, for a gentleman's library. Though Shakespeare was not the only 'modern' dramatist treated in this way, analogous to the acknowledged classics of Greek and Roman culture, no other writer was edited, re-edited, and exhaustively annotated in this way. And the historic incorporations of the great late eighteenth-century and Romantic-period editions included more than implications. What was supposedly superseded by new editions was also actively resurrected in their introductions, texts, and annotations.

Multivolume presentation of Shakespeare with a named editor began with Nicholas Rowe's edition (six volumes, 1709; revised

1714).[3] As the first editor not following in the seventeenth-century tradition of single-volume folio texts (F1, 1623; F2, 1632; F3, 1663; F4, 1685), Rowe established conventions of modern spelling and punctuation, added scene locations, entrances and exits, and other actions implied by the dialogue, a list of dramatis personae arranged according to a hierarchy of social status and gender, standardized characters' names (often variously spelled in early texts), and standardized (sometimes introduced) act and scene divisions—some features which return the reader to the theatre (locations, entrances and exits, other implied actions), some which disrupt theatrical continuity to emphasize more readerly perceptions of structure. Implicitly the Romantic debate about the proper location of Shakespeare (the theatre versus the study) began to be written into editorial procedures with Rowe. Rowe based his text on the Fourth Folio of 1685—the worst possible source, since, as Samuel Johnson saw,[4] the process of reprinting was largely a process of introducing new errors and no authoritative corrections (or at most—as a later debate between Steevens and Malone acknowledges—no authoritative corrections beyond those of the Second Folio, produced in a printing-house culture historically continuous with that of the First).

Rowe had been employed as a dramatist himself. As such he began an editorial tradition of presenting Shakespeare as a playwright only. His edition did not include the narrative poems or the Sonnets. These were printed in a matching format by the publisher Bernard Lintott (undated, 1709/10), with a text of the Sonnets based on the 1609 quarto. Lintott's edition, however, was largely displaced by that of the publisher Edmund Curll (1710, called 'volume the seventh', suggesting a completion of Rowe). Curll based his text on the edition of Shakespeare's poems by John Benson (1640). This reordered the Sonnets, added titles, and reworked the pronouns and other gender indicators so as to obscure the gender of the 'lovely boy' addressed in the Sonnets between 1 and 126[5]—thus initiating a double tradition: an apparently supplementary volume downgrading the poems to a secondary status, and a text obscuring the challenge of the Sonnets to heteronormative assumptions about love poetry. Lintott's edition dropped into obscurity. The Shakespeare of the Sonnets and the narrative poems disappeared to become a Romantic-period rediscovery— not always welcomed in the Sonnets' gender complications.[6] One final significant element of Rowe's edition was its life of the poet, written from material largely gathered by the actor Thomas Betterton from Warwickshire tradition and legend. Though often demonstrably false, and evidently shaped by myths of the all-conquering power of genius, it stood in place of better until Malone's researches showed it for what it was.

Shakespeare's next editor was Alexander Pope (six volumes, 1725; revised 1728). While Rowe was a minor dramatist, Pope was the greatest poet of the age. When he began his work on Shakespeare in 1721 he had just completed his translation of Homer's *Iliad* (1715–20), which set Pope up as the heir of Dryden (*Aeneid*, 1697) and the age's arbiter of poetic culture. With Shakespeare one editorial mission was to present his great predecessor purged of what he saw as the dross that Shakespeare's carelessness of fame, the unsophisticated criteria of his age, and the corrupt taste of his audience left embedded in his gold. Pope placed no great reliance on the First Folio, printed, he supposed, from playhouse copies 'cut, or added to, arbitrarily'.[7] He demoted material he judged non-Shakespearean (usually putting displaced text into a note, sometimes omitting it altogether) and emended the text with additions, omissions, and transpositions to suit Augustan views of metre and syntax. Where Rowe's emphasis was in part theatrical (scene locations, stage directions), Pope's was poetic—great passages pointed by quotation marks, great poetic scenes by asterisks (with corresponding daggers to mark bad scenes), with aesthetic criteria exercised in emendation. Implying readerly priorities, this is Shakespeare for the study. Pope initiated one change of editorial direction by beginning to use quarto texts (texts which, unlike the First Folio, were mostly published in Shakespeare's lifetime), but he knew only a few quartos, and he used them haphazardly, often to give an appearance of authority to readings he preferred. Despite this, partly perhaps because he was in the hands of the owner of publishing rights to the text, Jacob Tonson, Pope began a tradition, handed down to Samuel Johnson and beyond, of printing from a marked-up version of the preceding edition (Rowe's third edition, 1714). With whatever corrections, Pope thus passed on into the editorial tradition Rowe's mistaken choice of F4 as his base text.[8]

With conjectures based on taste rather than bibliographic evidence, other 'improvements', and in general an ahistorical freedom in his treatment of the text, Pope prompted what was to become a new and lasting tradition in Shakespeare editing: acrimonious controversy. In general among the least edifying forms of literary-scholarly debate, in this case it gave rise to some magnificent comedy. Lewis Theobald (1688–1744) responded to Pope's edition with *Shakespeare Restored, or a Specimen of the many errors as well committed as unamended by Mr Pope in his late edition of this poet; designed... to restore the true reading of Shakespeare in all the editions ever published* (1726). Pope regarded editing as a lowly business—as he called it, a 'dull duty' (Boswell–Malone, 1.16). Except in occasionally inspired conjectures, he was, as Theobald's confident title claims, an imperfect editor. Theobald was a genuine scholar. All he said of Pope's failings was true, and the pleasure he took in exposing Pope's errors was not muted by modesty. Pope responded with the full exercise of his abilities as a satirical poet. Theobald first appeared in the Pope–Swift *Miscellanies* (1727) as 'piddling Tibbalds: / Who thinks he reads, when he but scans and spells' ('Fragment of a Satire', 14–15). He soon reappeared as the epitome of contemporary corrupt learning in Pope's *Dunciad* (*Iliad* of Dunces, 1728), expanded as *The Dunciad Variorum* (1729), with notes by 'Martinus Scriblerus' (learning divorced from under-standing) and occasionally 'by' (parodying the manner of) Theobald, with others attacking him directly. It improves the comedy of all this to know that Pope nevertheless incorporated many of Theobald's corrections into his second edition, and that when Theobald came to produce his own edition of Shakespeare (1733), he used Pope's second edition as his base text—thereby again passing on Rowe's erroneous choice of the Fourth Folio. Theobald recognized the problem: in his table of editions he lists Rowe's and Pope's as 'editions of no authority'. His choice of base text may have been dictated by the fact that his publisher, like Pope's, was the rights' owner, Tonson—an early example of theoretical editorial principles in conflict with practical publishing necessities.

If Theobald scored against Pope in his time by pointing out real errors, Pope made Theobald a figure for all time of the scholar whose attention to minutiae displaces worthwhile knowledge. Theobald, whose scholarship was in its way truly sound and original, who can reasonably be seen as 'the first to edit Shakespeare systematically, and... the founder of modern scholarship devoted to Renaissance

English Literature',[9] was transformed by Pope into a personification of Learned Ignorance: the scholar who, knowing 'everything', understands nothing. Pope's satire implies an almost inevitable link: as 'knowledge about' is increased, so 'understanding of' is diminished. Attention to detail deflects from knowledge of the whole. The more vain the scholar of his scholarship—what Pope dubbed contemptuously 'all such reading as was never read' (*The Dunciad*, 4.250)—the more he will overvalue its relation to understanding. In an age when scholarship of vernacular literature was new, it would take the creative intelligence of Samuel Johnson to see that scholarship in a just relation to knowledge.

Theobald's edition (seven volumes, 1733) represents another highly significant change of direction, which was to be confirmed by Romantic-period editing: after a dramatist, after a poet, a scholar. Theobald was a dramatist too. He may even have rewritten a now lost play by Shakespeare and John Fletcher based on the Cardenio episode of Cervantes's *Don Quixote*.[10] But he was primarily a scholar, and his methods as an editor were distinctly different from those of his two predecessors. Like Pope, he regarded all the early texts as vitiated by the supposedly careless attitudes of the playhouse (not understanding that for much of his working life Shakespeare was a major member of the company for which he wrote). However, with access to more quartos than Pope, he also realized that quarto–folio differences could be rationally investigated, and his annotations sometimes imply (albeit not consistently) an idea of compositors working from reliable manuscripts. Like other editors of the period, Theobald's views of the texts appear to have developed as he worked, and views derived from later practice were not fully harmonized with the views from which he began. One should also bear in mind the practical difficulties for eighteenth-century editors in consulting multiple texts: though they might purchase early texts, they had no access to a complete range.

Training in the editorial methods applied to classical texts prompted Theobald to take a more disciplined view of the relationships of the early texts, the nature of textual corruption, and the methods of correction; and though the precise methods evolved for the textual criticism of manuscripts (in which he had been trained by the great classicist Richard Bentley) were not directly applicable to printed books, this led him to collate textual variants, in comparing which he could deploy a knowledge of Elizabethan handwriting to look behind corrupt print sources. His emendations show that he could be a good close reader; even his failures show an acute attention to meaning.[11] And the failures, though characteristic, are relatively few: Theobald is found in the collations of contemporary editions of Shakespeare more than any eighteenth-century editor before Malone. He was also the first thoroughgoing historical editor, making sense by reading sources and analogues, and understanding Shakespeare's vocabulary and syntax by relating it to contemporary usage, as evinced by parallel passages elsewhere in Shakespeare's work, and from wide reading in Shakespeare's contemporaries and predecessors. He initiated the movement from emendation by conjecture and taste to emendation by bibliographical and historical knowledge and research—the movement that, for the eighteenth century and beyond, culminated in Malone.

The clash between Pope and Theobald is in part simply a difference between a poet and a scholar, but it also has larger resonances which indicate how editorial practices are often embedded in broad cultural circumstances. It has been understood in terms of a Catholic–Protestant split reflecting the evolving authority of tradition and the Church versus the static authority of scripture understood in a historical context, and in Anglicanism specifically, mediated through a disciplined interpreter;[12] a version of Shakespeare our contemporary versus Shakespeare the Elizabethan, ultimately presentism versus historicism. Pope's dismissive view of Theobald's attention to minutiae can also be seen as congruent with neoclassical aesthetics: in Samuel Johnson's famous formulation, 'The business of a poet . . . is to examine, not the individual, but the species; . . . he does not number the streaks of the tulip' (Imlac, in *Rasselas*, §10). While it would be absurd to present Theobald as a proto-Romantic, his attitude to the expressive importance of the specific is more compatible with the aesthetics of Blake than of Johnson: 'strictly speaking all knowledge is particular' (Blake, annotations of Reynolds). In his practices of editing and annotating, of the earlier eighteenth-century editors Theobald is the most obviously a predecessor of Malone and the methods of Romantic-period editing.

The edition of Sir Thomas Hanmer (six volumes, 1743–4), though grandly printed by the Clarendon Press, is of no textual interest.

Hanmer largely took over Pope's text, incorporated emendations by Theobald and others, and freely added conjectures of his own. Johnson criticized the edition when it first appeared ('its pomp recommends it more than its accuracy'),[13] though he wrote of it with more respect in his *Preface* (Sherbo, 7.97–8). Malone dismissed it as worthless (Boswell–Malone, 1.234)—though he nevertheless incorporated its introduction into his final edition (1821). While Hanmer's edition might admit of different views, the edition of William Warburton had few defenders (eight volumes, 1747: according to its title page, 'the genuine text . . . restored from the blunders of the first editors, and the interpolations of the two last'—that is, Theobald and Hanmer, of whom Warburton's preface offers confident excoriations). Placing Pope's name before his own on the title page, Warburton took over Pope's text, he claimed at Pope's request, 'as he thought it might put a stop to the prevailing folly of altering the text . . . without talents or judgement' (Boswell–Malone, 1.54). Warburton apparently thought his own talents and judgement a preventative of folly, since in many places he altered the text, replacing good sense with conjecture.[14] As with Pope and Theobald, though more one-sidedly, the edition prompted comic controversy in Thomas Edwards's *A Supplement to Mr Warburton's Edition of Shakespeare. Being the Canons of Criticism* (1748). Edwards's 'canons of criticism', editorial principles supposedly extrapolated from Warburton's practice, are in fact a series of ironic absurdities: an editor has 'a right to declare that his author wrote whatever he thinks he should have written'; an editor 'has a right to alter any passage which he does not understand'; the function of annotation 'is not so much to explain the author's meaning as to display the critic's knowledge'; and so on.[15] Warburton's evidence that Pope urged his editorial labours—'see his [unpublished] letters to me'—prompted from the intemperate theologian Styan Thirlby, 'you might as well have said See my arse in a band box'.[16] Uniquely among the eighteenth-century editions, Warburton's was not reprinted. Nevertheless its introduction, like Hanmer's, was incorporated into Malone's 1821 edition, thus transmitting into the Romantic period the work of the worst of predecessors alongside the best. In a bizarre twist of textual transmission comparable to Theobald's use of Pope, and despite his appreciation of its weaknesses, Johnson used Warburton (heterogeneously intermixed with text from the fourth edition of Theobald, 1757) as the base text for his own edition.

Johnson's edition (eight volumes, 1765) is the most obviously influential for Romantic criticism. Its magisterial *Preface* was a provocation to contradiction. Hazlitt begins his *Characters* from its supposed simplicities and errors. Nevertheless, the *Preface* is no straightforward summary of neoclassical ideas. Particularly in its forcefully argued common-sense rejection of the unities, it is anti-Voltairean. As an editor Johnson was, or at least became, conservative. Though he shared Pope's low assessment of the early texts, he came to distrust conjectural emendation as practised by Pope and extended by Hanmer and Warburton, seeing it as a delusive pleasure. He likewise condemned Pope's practice (taken over by Warburton) of marking beauties and faults ('critical officiousness': Sherbo, 7.57). As a critic, however, Johnson is independent, and in the edition as a whole faces in more than one direction. Despite the magisterial rhetoric of weighing opinion and pronouncing judgement, one effect of his new practice of 'variorum' commentary, along with his frank admission that over time he changed his mind about both emendations and meanings, was quite opposite to closing down interpretation: his annotations often admit and legitimate range and variety, even allow the reader to entertain or synthesize alternative interpretations. Johnson was not simply exhibiting his predecessors for contradiction but including 'all that is valuable . . . from every commentator, that posterity may consider [this edition] as including all the rest, and exhibiting whatever is hitherto known of the great father of the English drama' (Sherbo, 7.58). While the rhetoric of annotation leading to a Johnsonian 'right reading' might seem closed, its content of informed multiplicity defied or evaded closure.[17]

The edition has been presented as signalling the advent of a new age of cooperative editing.[18] Johnson did indeed (as earlier editors had) solicit and incorporate annotation from literati he knew, and he began the close working relationship with George Steevens, extended in the 1770s in revisions of 1765. However, he was only less severe than his predecessors had been to what he considered error as a result of his perception of the melancholy evanescence of all such disputes: as he puts it, with the magnificent simplicity his magisterial rhetoric occasionally allows, 'we shall soon be among the dead ourselves'

(Sherbo, 8.219). His recognition of the failings of Warburton, though muted, is clear (Sherbo, 7.98–9). His account of Theobald ('weak and ignorant, . . . mean and faithless, . . . petulant and ostentatious'; Sherbo, 7.96) is extreme, and fails to recognize Theobald's genuine distinctions, including as a precursor of the methods of editing and annotation that Johnson himself adopted. The main research tool of Johnson's annotations was his own *Dictionary* (1755), for which he read widely in Elizabethan and Jacobean literature, and which equipped him superbly to comment on meaning and usage and adduce parallels from Shakespeare, his contemporaries, and his predecessors. But for this range of reading in vernacular literature Theobald was a serious predecessor. Johnson's view of Shakespeare's next editor, Edward Capell, was likewise ungenerous. Capell was not a distinguished writer—meaning can sink under his sometimes confused expression—but he actually performed what Johnson proposed in theory and edited afresh on the basis of the earliest texts. Johnson's implication that he is the scholar as Caliban replicates his injustice to Theobald.[19] As for a new age of cooperation, such alliance as there was between Malone and Steevens soon collapsed in their rival editions of 1790 and 1793. In attempting a grand synthesis Johnson is a significant precursor of Boswell–Malone, but debate in editions, and in the books, pamphlets, and articles they prompted, often remained as it had been: satirical, querulous, acrimonious. Aggressive rivalry continued to be at least as important as cooperative collaboration. 'This is *Paddy from Cork*, with a vengeance!', the antiquarian and controversialist Joseph Ritson exclaimed over a note about a stage direction by Malone (who was Irish).[20] For a modern reader of eighteenth-century editorial disputes—which (given that the participants have long ceased to suffer from whatever wounds may have been inflicted) are often very funny— what is most striking is their unbridled vehemence and violent assertiveness, completely out of scale with any real importance that might conceivably be attached by a sane person to the minutiae in hand.

Alongside 'variorum' annotation, Johnson also proposed the practice—again initiated by Theobald insofar as his resources permitted—of collating and recording differences between the readings of early texts, and working from the earliest texts as having highest authority. It proved beyond Johnson actually to do this, in part because he did not work afresh from early texts but from

Warburton and Theobald, in part because he was not given the access he wanted to early quartos. Nevertheless, the principle of potentially arranging early texts in a hierarchy of authority was a significant stage in the history of editorial practice. Also the edition contained a list of quartos known to Johnson (compiled by Steevens), and this, combined with immediately following publications using these texts by Steevens (1766) and Capell (1768), stimulated an interest in textual variants and their use, significance, and authority that became an increasingly important issue with Romantic-period editions.

Despite the variorum annotation, and the impression this may give of address to a scholarly reader, Johnson is fundamentally a democratizing editor. His notes are often anthologized as classics of downrightness and clarity for the common reader. The needs of the common reader are also foremost in his clarification of the text by punctuation. He remembers that 'parts are not to be examined until the whole has been surveyed' (Sherbo, 7.111). Whatever the rewards of informed and studied reading, its proper basis is reading uninterrupted and engaged. Johnson's focus is on literary pleasure, not scholarly mastery.

George Steevens first appeared in Shakespeare scholarship as an assistant to Johnson. To the edition of 1765 he contributed a list of extant quartos and some notes, and is said to have helped Johnson complete his work more promptly than the self-styled 'Idler' might otherwise have managed. He then turned immediately to a quite different and original form of Shakespeare publication, *Twenty of the Plays of Shakespeare . . . printed in Quarto during his life-time, or before the Restoration* (four volumes; London, 1766). These volumes included *The Contention* (1594) and *The True Tragedy* (1595: versions of Parts 2 and 3 of *Henry VI*), the 1597 *Romeo and Juliet*, the 1604/5 *Hamlet*, the 1608 *King Lear*, the 1609 *Sonnets*, and the 1622 *Othello*. It was the first systematic publication of quartos, and a new mode of editing—unannotated diplomatic transcription, retaining Elizabethan spelling and punctuation, which gave a more historic sense of the texts. It showed how different some quarto texts were from the received and in some cases conflated versions of the tradition of editing inherited from Rowe, facilitated a new interest in the problems of Shakespeare's text, and acted as a spur to more detailed collation at a time when the early copies on which collation depends were variously distributed in private collections.

Steevens continued working with Johnson, producing two revised versions of the 1765 edition in 1773 and 1778 (both in ten volumes). An addition by Johnson to the 1773 Preface implicitly attributed much of the new work to Steevens, 'who might have spoken both of his own diligence and sagacity, in terms of greater self-approbation, without deviating from modesty or truth' (Sherbo, 7.113). Edward Capell's edition had meanwhile appeared (ten volumes, 1768). The first to break with the tradition of editing from a text based ultimately on Rowe and F4, Capell had gone back to the early texts and transcribed them afresh. To pre-empt charges of plagiarism in relation to his own claim that the revised text had been 'constantly compared with the most authentic copies' ('Advertisement', 1773 text; 1778, 1.69), Steevens dismissed Capell's text on what he claimed was a cursory inspection of *2 Henry VI*, commenting that 'what is called plagiarism is often no more than the result of having thought alike with others on the same subject' ('Advertisement', 1773; 1778, I.78). In *A Letter to George Hardinge* (dated 1774, published 1777) Capell's friend, John Collins, showed how much of Steevens's argument about the text was in fact taken from Capell. Unable to refute Collins, Steevens, who often engaged in violent humour variously estimated from puckish to malicious, added to later editions explications of abstruse bawdry which he attributed to Collins, who was an Anglican clergyman. These are most extensively exemplified by a note which is in effect a short essay on Thersites' 'How the devil Luxury [lust], with his fat rump and potato finger, tickles these together!' (*Troilus*, 5.2.55–6)—a wide-ranging discussion of potato-based recipes for aphrodisiacs, and (in the absence of potatoes) a range of other fruits and vegetables by no means required to gloss Thersites' exclamation, with recipes from Gerard's *Herbal* and *The Good Huswives Jewell* indicating an unduly lively interest (1778, 9.166–70). This puckish-malicious masterpiece of learned parody had a long life, reappearing (still signed 'Collins') in the Boswell–Malone edition of 1821 (8.450–4).

Much of Steevens's editing, and one of its great strengths, involved real explication of difficult passages on the model of Theobald, illustrated by wide reading in Shakespeare and his contemporaries. Like Johnson, Steevens also offered critical comments, among the most striking of which is his unusual antipathetic view of Hamlet and 'the immoral tendency of his character'.[21] This is a developed version of observations by Johnson on Hamlet's reasons for not killing Claudius at prayer and his reconciliation with Laertes (Sherbo, 8.990, 1010). Pursued through a greater variety of incidents, Steevens's critique is antithetical to the typically Romantic sympathetic identification with Hamlet of Goethe, Coleridge, and Hazlitt. While his view might be seen as an oblique adumbration of the Romantic preoccupation with Hamlet's delay, its complete rejection of the perplexed admiration that usually accompanies that prefigures rather twentieth-century views such as that of Charles Marowitz: 'frankly, [Hamlet] gives me a pain in the ass'.[22] Whether this shows Steevens out of step with his age or aberrantly prescient, he was cogently answered at the time by the later scourge of Malone and Steevens's ally, Joseph Ritson.[23]

Steevens followed the second revision of Johnson's edition with another new direction in *Six Old Plays* (1779), printing source dramas which provided evidence of Shakespeare's artistic judgement in shaping his material, on which Coleridge was later to insist. He also began his association with the self-effacing Isaac Reed, helping with Reed's revision of Robert Dodsley's *Select Collection of Old Plays* (originally published in twelve volumes, 1744; revised 1780 by Reed with the assistance of Steevens, whose copious notes made him virtually a co-editor). The revised collection included work by Marlowe, Dekker, Marston, Heywood, Webster, Middleton, Massinger, and Ford, among others.[24] In keeping with the evolution of Shakespeare editing, the revision used earlier, more authoritative, texts. It also attempted a more chronological arrangement. Again this is material that figured in Romantic criticism, one basis for Lamb's *Specimens of English Dramatic Poets* (1808), which gave a new sense of the literary contexts in which Shakespeare worked.

After the 1778 revision of Johnson, Steevens presented himself as a 'dowager' editor, retired from work on Shakespeare, and turned to his love of Hogarth, assisting John Nichols with his life and catalogue of Hogarth's works (1781; revised 1782 and 1785). What prompted Steevens to a final edition of Shakespeare was probably a desire to demonstrate his superiority to Malone. Though his new edition (fifteen volumes, 1793) still bears Johnson's name, and is described on its title page as 'revised and augmented...by the editor of Dodsley's...Old Plays' (Isaac Reed), it is almost exclusively the work of Steevens. In something of a recantation of his views as expressed in the 'Advertisement' to 1773, the Preface defends practices of eclectic emendation (from 'a Warburton, a Johnson, a Farmer, a Tyrwhitt', 1.xii), on grounds of what Steevens now argues is the certain corruption of early editions, quarto and folio. 'We do not therefore hesitate to affirm, that a blind fidelity to the eldest printed copies, is on some occasions a confirmed treason against the sense, spirit, and versification of Shakespeare' (1.xvi)—that is, the practices of emendation inherited from eighteenth-century editorial tradition are superior to the more conservative practices urged by his contemporaries (and, in his view, rivals), Capell and Malone—though also by Johnson, whose cautious conservatism is not so easily to be associated with Warburton's fanciful conjectures as Steevens's breezy list implies. Steevens also dissents, as Ritson had done, from Malone's dismissal of the Second Folio and his views on supposed historic pronunciations which (Malone argued) regularize apparently defective metrical structures. Steevens's view in 1793 that 'irregularity of metre ought always to excite suspicions of omission or interpolation' (3.68) is a general principle that might justify a wide variety of practices. His sense of the importance of hearing metrical shapes had one crucial effect: he was the first editor to set out lines shared between more than one speaker so as to exhibit typographically their structure as single lines of verse. With Steevens in 1793 the principle also, however, justified a freedom to emend that the conservatism of Johnson and the textual disciplines of Capell and Malone had rendered anachronistic; and, congruent with this (for example, when dismissing Feste's closing song in *Twelfth Night* as 'some buffoon actor's composition' (4.173)), exercises of taste more in tune with the aesthetics of Pope than the age of *Lyrical Ballads*.

The 1793 edition is of the plays only. Unlike the editions of Malone, it does not include Shakespeare's non-dramatic poems because, in Steevens's view, 'the strongest act of Parliament that could be framed would fail to compel readers into their service' (1.vii). In this Steevens follows the assumptions of Rowe developed from the seventeenth-century folios and confirmed by Johnson (who also excluded the narrative poems and sonnets), but out of tune with Romantic-period interests. Though in general Hazlitt thought the poems not on the level of the plays, he was unfazed by the Sonnets' address to a 'lovely boy' ('the subject . . . seems to be somewhat equivocal'), and considered them 'interesting as they relate to the state of the personal feelings of the author' (*Characters*, 'Poems and Sonnets')—that is, like Malone, he read them as lyric autobiography. Coleridge saw in the narrative poems striking early intimations of Shakespeare's greatness as a poet (*Biographia*, ch. 15), and Keats experimented with the sonnet form partly by taking Shakespeare as an admired model.

For his clarity, verve, and wit, like Johnson, Steevens is often a pleasure to read, though his brilliance as a polemicist sometimes contrives to make his undoubtedly sharp sense of logic appear more convincing than clear-eyed evaluation of the facts shows it to be. In his later (post-Johnson) editorial practices, and in some of his ventures into criticism, Steevens was out of step with his age. He may at times have been misled by his pugnacious temperament into adopting views which allowed him to assert himself against those he considered rivals, especially Capell and Malone. His real contributions were in drawing greater attention to textual diversity and the problems this raises, and above all in annotation, with the acute sense of historical meaning and usage he derived from wide reading in Shakespeare's contemporaries.

Editing Shakespeare precisely contemporary with Johnson and Steevens was Edward Capell. Capell's influence was as inferior to that of Johnson and Steevens as his editorial practices were superior. A well-informed modern view sees his work as having 'revolutionized both the theory and practice of editing Shakespeare'[25]—which is rather what he might have done, had his work not been ignored by his contemporaries.

Capell was the first editor fully to break from the tradition inherited from Rowe of preparing a new edition from a marked-up copy of its predecessor—hence ultimately from F4. Capell began again. He transcribed the early copies. Prompted by his view of the fundamental errors of Hanmer's edition, he collected quartos and folios and began the work of transcribing Shakespeare's text afresh in 1749 (that is, before, but broadly contemporaneously with, Johnson), working through the entire dramatic oeuvre (like others before Malone, he did not include the poems) until 1766. His text began to be printed in 1760, and its first eight volumes (of ten) were set up before Johnson's edition appeared. The edition was published in 1767–8. In it he vindicated the early texts from the assumptions about playhouse corruption which passed from Pope to Johnson. He argued that some quartos were derived from authorial manuscripts, and saw that some folio texts were based on quartos. He therefore (as Johnson proposed, but did not) collated quarto and folio texts systematically. He was the first editor to do so, and the first to construct a reasoned hierarchy of textual witnesses. Where earlier editors had corrected mainly from the First Folio, emending haphazardly from later folios and such quartos as they happened to possess, Capell edited from what he judged the 'best' text (the text he supposed nearest to Shakespeare's manuscript) when he had it. (With *Romeo and Juliet* he knew he did not: he owned only Q3, 1609; like all his contemporaries, he knew only Q3 of *Titus Andronicus*, 1611, though he knew there had been at least one earlier text.) He deduced from folio texts set from quartos that folio texts commonly showed errors—not on the radical grounds supposed by Pope and others but on the limited grounds that simple compositor errors were not subject to exigent correction of proofs. From this he developed an argument for limited, disciplined emendation. It is a thoroughly reasoned editorial programme, set out in his introduction (1.1–74). He also gave an account of Shakespeare's sources. He defended Shakespeare's authorship of *Henry VI*, *Love's Labours Lost* (often doubted in the period, out of an Augustan distaste for Shakespeare's love of complex puns and verbal play), and—almost uniquely in the period, with a good account of its relation to the brief but powerful fashion of the 'tragedy of blood'—*Titus Andronicus*, for which critics well into the Romantic period felt a distaste which led to their denying the play was by Shakespeare. And finally he proposed the need for a history of the Shakespearean theatre and a properly documented life of Shakespeare, which became the main focus of Malone's research over the following decades.

One other major innovation of Capell's edition was the 'clean' text page, free of annotation. While working on his Shakespeare, Capell published a volume of *Prolusions; or, select pieces of ancient poetry* (1760), which offered examples of 'the integrity that should be found in the editions of worthy authors' (title page). It exemplified the beauty and clarity of the unannotated text.[26] Johnson had adumbrated one value of this in his 1765 'Preface' when he argued that, in reading notes, 'the mind is refrigerated by interruption' (Sherbo, 7.111).

Nevertheless, in Johnson's own edition (and increasingly in the editions of Steevens and Malone) half or more of a page may be taken up with annotation to which, however unwillingly, the eye is constantly drawn and the reader thereby distracted from the experience of the drama: that is, the convenience of the arrangement (the material is readily accessible, should it be needed) is outweighed by its real effect (the material constantly disrupts the experience, understanding of which it is intended to deepen).

The clean page, however, brought its own problems. Capell promised 'some other volumes, notes, critical and explanatory, and a body of various readings entire' (title page) to be published in due course. These appeared as *Notes and Various Readings to Shakespeare* (three volumes, 1779–83; the third volume published posthumously, and in part edited from Capell's notes, by John Collins). The first two volumes are annotations and (printed separately) collations for each play.[27] These annotations have sometimes a typically eighteenth-century aspect as when (like Johnson) Capell objects to the ordinariness of Lady Macbeth's diction: 'the blanket of the dark' (II.i.7); or, more extremely, when he removes from the text of *Hamlet* Claudius's 'in hugger-mugger' as a 'low and base' compound (I.i.143). But he understands that inelegance may be power, that 'the poet's force of expression is the cause that many parts of these speeches want interpreting' (I.ii.174), and in the explication of that compression he is often excellent—as with the 'mad' speeches of Edgar and Lear, where he sees that neither Shakespeare's 'real nor his counterfeit madmen throw out nothing that has not a vestige of sense, nothing quite unintelligible' (I.ii.167), and so makes sense of fragmentary utterances by grasping the implied but suppressed connections that show 'reason in madness'. The second volume of *Notes* also contains a chronology, superior to Malone's first attempt (1778), of which it was independent, and a subtle but archaically expressed essay on Shakespeare's metrics designed in part (like the much later essay of Malone) to pre-empt regularizing emendation. The third volume is 'the school of Shakespeare . . . authentic extracts from divers English books that were in print in that author's time', that is, a collection of source texts and illustrative quotations—excellent in its material, but the most difficult part of the volumes to use because the presentation (apparently Capell's; the completed manuscript is dated a month before his death) is, to say the least, complex in ways scarcely resolved by its index and systems of cross reference.

For a variety of reasons Capell's editing, though ahead of its time and congruent with sophisticated later practices, was limited in its effects. In part its effect was muted by Capell himself. His unusual insistence on a printed page with text only, which led him to publish his annotations and collations separately, made the edition as a whole difficult to use. He also devised a special scheme of punctuation, signs for asides, changes of addressee, textually prompted gestures, and (somewhat bizarrely) irony, which were explained in the *Prolusions*, but not in the edition. In all this Capell did not entirely help himself. But his work was also denigrated variously by Johnson, by Malone, and especially by Steevens. Johnson seems simply to have failed to appreciate Capell's originality. Steevens may have been motivated by a desire to assert his superiority and to cover his plagiarism. If he is, as has been supposed, the author of a series of abusive (anonymous) pieces in *St James's Chronicle* in 1773, he seems to have acted towards Capell with a malignity unusual even for him.[28]

Capell was a scrupulous and exact predecessor of the twentieth-century 'New Bibliography' of Pollard, McKerrow, and Greg—more so even than Malone; but he was ignored, and not recuperated until virtually the eve of the New Bibliography's overthrow by the quite different contemporary movement in Shakespeare editing.[29] While his work was in some ways notably original, his effect on Romantic-period views of Shakespeare was limited—either filtered surreptitiously through others (Steevens), or through congruent work carried out independently (by Malone).

A figure no less outside the main currents than Capell, whose work was equally original, though in a different way, was Charles Jennens (1700–73). Long before he turned to Shakespeare, Jennens was well known as a librettist. He had arranged and written the texts for four of Handel's English oratorios, including *Messiah*. Jennens was also a notable patron of music and the visual arts, and a collector of paintings and sculpture. He began editing Shakespeare late in life, publishing in all individual editions of five plays—*King Lear* (1770), *Macbeth*, *Othello*, and *Hamlet* (1773), with *Julius Caesar* appearing posthumously (1774). Jennens claimed that 'no fair and exact collation of Shakespeare hath yet been presented to the public' (Preface to *King*

Lear). The purpose of collation, he argued, was to show precisely how editions differ so that the reader may see and judge how the choice of a reading has been made. He was a careful and exact collator, but, unlike Capell, he did not attempt to arrange the early texts in any order of authority: he simply printed the variants of the early texts known to him, and the emendations of the eighteenth-century editors, at the bottom of the page—thereby, with *King Lear* and *Hamlet* especially, revealing how much the received texts were in substantial ways conflations of quarto and folio sources. He shares little with other Shakespeare editors of the period beyond being the subject of abuse by George Steevens, who attacked him for being 'too exact'—an objection indicative of Steevens's limitations, since, as Jennens replied, what is the worth of an editor who is not exact? Like Capell, however, he was ignored by his contemporaries, though he is unique in the period in making peculiarly clear how much some received texts were conflations of early sources.

Malone, who abandoned his training as a lawyer for literature with an edition of his compatriot Oliver Goldsmith (1777), began his Shakespearean work at the invitation of Steevens in relation to the third edition of Johnson–Steevens (1778). To this Malone contributed 'An attempt to ascertain the order in which the plays attributed to Shakespeare were written'—a venture with limited antecedents in Theobald and Capell, and a first step towards one of Malone's major contributions to Shakespearean scholarship, a fact-based life of Shakespeare. The careful phrasing of his title is indicative of Malone's approach: 'an attempt', recognizing that this was a first step, and fuller information might become available; 'attributed to', probably meaning that he was already doubtful about the authorship of the *Henry VI* plays (which he later contested at length). The chronology is not simply a list of dates: it incorporates for each play the wide range of evidence (external and internal, documentary, contextual, and stylistic) on which each dating is based. In the event Malone revised it twice (in his editions of 1790 and 1821), in his second revision establishing an order of composition broadly in line with modern views.

Despite some differences with Steevens, prompted in part by notes correcting Steevens's inaccuracies, Malone's supplement to the edition appeared in two volumes in 1780. Volume 2 contains the seven apocryphal plays attributed to Shakespeare in the Third Folio. Like

Steevens, Malone judged five of these spurious. On *Pericles* he concludes a debate with Steevens (who thought the play not by Shakespeare) with the muted affirmation of a double negative: 'I am ... unconvinced that the drama was not written by our author' (2.186). On *A Yorkshire Tragedy* (now sometimes also seen as a Shakespearean collaboration) he reports himself half-persuaded by Steevens's view that it is 'a genuine but hasty production of our author' (2.675). Far more important was Volume 1. This contained 'an imperfect account of our ancient theatres' (1.1–60; the basis of his later, greatly extended, History of the English Stage), a reprint of a major source, Arthur Brooke's translation of *Romeus and Juliet* (1562), and annotated editions of Shakespeare's non-dramatic poetry—the narrative poems, 'A Lover's Complaint', and above all the Sonnets. For the Sonnets he returned to the 1609 Quarto, and thus displaced the usual adapted text derived from Benson's edition of 1640. Malone's annotation opens up the possibility (severely contradicted by Steevens) of understanding the Sonnets as in part autobiography: '[Shakespeare] appears to me', he wrote of Sonnet 93, 'to have written more immediately *from the heart* on the subject of jealousy' (1.654), adding tentative conjectures about supposed marital infidelity that might lie behind Shakespeare's bequest to his wife of their 'second best bed' (his own correction to former misreadings of Shakespeare's will).[30] The Supplement thus announced major themes of Malone's work: analysis of collaborative authorship, theatre history, source study, editing directly from early texts, a reinstatement of Shakespeare the non-dramatic poet, and a way of reading lyric as personal expression congruent with the poetry of the period.

He took another significant new direction with his next major Shakespearean work, *A dissertation on the three parts of King Henry VI, tending to shew that those plays were not written originally by Shakespeare* (1787). This argues that Part 1 of *Henry VI* is not by Shakespeare but by Robert Greene and George Peele, and that Parts 2 and 3 were reworked by Shakespeare from plays first published as *The First Part of the Contention betwixt the ... Houses of York and Lancaster* (1594) and *The True Tragedy of Richard Duke of York* (1595), also (he supposed) by Greene and Peele. The theory raised what has proved to be a permanent issue in Shakespeare authorship debates, with arguments for and against rival ways of accounting for the plays' textual problems, including collaborative authorship, that continue to prompt controversy.[31] The dissertation was reprinted with the *Henry VI* plays in Malone's two editions (1790, 1821), and while the idea of collaboration was not straightforwardly congruent with Romantic ideas of Shakespeare's transcendent genius (Hazlitt, for example, entirely ignores it in his *Characters of Shakespeare's Plays*), two centuries later Shakespeare as collaborator has proved amenable again to a variety of perspectives.[32]

Meanwhile Malone had continued working on two other projects: a documentary life of Shakespeare, and an expanded history of the stage focussed similarly on documentary evidence about the contexts and conditions in which Shakespeare worked. Both were published with a new edition of Shakespeare's texts, using more rigorously the First Folio and the early Quartos (ten volumes, 1790; the first volume divided into two parts). For the life Malone worked in archives of many kinds to turn up documents in any way connected with Shakespeare. Many of these were public and of a purely factual nature (registers of baptism and marriage, wills), but they also included documents of other kinds, such as the biographical sketches written by the antiquarian John Aubrey (1626–97), whose manuscripts were in the Ashmolean Museum, Oxford. In his usual scholarly manner Malone transcribed Aubrey's anecdotal Shakespeare notes verbatim and discussed them to test and illustrate their probability. On the basis of all this material he wholly displaced the largely legendary life by Nicholas Rowe hitherto reprinted in all eighteenth-century editions (and reprinted by Malone with notes and commentary exposing its fictional nature), and replaced it with an extended scholarly biography containing a mass of new material. 'An Historical Account of the Rise and Progress of the English Stage, and of the Economy and Usages of our Ancient Theatres', leading up to accounts of Shakespeare's main theatres, the Globe and the Blackfriars, deals with the social, economic, and practical history of the stage.[33] It is perhaps Malone's most original piece of work, elaborately documented from an immense range of sources and drawing on newly researched materials, including a manuscript of 1599 giving the 'dimensions and plan of the Globe Playhouse' (I.ii.325). In relation to the History he turned up two of his most notable discoveries: the Office Book of Sir Henry Herbert, Master of the Revels to James I and Charles I from 1622 to 1642;

and—most significant of all—the diary of Philip Henslowe, proprietor of the Rose Theatre (near the Globe, on Bankside), from 1592 to 1603. Though it deals with the period after Shakespeare's death, Sir Henry Herbert's Office Book is an important source because the Master of the Revels was concerned not only with performances at court but also with public theatres, including licensing plays.[34] Far more important, however, especially because it was precisely contemporary with Shakespeare, is Henslowe's diary. Though not concerned with Shakespeare's company, this reflects the working conditions of a Shakespearean theatre during the first half of Shakespeare's career. It also records details of plays performed by two other companies between 1592 and 1597, and Henslowe's dealings with or related to Marlowe, Ben Jonson, Thomas Middleton, and George Chapman.[35] Both discoveries came too late for Malone to incorporate them into his History of the Stage, already prepared for the press. He therefore added transcriptions of the material, which were retained in similar form when the edition was revised in 1821. The material opened up new possibilities for the contextual study of Shakespeare, possibilities not much developed in criticism before the twentieth century, though knowledge of Shakespeare's bare-stage theatre influenced performance earlier.

Malone's edition of 1790 is described on its title page as 'collated *verbatim* with the most authentick copies'. Its texts were indeed edited in some new ways, though, like other editors apart from Capell, Malone did not begin entirely afresh: his printer's copy was a marked-up version of the Johnson–Steevens–Reed edition of 1785 (still a text based ultimately on Rowe and F4). Malone corrected this, however, from the earliest copies—F1 for plays only in the Folio, and, where appropriate, the earliest Quartos—that is, for all but *Henry V*, 1600, and *Merry Wives*, 1600, which he judged 'either sketches or imperfect copies' (I.i.xliv), and *Richard III*, 1597, which he was only able to obtain when his F1-based text had gone to press, and which he collated in an appendix. (Malone did not know Q1 of *Hamlet* (1603), which was not discovered until 1823.) The Second Folio he in theory rejected because its differences from the first showed, he thought, its editor's 'profound ignorance of our poet's phraseology and metre' (I.i.xix). An extended demonstration of F2's errors ends with his complete condemnation of it as without any authority (I.i.xix–xliii). In an attempt to ensure that he corrected the Johnson–Steevens–Reed text fully by folio and quarto sources, Malone subjected it to an extraordinary correction process. 'Having often experienced the fallaciousness of collation by the eye' (I.i.xliv), he had each proof sheet read aloud to him while he checked it against its source (F or Q) and his tabulation of F and Q variants. By this he hoped insofar as humanly possible to obviate error. Among what he claimed were 1,654 emendations of the received text, in controversy with Joseph Ritson he admitted to eight errors over which his vigilance had lapsed.[36] Nevertheless, despite his insistence on the validity of historic usages, Malone continued silently to 'correct' for some expectations of eighteenth-century grammar, and (as Steevens vigorously pointed out) he also incorporated a number of F2 corrections.[37] His editorial practice—like that of all other eighteenth-century editors—was thus more eclectic than his editorial theory admitted.

For Malone, 'the two great duties of an editor are, to establish the genuine text of his author and to explain his obscurities' (I.i.liv). His explanations of difficulties are exemplary for their period—concise relative to the practice of including evidently mistaken 'elucidations' and discussing (or triumphing over) their errors, illustrated cogently from existing scholarship and his own wide reading. It is a practice which allowed him to claim justly (following Johnson) that 'not a single passage in the whole work has appeared to me obscure, which I have not endeavoured to illustrate' (I.i.liv). Malone's are annotations which later editions (down to the present) would often cite.

As early as 1792 Malone announced plans for a revised and enlarged reworking of 1790, but in the ensuing decade he turned from work on Shakespeare to other literary projects. Since the early 1780s he had been assisting James Boswell with Johnsonian writings (*A Tour to the Hebrides with Samuel Johnson*, 1786; *Life of Johnson*, 1791, and later revisions, edited, after Boswell's death, by Malone). He edited, with a biography, the works of Sir Joshua Reynolds (two volumes, 1797), and similarly, also with a biography, the critical and miscellaneous prose of Dryden (four volumes, 1800). Directly connected with Shakespeare, though not to his edition, was his exposure of Shakespearean forgeries by William Henry Ireland (1796; a cache of documents including what purported to be four play manuscripts). Malone's training as a lawyer and his reliance on the validity of genuine Shakespearean documentary material were both engaged. Malone had earlier demonstrated the forgery of poems by a supposed fifteenth-century monk, William Rowley, by Thomas Chatterton (1782), and he deployed the same forensic skills, plus his knowledge of Elizabethan language and handwriting, on Ireland's documents. His last work directly on Shakespeare was a further source study, *An Account of the incidents, from which the title and part of the story of Shakespeare's Tempest were derived* (1808), new information which helped him date the play more precisely to 1611.[38]

When he died in 1812, Malone left the manuscripts for his proposed revision of his 1790 edition to James Boswell Jr, who handsomely repaid Malone's efforts with his father's writings on Johnson by editing the material into Malone's Shakespearean summa, the twenty-one-volume edition of 1821, the so-called 'third variorum'. This is the most developed form in which Romantic-period readers encountered eighteenth- and early nineteenth-century traditions of editing as developed before and after Johnson. 1821 is in part 1790 extended. Much of its material was present in some form in 1790, and so was known throughout the Romantic period. Like earlier 'variorum' editions (Johnson, 1765; Reed, 1803) it included the introductions of all the main eighteenth-century editors and some other eighteenth-century writings, including Farmer's pamphlet on Shakespeare's knowledge of classical literature. The annotation was expanded, and the plays were printed for the first time in their order of composition according to a newly revised chronology, though with the histories printed separately in the historical order of their subjects, from *King John* to *Henry VIII*.[39] A new 'Essay on the Metre and Phraseology of Shakespeare and his Contemporaries' (I.505–85), written by Boswell from Malone's notes, was designed primarily to pre-empt modes of 'emendation' practised by editors (including Steevens) who did not understand Elizabethan usage and syntax and Shakespeare's metrical freedoms. How much this was in tune with the spirit of the age may be judged by comparing Pope's Augustan regularization of Shakespeare's metre in the 1720s with Wordsworth's Romantic-period view of verse rhythm: 'I can scarcely say that I admit any limits to the dislocation of the verse, that is, I know none that may not be justified by some passion or other.'[40] The life is supplemented by new documentary materials and new conjectures, though it still included no account of Shakespeare's years writing for the theatre.

Malone had distinguished admirers and supporters. Supporters included Thomas Tyrwhitt (1730–86), classical scholar, editor of Chaucer (*Canterbury Tales*, 1775–7), and curator of the British Museum, who contributed copiously to his annotations;[41] and Richard Farmer (1735–97), classicist and antiquarian, Master of Emmanuel College, Cambridge, whose *Essay on the Learning of Shakespeare* (1767), arguing that Shakespeare acquired his knowledge of classical writers largely through translations, was broadly accepted well into the nineteenth century.[42] Admirers included the conservative statesman and philosopher Edmund Burke (1729–97), who praised Malone's historical study of English theatrical culture, uniting different strata of society, as congruent with his own political views on the importance of stable traditions of social and political institutions.[43]

Malone also had detractors. With characteristic intemperance but not without justice, Joseph Ritson both impugned his ear for verse and attacked the accuracy of his collations. In *The Essence of Malone* (1800), George Hardinge, an MP and major figure in the legal profession, adopted the ironic mode of Thomas Edwards with Warburton, offering 'canons' supposedly extracted from Malone's practice: 'The Life of A should be the lives of B, C, D, etc. to the end of the alphabet'; 'A biographer cannot be too minute in what he relates to his Hero'; and so on.[44] Hardinge's point was that Malone lacked perspective in presenting his material: whatever he discovered that could be connected with Shakespeare, however remotely, he presented in the fullest possible detail. Malone was ignored by the great Romantic critics of Shakespeare, partly perhaps because they associated him with Johnson, and so with critical views they regarded as superseded. Malone had first appeared as a Shakespeare scholar in association with the 1778 revision of Johnson–Steevens, and it was indicative of his critical allegiances that he placed Johnson's *Preface* at the beginning of his 1790 edition. But Hardinge's critique may indicate a less contextual problem: Malone's presentation of his scholarship was hardly of a kind to draw in the enthusiast seeking to deepen knowledge, love, and wonder. Where, for all his erudition, Johnson wrote for the intellectually inclined lover of Shakespeare, Malone's methods are designed to assert his position as the doyen of Shakespeare scholars.

This is no simple historical development: Theobald has more in common with Malone than with Johnson. It is, however, indicative of a broad shift. Johnson was the last major writer to edit Shakespeare. From Malone onwards editing became increasingly the province of a professional clerisy.

In many ways Malone took up from his eighteenth-century predecessors—Theobald (annotating Shakespeare from himself and his forebears and contemporaries), Johnson (the 'variorum' edition, with multiple voices in the annotation), Capell (editing from the earliest copies), and Steevens (who also returned more emphatically than others to the quartos and annotated in the manner of Theobald). He also showed ways for his successors, establishing the main elements of what, codified and sophisticated, became in the twentieth century the 'New Bibliography'. In so doing he set patterns for Shakespeare editing for the next 150 years. In all this he gave new impetus to the gradual professionalization of literary studies, a movement away from the primarily aesthetic orientation of Pope and, in his way, Johnson; a movement, the origins of which lie earlier in the eighteenth century, that conferred a new prestige on studies more fact-based and historical. It is indicative both that the part of the long-meditated life of Shakespeare that Malone did not write was for the years in which Shakespeare was an active poet-dramatist, and that his work was largely ignored by the Romantic writers most concerned with Shakespeare—Coleridge, Hazlitt, Lamb, and Keats.[45] Malone helped to create a new caste of literary-historical professionals which came gradually to displace the centrality to literary-critical culture of the aesthetic conveyed by writer-intellectuals—the tradition of Dryden, Pope, and Johnson. Malone's researches saved from oblivion a range of Shakespeareana that might have been lost without his efforts, and he led the way in establishing new fields of literary-historical enquiry. But, to adopt his equivocal double negative, it is not clear that Pope would not have found for him a place in a new epic of the end of culture.

The English Stage

The Age of Siddons

> Manifestations [of the art of the stage] fleet away like a shadow, leaving
> no trace behind; and an unsatisfying remembrance of the great
> moments of delight and rapture fills us with sadness, for no memorial
> can restore these fleeting phenomena for those who have hung upon
> them with transport, because all that language or the painter's skill can
> do are inadequate to portray what the rapt spectator has seen and heard.

Thus Ludwig Tieck, commenting on the farewell performance of John
Philip Kemble as Coriolanus at Covent Garden in 1817.[1] Ten years
later Heinrich Heine saw his successor as the dominant Shakespearean
of the age, Edmund Kean, in some of his greatest roles—Shylock,
Othello, Richard III, and Macbeth. Like Hazlitt, Heine saw performance as an especially suggestive form of criticism: Kean's acting 'said
more than a four-volume commentary by Franz Horn'.[2] But like
Tieck, when he attempted to 'translate' the meanings of Kean's performance of Shylock—his Shylock as 'a hero' who struggles between
'outward humility and inner rage', with details of the tones, expressive
gestures, and embodied movement by which this was conveyed—even
so great a writer as Heine concludes, 'all this is vain. The best description cannot bring the essential Edmund Kean before you.'[3] This is not
only a difference between the age of mechanical reproduction and the
more distant past, the forever lost, moment-by-moment subtlety of
vocal tone and inflection, bodily deportment and gesture, the detail of
which no description of performance from before the age of film can
fully evoke. Neither is it the difference between a living reality and its

Shakespeare and the Romantics. David Fuller, Oxford University Press (2021). © David Fuller.
DOI: 10.1093/oso/9780199679119.003.0006

electronic preservation evident in film. It is a difference between live theatre and even the 'live' theatre of simultaneous broadcast, between the living body of the actor and any form of its representation. What cannot be recovered is being part of the moment in which the actor's mental and physical charisma communicates a reciprocal intensity with a present audience, being a part of the arena in which the actor's voice and body are a 'real presence'. The idea of a secular sacrament implied by the phrase is not inappropriate. It is wonderful that we can see Laurence Olivier and Peggy Ashcroft, Margot Fonteyn and Rudolf Nureyev, Maria Callas and Luciano Pavarotti; but no reproduction can give the effect of their living presence. Though the objective solidity of documentary evidence can be so persuasive, no account of theatre should forget that it is in part the irreproducible ephemerality of the performing arts—that they have their full being only in the life of the present moment—that gives them their intensity. Heine's despair of bringing Kean before the reader who was not present is salutary.

With the reservation that to recreate outward forms is not to bring back into being that living essence of theatre, there is nevertheless a great deal of material from which the nature of Romantic-period performance of Shakespeare can be recreated: texts, which were often highly adapted, prompt books, which show movements and music, reviews of performances, actor biographies, paintings and engravings of actors and sets, and accounts of theatres and of theatre-related events in their social and political contexts—copious material which provides bases from which something of that once living reality can be imagined.[4]

The age following the retirement in 1776 of the dominant Shakespearean actor of the mid-eighteenth century, David Garrick (1717–79), was in some ways a period of transition, moving away from control by the licensed theatres established in the reign of Charles II. By a law dating from 1660 and reconfirmed in 1737, in London only the 'royal' theatres of Drury Lane and Covent Garden were licensed to present spoken plays during the main theatrical season (autumn to spring). To this the Haymarket was added in 1766 for a summer season while the main theatres were closed. In the early post-Garrick period these licensed London theatres were dominated by two performers, Sarah Siddons (1755–1831), and her brother, John Philip Kemble (1757–1823). There were many other actors of note, several of them famous in Shakespearean roles: the charismatic but erratic George Frederick Cooke (1756–1812), particularly for his performances of Richard III; Dorothy (Dora) Jordan (1761–1816), unusually in the period better known for her performances in Shakespearean comedy; Eliza O'Neill (1791–1872), famous as Juliet, whose brief career (1814–9) was curtailed by marriage; Harriet Smithson (1800–54; later Mme Berlioz), best known as Ophelia, and more for Shakespeare performances in Paris than in London; William Charles Macready (1793–1873), whose career began at the time of Kemble's retirement, notable for restoring the Shakespearean text of *King Lear*, displacing the adaptation by Nahum Tate which held the stage from the late seventeenth century until the 1830s.[5] But Siddons and Kemble dominated the London stage from the 1780s until the arrival of Edmund Kean shortly after Siddons retired (1812) and just before the retirement of Kemble (1817). Though the period has been called 'the Age of Kemble' (Odell) and 'the Age of Kean' (Donohue), it is more properly 'the Age of Siddons'. Sarah Siddons was its dominant figure, celebrated in high art and popular culture, with a quasi-mythic status in her own lifetime and in the history of British theatre.

Edmund Kean (1787–1833) was the period's other great performer. Kean brought a striking new naturalism from the 'illegitimate' (unlicensed) theatres, the increasing influence of which is an important context of the transition from classic to Romantic, elite to democratic, epitomized by his antithetical relation to Kemble. To an extent unusual even for this most social-facing of the arts, Shakespearean performance in the period was often political: *Coriolanus*, problematic in the French Revolution and war-and-food-shortages context of the 1790s, *Macbeth* in the context of French Revolutionary regicide, *King John* and *Henry V*, their anti-French nationalism resonant in the context of the Napoleonic Wars, *King Lear* not performable during the period of the madness of George III—forms of topicality with which performers interacted in a variety of ways.

Politics affected some plays, architecture affected all. The structural environments of the main theatres played an important part in determining the style of Shakespearean production in the period. Small theatres, which from an artistic point of view might have been preferable, would have been available only to a high-paying, socially elite audience. Both Drury Lane and Covent Garden were large theatres with socially diverse audiences, and both became larger following reconstructions prompted by fires. The new Covent Garden, opened in 1792, held an audience of about 3,000. The new Drury Lane, opened in 1794, held just over 3,600. This was verbal theatre performed in buildings on, and mostly beyond, the scale of the largest modern opera houses. (The Metropolitan Opera, New York, the largest repertory opera house in the world, holds 3,800; Covent Garden, London—not the same building as the late eighteenth-century theatre—2,250; the Palais Garnier, Paris, 1,900.) These late eighteenth-century theatres required styles of production and performance proportionate to their large stages and immense audience spaces. Performers could be heard only with vocal projection, and seen only with gesture and physical expression, that militated against modern forms of subtlety. Spectacle was important for appealing to those parts of the house from which hearing could be problematic. Only the Haymarket Theatre, holding around 1,500 people, was near to the scale of a modern theatre designed for verbal performance. (The reconstructed Globe Theatre, London, holds 850 seated, with 700 'groundlings' standing round the thrust stage; the Royal Shakespeare Theatre, Stratford-upon-Avon, has an audience capacity of just over 1,000.) In virtually requiring spectacular sets, usually realist in style, with a comparably large cast of extras, changes of scenery (albeit swiftly executed by the wing-and-flat mechanism), and acts separated by orchestral interludes (with the curtain dropped to reset the next sequence of scenes), these immense theatres were antithetical to the Shakespearean expectation of verbal scene painting, minimal sets, quick and fluid transitions, and a relatively intimate relation between actors and audience. The theatre of Kemble, Siddons, and Kean was epic theatre. It was nearer in scale and mode to modern Shakespearean cinema than to the theatre for which Shakespeare wrote, but without cinema's instantaneous juxtapositions, close-up for intimacy, and easy audibility to complement its conventions of un-Shakespearean realism and panoramic scenic scale. Not the Shakespearean injunction 'on your imaginary forces work', but rather 'expect, when we talk of armies, you will see them'—or at least, often with massed supernumeraries, something as like an army as a stage could accommodate.[6]

While Siddons and Kean were the most important to their contemporaries for their charisma and intensity as performers, and also the most interesting in their influence on later styles of performance, Kemble is in some ways the more significant figure in the period in that, unlike them, he became an actor-manager—in effect an actor-director, in the mode in modern times of Laurence Olivier and Kenneth Branagh. After 1788, when he became the actor-manager of Drury Lane—a role which he took over in 1808 at Covent Garden after his move there in 1803—Kemble organized every major aspect of many of the Shakespeare productions in which he performed. He arranged the texts and their stage presentation, including the kind of scenery employed, historically researched costumes, and, as his punctiliously notated prompt books show, carefully choreographed movement, expressive groupings, and extensive use of music.[7] He performed in a greater variety of Shakespearean roles than most actors of the period—over twenty major parts in all. While his successes were not confined to tragic roles (he was notable as Hotspur and Posthumus), his most famous characterizations were of King John, Brutus, Hamlet, Macbeth, Prospero, Wolsey, and above all Coriolanus—often with Sarah Siddons in the corresponding female role: Constance, Lady Macbeth, Queen Katherine, Volumnia. Each of these productions is in some different way indicative about Kemble's aims and abilities, and all have been copiously reconstructed and studied.

As had been usual since the Restoration, 'Shakespeare' meant Shakespeare more or less radically reworked; not what until recently was the norm in modern performances, Shakespeare with cuts, often simply of material regarded as difficult to convey to a modern audience. Rather the norm was Shakespeare with cuts and with sometimes extensive additions, Shakespeare more or less transformed—as increasingly again in modern performances, whether to embody a directorial view or conform to contemporary presuppositions. In the Romantic period change to suit directorial emphasis, audience taste, or simply traditional expectations took many forms. The situation with regard to textual adaptation at the beginning of the Kemble era can be understood from John Bell's edition of Shakespeare (eight volumes, 1773–5), the twenty-four plays in the standard London repertoire, according to the title page, 'as they are now performed at the Theatres Royal... regulated from the prompt books of each house' (that is, Drury Lane and Covent Garden), with the other plays then thought authentic (not *Pericles*) in complete texts, with indications of how they might be cut for performance. These texts indicate the kind of bases which Kemble then reworked.[8]

Did most of Kemble's audience know that what they saw was only in part by Shakespeare? Except in extreme cases, most contemporary audiences perhaps have little idea how much what they see has been shaped by a director's cuts and other forms of intervention. Quite probably many of those who saw John Barton and Peter Hall's widely praised *The Wars of the Roses* in the 1960s did not realize how much of it was not only shaped by Barton and Hall's huge cuts and reworkings but also by their additions.[9] Kemble's texts were based on versions well known to theatregoers, many of them dating back to Restoration adaptations, further rewritten to suit later tastes by eighteenth-century playwrights, actors, and managers. While this was anathema to Coleridge, Lamb, and others, it would have astonished Romantic-period audiences if they had seen Shakespeare without 'improvement'—which they never did.

Kemble's *Hamlet* is textually his least adapted. It is broadly the usual eighteenth-century version, exceptionally with no non-Shakespearean additions, but with multiple cuts, broadly along lines sanctioned by stage tradition, to streamline the action. These include most of the Fortinbras material, most of the Act 2 soliloquy ('O, what a rogue and peasant slave am I!'), Claudius's prayer of penitence and Hamlet's decision not to kill him at prayer, the Act 4 soliloquy 'How all occasions do inform against me', and almost everything that follows the death of Hamlet. While these are not different in extent from cuts often introduced into eighteenth-century and modern performances, they are different in kind: taken all together they very much diminish the issue of delay, and make Hamlet the more straightforwardly Romantic figure depicted in Sir Thomas Lawrence's famous portrait (Figure 6.1).[10]

At the opposite extreme of cuts with adaptation is Kemble's *The Tempest, or The Enchanted Island*. For this, unusually, Kemble staged two substantially different versions; and, again unusually, though Garrick had returned to Shakespeare (and his text was printed in Bell's edition), Kemble reincorporated major elements of the Restoration adaption by Dryden and Davenant (1670). For Kemble's first version (1789) this meant that he could also avail himself of music by Purcell, Thomas Arne, and Matthew Locke, thereby very much

Figure 6.1. John Philip Kemble as Hamlet ('Hamlet with the skull of Yorick'). Painting by Sir Thomas Lawrence (1801). The Tate Gallery, London. Photo © Tate.

increasing the appeal of his staging, with spectacular visual effects of storms and spirits intensified by music.[11] Drawing on the Restoration texts, in both versions (1789 and 1806) Kemble added to Shakespeare Hippolyto, a man who has never seen a woman (parallel, therefore, to Miranda), and a sister to Miranda, Dorinda, with whom he falls in love—so the Miranda–Ferdinand plot is complicated by a gender-reversed parallel, with accompanying new plots.[12] The wedding masque of goddesses for Miranda and Ferdinand is cut in both versions, and in 1789 is replaced by a closing Masque of Neptune and Amphitrite.[13] If Coleridge witnessed a performance of this, it would in itself be enough to explain the 'pain, disgust and indignation' to which he was prompted by seeing Shakespeare in the theatre.

Everything else lies between this gamut from extensive cuts to extensive adaptation. Even a relatively limited adaptation such as Kemble's *Macbeth* used a text based on that reworked by Garrick from Davenant (1664), the version published in Bell's edition, including extra scenes for the witches, with a chorus of witches and songs and dances, also using music written for Restoration performances.[14] The staging was on the grandest scale, with elaborate backdrops for sixteen scene changes, special effects to enhance the supernatural, and costumes which, while not literally medieval, conveyed an idea of the Scottish.[15] Spectacular staging was not new. In the 1770s Garrick had employed the Franco-British painter Philippe-Jacques de Loutherbourg to create elaborate scenic illusions, but Kemble established spectacular setting as a regular feature and added to this an antiquarian interest in historical costumes, which he developed further in later productions.[16] Many of Kemble's cuts appear to any modern view of the play extraordinary. While it is unsurprising that the Porter, with his bawdy comedy, is entirely removed, as unsuited to Kemble's high view of tragedy, Kemble also omitted passages of the most intense poetry: 'pity, like a naked new-born babe' (1.7.21–5), 'Sleep that knits up the ravell'd sleeve of care' (2.2.34–7), and Macbeth's confrontation with apocalyptic destruction culminating in 'though the treasure / Of nature's germens tumble all together' (4.1.52–61).[17] In keeping with Kemble's usual attitude to onstage violence, though also with the specific effect of making Macbeth's violence less viscerally repugnant, there is no scene for Lady Macduff and her son between Macbeth's resolution to slaughter the Macduff household and Macduff's hearing that his wife and children have been murdered. A contested production innovation was to have no Ghost of Banquo appear at the banquet: attention was not to be diverted from Macbeth's guilty imagination—though objections apparently meant that in later performances the Ghost was reinstated. Kemble's most significant textual addition was a death speech for Macbeth, written by

Garrick, in which the penitent regicide draws a pious moral about 'ambition's vain delusive dreams' and sees himself being dragged to hell.[18] Despite these evident distortions, Scott thought Kemble as Macbeth 'unapproachable': his performances, with Sarah Siddons as Lady Macbeth, he judged 'the highest perfection of the dramatic art'.[19] Fundamentally, commentary praised Kemble's playing off the formal and stylized against moments of more natural expression to generate a dynamic between horror at and pity for Macbeth, a combination of heroic courage with guilt-ridden remorse which gave the tragedy its full effect.[20]

Similarly limited but crucial changes to *Julius Caesar* more radically transformed the play's meaning. The play was very little acted in the late eighteenth century, possibly because of what were perceived as republican implications, and Kemble did not stage it until 1811, though he then revived it each year up to his retirement. As with *Macbeth*, the sets were spectacular, showing Rome as in the imperial age—an idea of Roman grandeur rather than the actual Rome of the republican period, with historically informed costumes and a large cast of extras (up to a hundred people) for processional scenes. The 1811 prompt book shows lighting used to produce the sense of supernatural premonition which Kemble cut from the text. The similarly dressed principals were distinguished by movement: stoic calm for Brutus, nervous energy for Cassius, relaxed grace for Antony. Basing his text on the Bell edition (derived ultimately from a text again attributed to Dryden and Davenant), but with more extensive cuts, Kemble reduced the number of characters associated with Brutus and expanded the number of Antony's attendants to produce two balanced opposed groups. He similarly concentrated—and simplified—the central characters. Antony is improved, mainly by having the ruthless and manipulative realpolitik of Act 4, Scene 1 omitted.[21] Brutus—Kemble's own role—is similarly simplified. While the 'serpent's egg' soliloquy, in which Brutus slithers between honest appraisal and manipulative presentation of Caesar, is retained (2.1.10–34), the ritual, proposed by Brutus, of bathing in Caesar's blood is cut, and he kills himself without assistance, after a death speech derived from pseudo-Dryden–Davenant about 'the justest cause that ever men / Did draw their swords for'. The ambiguity of Shakespeare's character, acting with a mixture of idealism, pride of caste, naivety, and self-deception, is reduced; Brutus approaches more nearly the ideal of an anti-tyrannous philosopher-patriot. Over the play as a whole Shakespeare's Gothic patterning is trimmed to suit the aesthetics of neoclassicism, and his complex depiction of character and motive in political action is simplified to produce more moralized implications.[22]

While in this more diagrammatic version Kemble could play a noble republican, to play a noble patrician suited him much more. Coriolanus (Figure 6.2) was his signature role. He performed it in his first season as acting manager at Drury Lane in 1789, and while he did not

Figure 6.2. John Philip Kemble as Coriolanus. Painting by Sir Thomas Lawrence (1798). The Guildhall Art Gallery. Photo credit: City of London Corporation.

perform the play between 1797 and 1806, because political ideologies from the French Revolution and social conditions created by the Napoleonic Wars meant it was politically inflammatory, he marked its special position in his career by choosing it for his farewell performance on 23 June 1817.[23] 'Adapted to the stage, with additions from Thomson, by J. P. Kemble': thus the title page of the 1812 text. 'Thomson' is James Thomson (1700–48), the poet of *The Seasons*; the 'additions' are from his *Coriolanus*, first acted (posthumously) in 1749. This was not a version of Shakespeare's play but a neoclassical tragedy on the same subject. Kemble drew from this directly, and from an adaptation of it already combined with Shakespeare (1752) by Richard Brinsley Sheridan. The changes to Shakespeare evolved from this by Kemble are extensive.[24] Acts 1 and 2 are streamlined in the manner of his *Hamlet*. Coriolanus becomes a less extreme figure. Much of his irascibility and patrician contempt disappears: there is less in the mode of 'Bid them wash their faces, / And keep their teeth clean' (2.3.60–1). Acts 3 to 5 are a combination of Shakespeare and Thomson–Sheridan. With the inflammatory in Coriolanus's anger reduced, his banishment arises less from his provocations, though the climax retains his contempt for the common people unmitigated (3.3.120–35). Much of Volumnia's great plea (5.3.94–182) is omitted, as is Coriolanus's response, 'O mother, mother, / What have you done?'. From that point in the recantation Shakespeare is replaced by Thomson. Coriolanus yields not to Volumnia's words but to the melodrama of her drawn dagger and threat of suicide. The whole scene is written in a conventional eighteenth-century rhetoric which Kemble's performance evidently made more impressive than the printed page can show. What is astonishing about Kemble's text is how much of the plebeian-baiting autocrat it retains for performance before a socially heterogeneous audience in the era of the French Revolution, the radical-reformist London Corresponding Society, and the treason trials of its leaders. Kemble was apparently able to give a thrilling appeal to the heroic figure destroyed by his attempt to stand alone, 'As if a man were author of himself, / And knew no other kin' (5.3.36–7), an appeal that transcended contexts shaped by political opinion.

The prompt book alone is misleading, in part because it cannot convey Kemble's charisma in his favourite role, but also because performance in the period was a happening in which the audience was participatory. Exchange was not only from stage to audience: the audience joined in. It shouted and applauded for what gave it pleasure; it jeered and catcalled what gave it offence. Enthusiastic cheering is a phenomenon often reported—for a great speech, a grand procession, a *coup de théâtre*. On Kemble's first entry in one of his final performances as Coriolanus, 'in every part of the house the audience rose, waved their hats, and huzzaed, and the cheering must have lasted more than five minutes'.[25] Extended interventions of audience response are frequently mentioned in accounts of the period. The performance of a great speech could be like that of a bravura aria in Italian opera or a great *pas de deux* in Romantic ballet: the drama was brought to a standstill, the stage illusion disrupted, by the participatory audience— an effect utterly unlike that usual in contemporary verbal theatre, where the audience sits silent and the supposed illusion is interrupted only by the convention of an interval.

Kemble's pleb-baiting Coriolanus is especially remarkable in the context of his *Macbeth*, which was the occasion of the period's most notable example of theatrical politics, the 'Old Price' riots. Kemble chose *Macbeth* to open the new Covent Garden in 1809, after the 1792 building was destroyed by a second fire in the theatre the previous year. The new building had more exclusive accommodation (private boxes), less commodious and well-sighted accommodation in the cheapest area (the gallery, from which it was said only a performer's legs were visible), and proposed to charge higher prices for the regular boxes and for the pit. The first night's disruptive opposition to these innovations was kept up for sixty-seven nights. The protesters, with banners and slogans such as 'Old Prices' and 'John Bull against John Kemble', seen as disorderly mobs or carnivalesque defenders of popular rights depending on the commentator's point of view, became the subject of much journalism and the occasion of some brilliant cartoons. These include Isaac Cruickshank's 'Is this a rattle which I see before me' (Macbeth alarmed by the trajectory of an implement of disruptive protest), and Charles Williams's parody of the same soliloquy, 'Is this a seven-shilling piece I see before me' (referring to the new price of entry to a regular box), both of which, in their texts, imply a wider political resonance to the cultural battle. Eventually Kemble and the Covent Garden management capitulated to the demands of the protesters with an apology, a banquet in which

Kemble joined the protest leaders, signifying the conclusion of a peace, and the restoration of old prices in the major disputed areas of the theatre. The context was one in which opposition to patrician-class innovation was frequently expressed by organized dissent, sometimes with a measure of licensed authority in relation to popular defence of traditional practices and liberties. The objectors' defence of popular access to the theatre, and to Shakespeare, raised issues about the politics of culture. As a manifestation of political radical-ism in the period the theatre audience versus the management could also be seen as a synecdoche for the rebellious many versus the oppressive few.[26]

The fundamental mode of Kemble's acting was studied, not spon-taneous, paced and focussed to concentrate on great central effects. His manner has been connected with the classical principles exempli-fied by the annual Royal Academy *Discourses* of Reynolds (1769–90), and might be connected with the generalizing principles of classicism more broadly. In this, as in much else, he was the antithesis of the dynamic, spontaneous, idiosyncratic Kean.[27] His deliberation, in speech and in movement, was often remarked, and while for some this was properly expressive, for the sceptic it could seem comically pretentious: 'this artificial actor does so dole out his words, and so drop his syllables one by one upon the ear, as if he were measuring out laudanum' (Leigh Hunt); 'he manages the movement of his person with as much care as if he were a marble statue and as if the least trip . . . would be sure to fracture some of his limbs' (Hazlitt).[28] Kemble was an intellectual, as is indicated by his essay on the character of Macbeth;[29] a bibliophile, as Garrick had been, collecting early texts; a friend of the scholar Edmond Malone, contributing to the annotations of his edition (1821); the first actor systematically to publish his own acting versions, often in multiple revised editions as the productions developed, from 1789 to the end of his career. Even his critics were ambivalent: Hazlitt, who preferred Kean, nevertheless paid tribute to Kemble at the end of his career, embodying implications of all he had accomplished, as 'a stately hieroglyphic of humanity' (Howe, 4.155). The portraits of him by Sir Thomas Lawrence—as Hamlet (Figure 6.1), as Coriolanus (Figure 6.2), and in his own person— indicate the grandeur of his presence and epitomize the esteem in which he was held.[30]

In the view of Shakespearean character propounded by Coleridge as combining the individual and the type, Kemble stressed the type, the Platonic form, as Kean—more in tune with Romantic aesthetics and with modern preferences—stressed the idiosyncratic, the individual. He was successful within a narrow range, agreed not to be good in comedy (for example, as Benedick), and not to be good as a romantic lover (for example, as Romeo). He was not the kind of actor that disappeared, chameleon-like, into alien personalities. His grand portraits are suggestive: he expressed a character most powerfully by imposing his personality through roles to which it was suited.

As an actor-manager he aimed for a kind of Wagnerian *Gesamtkunstwerk*, a play as 'total art work' in which every element, including set and costume design and all the aspects of stage movement and grouping, contributed to the effect of a unified whole. This was not the dynamic, fast-moving drama of Shakespeare's stage; but, though moving in separate tableaux, it was a form of art theatre in which Shakespeare was brought vividly to life. Concentration on what documents tell of texts and staging cannot reveal more than the outer garments of that life. The eyewitness account by a great writer may do more, and in this period, in the hands of Lamb, Leigh Hunt, and above all Hazlitt, the theatrical review became a mode of artwriting. But, as Heine's 'I cannot' indicates, no writing can entirely bring back the life of theatre.

In a review of Kemble's farewell performance in 1817, Hazlitt—by then an admirer of Kean, a convert from 'the Kemble religion' in which (as he put it) he had been brought up (Howe, 5.345)—attempted to sum up the actor's abilities and his limitations. For Hazlitt Kemble's King John epitomized limitations: it was done 'according to the book of arithmetic', as if 'waiting for some complicated machinery to enable him to make his next movement, instead of trusting to the true impulses of passion' (Howe, 5.377). The impulses of passion were Kean's forte, not Kemble's. Similarly, as Macbeth, Hazlitt thought, Kemble did not sufficiently register the conflicts of will and imagination; as Hamlet he was too inveterate of purpose, 'like a man in armour', not able to convey the character's 'perpetual undulation of feeling'. Kemble's gift was for the character in whom 'all the passions move round a central point, and are governed by one master-key': his greatest and most characteristic achievement was as Coriolanus.[31]

Kemble's twentieth-century biographer presents him as 'the official voice of the national poet'.[32] For an age sceptical of official voices that more readily associates the arts with subversion, and an age likely to suspect that the idea of a national poet implies a superseded idea of the nation, this is not a straightforward recommendation. But contemporary reflexes are not the basis for a just estimate of Kemble. At his retirement he was celebrated by all classes of theatregoers. After his lament for the evanescence of theatre Tieck describes 'the plaudits ... cheers ... shouts of rapture and tears of emotion' that marked Kemble's farewell: 'The loudest outburst of applause I had ever heard, even in Italy, was but feeble, compared to the indescribable din, which ... arose on every side.'[33] The achievement thus celebrated was to recreate Shakespeare in performance as high art and as popular theatre. Kemble accomplished this in terms shaped by his context, but also against the grain in terms he himself in part shaped.

Sarah Siddons often played opposite her brother, but though her career was in many ways parallel to his, her fame was of another order. She became the most celebrated theatrical figure of her age, and one of the supreme figures of English theatrical history. For Leigh Hunt, in 1809, 'There is but one great tragedian living, and that is Mrs. Siddons.'[34] A tribute by Hazlitt, written in 1816 after her official retirement from the stage in 1812, conveys more elaborately the idea of her transcendent position.

The homage she has received is greater than that which is paid to Queens. The enthusiasm she excited had something idolatrous about it; she was regarded less with admiration than with wonder, as if a being of a superior order had dropped from another sphere to awe the world with the majesty of her appearance. She raised Tragedy to the skies, or brought it down from thence. It was something above nature. We can conceive of nothing grander. She embodied to our imagination the fables of mythology, of the heroic and deified mortals of elder time. She was not less than a goddess, or than a prophetess inspired by the gods. Power was seated on her brow, passion emanated from her breast as from a shrine. She was Tragedy personified. She was the stateliest ornament of the public mind. She was not only the idol of the people, she not only hushed the tumultuous shouts of the pit in breathless expectation, and quenched the blaze of surrounding beauty in silent tears, but to the retired and lonely student, through long years of solitude, her face has shone as if an eye had appeared from heaven; her name has been as if a voice had opened the

chambers of the human heart, or as if a trumpet had awakened the sleeping
and the dead. To have seen Mrs Siddons, was an event in every one's life.

(Howe, 5.312)

Not even Garrick had been so admired, and the details of Hazlitt's
report are reflected in numerous contemporary accounts. In the Age of
Sensibility Siddons's performances generated the kind of overt emotional responses, from women and men, from the crowd in the actual
and the reader in the imagined theatre, that in modern times have not
been the province of verbal performance. She was also 'the stateliest
ornament of the public mind', a woman recognized and admired over a
broad social range. Reynolds's portrait of her thirty years earlier as 'The
Muse of Tragedy' (1784) shows that she held this position for a
generation. As the diarist Henry Crabb Robinson put it, 'She is the
only actor I ever saw with the conviction that there never was and
never will be her equal.'[35]

Siddons' career was not an immediate success. She acted with
Garrick in his last London season (1775–6), playing roles such as
Portia to which her later career suggests she was not well suited. Like
her brother, her range was not wide: her transcendent talent was for
tragedy. But after a period working in provincial theatres, her return to
London in 1782 was a success, and thereafter, continuing to tour
widely outside the London season, she was the most important figure
in British theatre until her retirement in 1812.[36] As such, she achieved
a cult status, with hundreds of portraits, paintings, drawings, and
engravings as herself and in various stage roles by the greatest artists
of the age—Reynolds, Lawrence, Gainsborough, Romney, Westall.
There were also more popular memorabilia—caricatures, paintings on
porcelain, engravings on glass, and much more.[37] She thus transformed the social status of the actress and is a significant figure in
the history of women in public life in Britain. Before Siddons actresses
were associated with immoral living, albeit sometimes with a certain
cachet—as with Dorothy Jordan, the mistress of the Duke of Clarence
(later William IV) and mother by him of at least ten children.[38]
Siddons cultivated a different image: a wife and mother of unimpeach-
able respectability. With one scandalous reputed lapse safely behind
her (with a fencing master who, in Dublin, played Laertes to her
Hamlet), she never thereafter erred from a path that created a public

persona of such respectability that she could be invited to read to George III and Queen Charlotte.[39]

Siddons's public image of the actress as mother was most obviously taken onto the stage in Shakespeare in one of her most notable roles, as Constance, the mother of Prince Arthur, in *King John*, a role she first played opposite her brother as John in 1783 and continued to perform throughout her career. The play was more often performed than in modern times, in part because of its anti-French English nationalism in the context of the Napoleonic Wars, and its proto-Reformation attitudes to papal power expressed by John, congenial to pre-Catholic-Emancipation Protestantism. Kemble's text was based on Bell's edition (Garrick's acting version), cut in his usual streamlining manner, but with minor additions to heighten the anti-French attitudes.[40] The role of Constance is abbreviated but not reshaped. The part is difficult because Constance's two great scenes are opposite—a triumph of foreign alliance supporting Arthur's claim to the English throne, followed by defeat through realliance, with no transition: the change occurs while Constance is offstage. Siddons's account of her own performances as Constance to her biographer, the poet Thomas Campbell, showing how she addressed this difficulty, is indicative of the fundamental approach that made her so riveting a performer.

I never, from the beginning of the play to the end of my part in it, once suffered my dressing-room door to be closed, in order that my attention might be constantly fixed on those distressing events which, by this means, I could plainly hear going on upon the stage, the terrible effects of which progress were to be represented by me. Moreover, I never omitted to place myself, with *Arthur* in my hand, to hear the march, when, upon the reconciliation of England and France, they enter the gates of Angiers to ratify the contract of marriage between the *Dauphin* and the *Lady Blanche*; because the sickening sounds of that march would usually cause the bitter tears of rage, disappointment, betrayed confidence, baffled ambition, and, above all, the agonizing feelings of maternal affection to gush into my eyes. In short, the spirit of the whole drama took possession of my mind and frame, by my attention being incessantly riveted to the passing scenes.[41]

'The spirit of the whole drama took possession of my mind and frame': Siddons 'acted' by immediate involvement in the drama on the occasion of its performance. This is the Stanislavsky 'method' *avant la lettre*, not the contrived representation of feeling but the experiencing of that feeling in the moment by immediate participation. Siddons referred to this as 'abstraction', by which she apparently meant withdrawing herself from all circumstances other than those bearing on the drama. Unlike many earlier performers (Garrick's Lady Macbeth, Hannah Pritchard, declared that she had never read the end of the play), Siddons involved herself in the whole context by which her character was created and framed. As with Kemble, though by a different route, her aim was performance that recognized the integrity of the play as a whole. Emotional involvement in the moment was complemented by effects of art and control in voice and embodiment. Campbell reports the 'clear and intelligent harmony of unlaboured elocution, which unravels all the intricacies of language, illuminates obscurity, and points and unfolds the precise truth of meaning to every apprehension' (2.142): however impassioned her delivery, she never let the tones of passion compromise articulation of the sense by which the passion was expressed. Siddons's other contemporary biographer, James Boaden, describes how, in the scene in which Constance first appears with unbound hair symbolic of her distraught state and then binds up her hair as a symbol of her son's imprisonment, she 'dishevelled even her hair with graceful wildness'.[42] She became her character, but by a combination of passion and planning.

A part differently suited to Siddons's gifts, in which she was equally celebrated, was Queen Katherine in *Henry VIII*—also oppressed by politic craft, but restrained in adversity, with eloquence only occasionally flaring into bitterness. It is a magnificent role, complemented by that of her adversary, Cardinal Wolsey, hateful in the pride of vicious success, but sympathetic in the humility he extracts from his defeat and fall. Siddons first played Katherine in 1788. Kemble played opposite her as Wolsey from 1806. These are the great characters of a play which otherwise—as the unusually full Folio stage directions make clear—depends for its success on spectacle. This Kemble's production developed. The stage directions are among the most elaborate in all the Kemble prompt books. Though his cuts included the scenically grand coronation procession of Anne Boleyn, this gave only greater emphasis to his spectacular staging of the final action, the christening of Elizabeth I, for which the 1804 prompt book prescribes a hundred extras.

Kemble's grand staging can be sampled in the scene of Wolsey's banquet (1.4), for which he prescribes multiple extras, elaborate cues for music, eight couples for its masque dance, and 'drums and

Figure 6.3. Sarah Siddons as Queen Katherine ('The Trial of Queen Katherine'). Painting by George Henry Harlow (1817). The Royal Shakespeare Company Theatre Collection.

trumpets, and . . . some symphony cheerful and grand' for the final exit. It is also evident in one of the most famous Shakespeare illustrations of the period, George Henry Harlow's painting of Queen Katherine's trial, known as 'The Kemble Family', because as well as John (Wolsey) and Sarah (Queen Katherine) it contains their brothers Charles (as Thomas Cromwell) and Stephen (as Henry VIII) (Figure 6.3). For its combination of dignity and passionate wronged innocence the trial scene became one of Siddons's most famous performances, complemented by the pathos of the scene of the Queen's approach to death. For this Kemble omitted the dream vision of a dance of angels, replacing it with the aria 'Angels ever bright and fair' from Handel's martyrdom oratorio *Theodora*. With Handel to heighten the pathos of innocent suffering and imminent death, Siddons's performance was penetratingly based on actual observation of the dying.[43] As with Constance, the gamut encapsulated her approach: studied and stylized drama; carefully observed presentation from life.

These history plays show Siddons's ability to take an area of Shakespeare's work often thought of as male-dominated and bring out the interest of its great roles for women. Her most famous characterization, Lady Macbeth (Figure 6.4), shows her ability to rework a well-known woman's part in new terms. The sources of evidence about her performances as Lady Macbeth are more extensive

Figure 6.4. Sarah Siddons as Lady Macbeth. Painting by George Henry Harlow (1814). Courtesy of the Garrick Club, London.

and detailed than those for any other in the period—her own notes as given to Thomas Campbell, the extended discussion of her other biographer, James Boaden, detailed notes on tones, inflections, gestures, and movements recorded by the Edinburgh jurist and legal writer George Joseph Bell, who saw her in the role *c.*1809, the Kemble prompt books, and myriad reviews, reminiscences, paintings, and drawings.[44] Her performance effected a major critical revaluation: she made Lady Macbeth both more important in the play as a whole, less purely an instrument of the transformation of Macbeth, more his equal in their reciprocal interactions, and, as a victim of her support for his desires as of her own, a more sympathetic and tragic figure in her own right.

To project this, Siddons saw her task as to build from the text an embodied version of the character's suppressed but implied conflicts— not simply the 'fiendlike queen' of Malcolm's verdict, or the 'merely detestable' figure seen by Samuel Johnson, but, like Macbeth, a sympathetic character riven by conflicting feelings. Her notes show an exploratory approach that produces a version of the character drawn not from the words only but from the words and their possible implications. They exemplify the active and imaginative intelligence with which she searched every phrase of the text for tones and emphases that could register its most interesting meanings. These included implied relations with Macbeth, based on a similarly exploratory attitude to his conflicted character. The notes show a creative sense of all that can be drawn from the text of both roles in terms not only of verbal meanings but also of physical theatre. If this goes beyond what is usually thought of as the parameters of disciplined interpretation, it shows an art of acting in which the creative-exploratory is merged with the interpretive. There were dissenters, such as Coleridge: 'These might be the Macbeths of the Kembles, but they were not the Macbeths of Shakespeare' (Raysor, 2.230). But whatever the problems of Siddons's reading as a technique of literary criticism, as a basis for acting it enabled what was by almost universal agreement the greatest performance of the age. It was also a typically Romantic view of the character in which straightforward moral judgement was subverted by complexities read against the grain—an interpretation congruent with Blake's and Shelley's readings of *Paradise Lost* through a heroic Satan, or Byron's version of the biblical narrative of Cain and

Abel (*Cain: A Mystery*, 1816) from the viewpoint of Cain. As Lady Macbeth Siddons brought into theatrical performance the Romantic idea of the imagination as a test of moral categories, not a form of knowledge bound by their prescriptions.

The sources from which this performance can be reconstructed do, however, record a paradox: Siddons's account of the starting point of her conception ('fair, feminine, nay, perhaps even fragile... captivating in feminine loveliness', Campbell, 2.11) contrasts directly with the extraordinary and diabolic force reported by eyewitnesses of its performance. Siddons played the part for thirty years (from 1785 to 1812, and occasionally thereafter), with different Macbeths, with whom she interacted differently, and, as with all her famous roles, with each new performance she reread and reworked it. Aspects of her conception of Lady Macbeth changed, on some issues distinctly. In the notes given to Campbell she records an unusual idea of the guilt of Lady Macbeth. Her response to Macbeth's 'Thou know'st that Banquo and his Fleance lives'—'But in them Nature's copy's not eterne' (3.2.37–8)—is understood not as general reassurance but as a hint which makes her in part guilty of Banquo's murder. Sharing the guilt of his murder, in the banqueting scene she, like Macbeth, sees his Ghost (Campbell, 2.29–30). The conception gave rise to what she called 'one of the greatest difficulties of the scenic art' (2.28): when the Ghost appeared, she acted the double part of attempting to still Macbeth's terrors while showing in barely suppressed forms her own. If Siddons acted this conception in the performances witnessed by G. J. Bell, he did not see it, nor is it recorded in Boaden's account of her performance in the scene (2.140–2). With whatever changes of detail, however, Siddons's conception of the part remained fundamentally that described in the Campbell notes: 'smothering her sufferings in the deepest recesses of her own wretched bosom... she devotes herself entirely to the effort of supporting [Macbeth]' (2.24). It was the wretchedness of suppressed guilt and suffering that emerged vividly in the most famous aspect of Siddons's performance, in which her sense of Lady Macbeth as a tragic figure was fully displayed: the sleepwalking scene. The pathos of this was created by Siddons's expressive range and intensity in every aspect of presentation: 'the death-like stare of her countenance, while the body was in motion', which Leigh Hunt thought 'sublime';[45] the vigorous handwashing, for which, defying precedent, she put down her candle, basing her action on observation of actual somnambulists (Campbell, 2.37–9). Her costume of shroud-like white suggesting a sepulchral being, living in a world of the dead that possessed her during the unrestrained fantasies of sleep; her spectral whisper to the absent-supposed-present accomplice ('to bed, to bed'), recalling in tone as in words the relative innocence of the moment after the murder of Duncan when they were 'yet but young in deed': vocal expressivity combined with imaginative embodiment. Precise accounts differ, but, *pace* Coleridge, most commentators followed Hazlitt (Howe, 5.373–4) in finding it one of the great performances of British theatrical history.

Siddons played most of Shakespeare's other tragic heroines—Juliet, Ophelia, Gertrude, Desdemona, Cordelia (in Tate's adaptation), though never Cleopatra (which she played only in Dryden's adaptation, *All for Love*)—but in none of these roles did she achieve the celebrity of her most famous characterizations. In comedy, though she played many of the major roles (Portia, Beatrice, Rosalind, Olivia, Imogen), she was regarded as successful only in the more serious or semi-tragic roles of Isabella and Hermione. Hermione is one of the roles that prompted Hazlitt's other extended tribute to Siddons as 'the Muse of Tragedy personified'. Contrasting her with the more impetuous Kean, Hazlitt stressed how 'transitions ... rapid and extreme ... were massed into unity and breadth' (Howe, 18.407–8).

Underlying her variety was a unified conception which gave greater force to the individual moments. This was fundamental to a performance style that combined the classical formality of Kemble with the Romantic spontaneity of Kean—spontaneity in appearance at least, though, as Anna Jameson observed, 'what ... appeared like sudden inspiration ... was the result of profound study and unwearied practice'.[46]

Siddons acted with every aspect of her being, but she was in part a voice. Many commentators describe the musicality of her delivery, thrilling in its force, subtle in its variation. Coleridge's sonnet about her is focussed on the sound of her voice, which he associated with Gothic horror and an emotional range from sublimity to pathos: its tones produced 'shivering joys'; their emotional effect melted the heart.[47] The dramatist Joanna Baillie also focussed on her voice, its variety of pace ('rapid, fitful, slow') and of timbre ('loud rage and fear's snatched whisper'), and ability to clarify complex structures by expressive intonation ('as if some secret voice, to clear / The ravelled meaning, whispered in thine ear').[48] But for all that could be said about how Siddons used her voice, all that Bell annotated and Boaden described of the emotional and imaginative intelligence with which her vocalizations could search and project a text, part of her power lay in what is unrecoverable, the voice's sheer sound. What Byron could not describe, he evoked: its 'tones were superhuman, and power over the heart supernatural'.[49]

Siddons also acted with her whole body: as Campbell put it, 'her very body seemed to think' (1.210). Some of her most admired effects were textless. She could dominate a stage with movement and with statuesque silence. Gilbert Austin's *Chironomia; or, A Treatise on Rhetorical Delivery* (1806), addressed not only to speaking but also to 'the language of the body' and 'corporal eloquence' (Introduction, sig. B), uses engravings of Siddons in some of her most famous roles to illustrate her use of conventions of expressive posture.[50] These illustrations inevitably appear sculpturally static, and by modern standards they also appear excessively histrionic. How Siddons animated these postures it is impossible to know, but, since her acting was often praised in terms of its relative naturalism, it seems likely that the static postures are misleading, except insofar as they imply an absence of inhibition about emotional extremes suited to the vast scale of the theatres in which she spent the last twenty years of her career. As with Kemble's more statuesque performances, conventions of this kind were one basis of Siddons's training, but all accounts of her on stage indicate that there was an alpha to this omega, that she combined use of convention with more naturalistic effects drawn from observation. As a complement to effects of art, as her account of performing Constance testifies, she participated in the feelings of the living moment. 'Her audience', wrote Anna Jameson, 'almost lost the sense of impersonation in the feeling of identity'—so much so that Campbell reports an incident in which she so interiorized the passions she was performing that she fainted on stage.[51] The unprecedented intensity that made her for Hazlitt 'the Muse of Tragedy', and seeing her performances 'an event in every one's life', drew on all these resources of the voice and the body, observation of nature, and effects of art.

When Yeats calls in tragedy for 'gaiety transfiguring all that dread', he expects the transfiguration to emerge from stylizations inherent in poetic drama, especially the structure of the verse line. Great actors 'do not break up their lines to weep': on the contrary, they use the structures of verse as the basis of their expressivity.[52] Yeats's desiderata suggest how the acting style of Sarah Siddons should be imagined—a range which for her contemporaries combined stylization of speech and gesture for extremes of feeling with actions observed from life and participation in feeling in the present moment that carried across into the auditorium the exhibition of concentrated passion; as Leigh Hunt put it, 'those exquisite touches in Mrs Siddons, which in the very midst of tragedy introduce a noble and natural familiarity, utterly unknown to declaimers'.[53] Her style was a unique combination of apparently antithetical methods, the classical and the proto-Stanislavskian—a studied and calculated view of a whole role, in its full context, projected in part through conventions of embodiment which generated its apparent antithesis, fidelity to the passion of moment-by-moment lived experience: heightened emotion by complementary means.

While Siddons was celebrated as analogous to a divinity, the other outstanding actor of the period, Edmund Kean (1787–1833), was celebrated as a demon. The age of Byron and Shelley was an age for celebrating demons, and Kean had all the necessary qualities—which included many antithetical to those conventionally thought appropriate to a tragic hero, not least that he was slightly built and short (five feet seven inches tall). While the Kemble family background was theatrical, it was also aspirational. Kemble had been sent to the great Catholic college at Douai with a view to following his family's traditions and going into the priesthood. At Douai he was taught classical languages. He had the education of a scholar and a gentleman, an education which prepared him to be the associate of Johnson and Malone. Kean's theatrical background was quite different. He came from lower than below. It is not entirely certain which of three brothers—Aaron, Moses, and Edmund Kean—was his father. His mother, Anne Carey, was an actress who also earned a living as a prostitute. Edmund, the actor's putative father, committed suicide in 1793. Kean was brought up between his uncle Moses's mistress, Charlotte Tidswell ('Aunt Tid'), and his mother's sister, Mrs Price. He was trained in multiple aspects of the 'illegitimate' theatre, and brought from it to his career in the royal theatre of Drury Lane both specific skills of physical performance and a more general sense of being the invader from an underworld. Working as a child in drinking houses and fairgrounds, in pantomime, melodrama, and other entertainments where his abilities as mime, tumbler, tightrope walker, boxer, fencer, or dancer could be put to use, he also knew the royal theatre as a visitor—part of the Drury Lane children's chorus (in which he appeared on stage with Kemble).[54] Aunt Tid's liaisons may have included Charles Howard, Duke of Norfolk, from which Kean developed a fantasy of aristocratic lineage. He named his sons Howard and Charles.

After twenty years, from childhood, in the irregular theatre, eventually in provincial companies, sometimes playing principal parts—but also Harlequin—Kean's projection into fame was sudden and meteoric. He was engaged to perform at Drury Lane, where he made his debut on 26 January 1814 in his own choice of role, Shylock (Figure 6.5). He played to a half-empty house, but this first London performance was reviewed by Hazlitt, writing his first London theatrical review. Hazlitt instantly saw Kean's genius, and said so in the clearest terms: 'For voice, eye, action, and expression, no actor has come out for many years at all equal to him' (Howe, 5.179). Hazlitt saw and described the originality of Kean's conception of Shylock and the intensity of his engagement. He also saw that his acting had a subtlety which in the huge Drury Lane auditorium was 'intelligible only to a part of the house'. Kean's second performance was to a packed theatre. Hazlitt went to check his impressions and enthused yet further:

His style of acting is ... more significant, more pregnant with meaning, more varied and alive in every part, than any we have almost ever witnessed. The character never stands still; there is no vacant pause in the action; the eye is never silent. For depth and force of conception, we have seen actors whom we should prefer to Mr. Kean in Shylock; for brilliant and masterly execution, none. It is not saying too much of him, though it is saying a great deal, that he has all that Mr. Kemble *wants* in perfection. He reminds us of the descriptions of the 'far-darting eye' of Garrick. (Howe, 5.180)

The contrast between Kean's constant movement and Kemble's statuesque classicism; the comparison with Garrick's intensity of performance in the moment: Hazlitt identified central features of the style

Figure 6.5. Edmund Kean as Shylock. Engraving by Henry Meyer (1814), after a painting by Walter Henry Watts (1814). The National Portrait Gallery, London.

that made Kean the quintessentially Romantic actor. The most famous comment on this style comes from a report of Coleridge's conversation: 'His rapid descents from the hyper-tragic to the infra-colloquial, though sometimes productive of great effects, are often unreasonable. To see him act, is like reading Shakespeare by flashes of lightning'—apparently a criticism of Kean's famously abrupt changes of tone and the overall of effect of these, moments of intense insight not adequately connected into any total significant design. Less well known, but Coleridge's *ipsissima verba*, is a letter written just two months earlier in which his praise is less equivocal: Kean's 'Genius in re-creating the creations of the World's first Genius' (Shakespeare) is recognized, he reports, even by those opposed in theory to his methods.[55]

Kean's dominance of the London stage was turbulent and brief. Though he acted in London, with two brief seasons in America (1820–1, 1825–6), from 1814 until his death in 1833, the toll on energies that fuelled onstage intensity by offstage drinking and a colourful sex life meant that the years of straightforward success scarcely extended beyond 1820. The diaries of James Winston (the acting manager of Drury Lane from 1819 to 1827) record Kean's boast of or need for sex before, after, and (offstage) during performances. ('Send me Lewes or the other woman. I must have a fuck', and so on.)[56] He was also a great drinker, sometimes performed when drunk, and occasionally missed performances as a result of drinking. His sexual intrigues became a matter of public notice through his liaison with the wife of a London alderman, Charlotte Cox, with whom his 'criminal conversation' (adultery), beginning around 1820, became the subject of legal proceedings brought by her husband in 1825. Over the following season, in London and in the provinces, Kean's performances were interrupted and sometimes drowned out by both moral objectors and vociferous supporters. Drink did Kean as much harm with his audiences as scandal because it adversely affected his voice and the physical energy required for his mode of being on stage. Drink and sex both stimulated Kean's genius and, in different ways, compromised his ability to perform. After 1825, though he continued to act, and was part of the English company that performed in Paris in 1827–8, he had no successes to equal those of his great days.

Kean played a variety of Shakespearean tragic roles: Romeo, Richard II, Hamlet, Lear, Timon, and Coriolanus. Like Kemble, he usually played these in adaptations. Sometimes, as with Cibber's *Richard III* and Tate's *King Lear*, these were standard versions. Sometimes, as with *Richard II* and *Timon of Athens*, they were versions specially made for Kean's performances, which Kean probably had a hand in shaping.[57] Kean also began a movement, which advanced more fully in the next generation, towards reinstating Shakespeare's texts on the stage. He removed the Thomson and Sheridan interpolations used in *Coriolanus* by Kemble; his *Timon of Athens* stripped out eighteenth-century mutilations (though he still performed the play without the whores Phrynia and Timandra, unsuitable to polite taste even in the Age of Revolution); and on a small number of occasions he played *King Lear* not in Tate's version but with Shakespeare's tragic ending.[58] Kean also played Richard, Duke of York (in a compilation from *1–3 Henry VI*), King John, Hotspur, Posthumus, Wolsey, and (disastrously, late in his career, when he was no longer able to memorize new parts) Henry V. In none of these roles was he notably successful. Kean's best acting regularly came from exploiting something in his own personality to create the character he played: 'he could play all sorts of parts, but in those parts he always played himself', or so thought Heine.[59] For whatever reason, the innocent idealism of Romeo and the meditative intellectuality of Hamlet were widely judged not within his range. Hazlitt thought Coriolanus antithetical to Kean's very being as 'one of the people...a *radical* performer' (Howe, 18.290), an incarnation in politics of the revolutionary spirit of the age: that he should not be a good Coriolanus was for Hazlitt a republican badge of honour. Of his Romeo, Hamlet, and Lear Hazlitt was more equivocally critical: even when he did not accept Kean's fundamental idea of a character, he regularly admired his performances for their 'spirit, ingenuity, and originality...energy and depth of passion' (Howe, 5.208); and, as often with Hazlitt's reviews, disagreement about the fundamental conception prompted some brilliantly engaged, exploratory criticism.[60]

The roles that made Kean one of the great theatrical figures of the age and one of the great Shakespearean actors of all time were outsiders: Shylock, Richard III, Macbeth, Iago, and above all Othello (Figure 6.6). For these characters, as he played them, Kean was the authentic voice, the underdog in person, the Romantic spirit incarnate: outsiderdom, nonconformity, rebellion.

Shylock both established Kean's mode and remained a signature role throughout his career—a personal, probably original, certainly unusual, conception of the part. One witness was Heine, who saw Kean's Shylock as a heroic figure, not at all broken down by the

Figure 6.6. Edmund Kean as Othello. Hand-coloured lithograph by William Sheldrick (*c.*1830), after a painting by E. F. Lambert. Royal Collection Trust/ © Her Majesty Queen Elizabeth II 2020.

injustices by which he is embittered and oppressed; and beyond the specifics Heine saw Kean not as acting a part but becoming the character.[61] It is probable that Kean was himself part Jewish (if neither Moses nor Aaron Kean were his father, both were his uncles); it is certain that he saw himself as unjustly oppressed and excluded—a Shylock figure in his own experience: part of him could be released into his assumption of the role. One centrepiece of his performance was Shylock's bitterly enraged rejection of othering that sustains cruelty and injustice, 'Hath not a Jew eyes?'[62] Heine offers vivid detail of his opening scene. In exchanges with Bassanio and Antonio (1.3), 'you think you are hearing, not a role learned by heart, but a speech made up, thought out with effort, then and there'; and when Shylock addressed Antonio directly, for Heine Kean conveyed a 'struggle of outward humility and inner rage' by contrasts between the body (expressing submission), the eyes (expressing rage), and the voice (expressing hatred cloaked in submission). Like other commentators, Heine saw Kean's eyes as especially expressive: 'a magic lightning flash, a fiery flame'.[63] Though Heine declares his account inadequate ('the best description cannot bring the essential Edmund Kean before you'), it is wonderfully vivid. Hazlitt had seen the same conception of the role a decade earlier: at first he judged it wonderfully performed, though not entirely true to the play; later more true to the play than he had recognized, and showing an intensity of engagement that challenged the idea of 'acting'.[64] Only the Stanislavskian mode of Sarah Siddons gave a similar sense of the actor as a transformed being. Hazlitt was explicit about the comparison (Howe, 4.211), and also about how Kean's performance—like Siddons's Lady Macbeth—helped him to see Shakespeare's play more clearly (Howe, 5.314). Siddons and Kean uniquely 'have raised our imagination of the part they acted' (Howe, 4.222).

Within three weeks of his Shylock debut, Kean's Richard III followed in the same mode. The conception was, Hazlitt wrote, 'entirely his own'; 'every scene had the stamp and freshness of nature' (Howe, 5.180). Again Hazlitt was doubtful that the role as acted (even allowing that this was the 'miserable medley' concocted by Cibber) was entirely the role as written by Shakespeare. But while in 1814 Hazlitt detected an excess of lightness in Kean's Richard's enjoyment of his villainy, in 1819 Hunt, contrasting Kean with Macready, praised his gloom, melancholy, and reflectiveness as having 'more of the serious-ness of conscious evil' (Houtchens, 220). And again Hazlitt celebrated the genius of Kean's execution, stressing a new element of purely physical theatre, the absolute theatre of embodiment without text, or in which text is secondary to embodiment: his graceful movements in the seduction of Lady Anne ('he seemed like the first tempter'); his abrupt transition to daylight consciousness highlighting a moment of abstracted reverie before the final battle, which 'received shouts of applause';[65] and the dumb show of his death:

He fought like one drunk with wounds: and the attitude in which he stands with his hands stretched out, after his sword is taken from him, had a preternatural and terrific grandeur, as if his will could not be disarmed, and the very phantoms of his despair had a withering power. (Howe, 5.182)

As Hazlitt put it in a later review, 'if Shakespeare had written marginal directions to the players...he would have directed them to do what Mr. Kean does' (Howe, 5.202).[66]

Kean's Macbeth Hazlitt judged in its overall conception unsuccess-ful, 'deficient in the poetry of the character' (Howe, 5.206), not sufficiently differentiating Macbeth's intense imaginings of horror and guilt from Richard III's cold-blooded cruelty. Kean's Macbeth was a more isolated figure than Kemble's, and, perhaps for want of a strong Lady Macbeth, he took the lead from the first, simplifying the interplay of moral struggles by which Kemble and Siddons intensified the tragedy.[67] Nevertheless, in its portrayal of traumatized guilt Hazlitt thought the scene after Duncan's murder 'heart-rending': Kean's combination of vocal tone, facial expression, eyes, and gesture 'beggared description'. It was, Hazlitt thought, one of 'the finest things Mr. Kean has ever done'. This is performance as Romantic ruin—a fragment, but great beyond a more regularly accomplished whole: 'no one who saw it can ever efface [the scene] from his recollection' (Howe, 5.207). Though Hazlitt judged later performances more con-sistently brought up to this level (Howe, 18.260–1), Kean performed again with a Lady Macbeth Hazlitt thought weak: retaining the dominance of Macbeth throughout, he kept the balance of the two roles as it had been, Macbeth more isolated, more the author of his own destruction.[68]

In *Othello* Kean played Iago as well as Othello. In different ways both roles suited him—the class outsider, passed over for promotion, and with a more general grudge against the world; the cultural outsider, uncertain of his place in the society that has taken him in. As with Richard III, Hazlitt felt Kean failed sufficiently to register the dark side of Iago; but Kean's unusual idea of the character is evident in Hazlitt's criticism: exhilarating delight in asserting dominance through deception, delight in demonstrating the credulity of honesty and nobility, and delight simply in destroying—'Pleasure and action make the hours seem short' (2.3.374). This Iago was also attractive to at least part of the audience—to the gallery if not the boxes: a man of the people, one of their own, badly treated by the patrician classes; as Hazlitt perceived, 'a true prototype of modern Jacobinism' (Howe, 5.212). The evil in this is left for the audience to see, but an important part of that evil is the delight in power and destruction that Hazlitt's account of Kean's performance registered even as Hazlitt repudiated its execution. Hazlitt took great pains precisely to articulate his critique of Kean's performance: taken together, his reviews, and rebuttal of objections to his reviews, constitute his longest piece of theatrical criticism.[69] As usual, Kean's genius and originality engaged Hazlitt intensely even when he did not approve the results. Though he thought the performance underplayed what he called Iago's 'diseased intellectual activity' and his 'perfect indifference to moral good or evil' (Howe, 4.206), nevertheless he judged it 'one of the most extraordinary exhibitions on the stage' (Howe, 5.212).

If Kean's Iago showed his genius misapplied, his Othello showed it fully realized. Othello was for Kean what Coriolanus was for Kemble and Lady Macbeth for Siddons, the role in which he excelled above all others; and as with Siddons as Lady Macbeth, Hazlitt thought his performance revelatory. While in early reviews Hazlitt expressed reservations, he later called it 'the finest piece of acting in the world. . . . almost every scene or sentence in this exhibition is a masterpiece of natural passion'.[70] Hunt concurred: 'We never saw anything [he includes Siddons] that so completely held us suspended and heartstricken, as Mr Kean's Othello. . . . Mr Kean's *Othello* is the masterpiece of the living stage.'[71] The performance was wholly sympathetic to the agonies of Othello's delusions and the actions derived from them, building from the sense Kean so sharply and intimately shared of the vulnerability of the cultural outsider. On this reading, Othello is most of all Iago's victim when he violates the ideals that love of Desdemona has revealed to him by turning with such terrible violence against their source. In this performance Othello was as sympathetic and as innocent a victim as Desdemona herself. One climax of Kean's performance was the temptation scene of Act 3, which Hazlitt judged 'perfect tragic acting' (Howe, 5.357). Here the two sides of Othello's conflicting feelings were brought to the highest pitch: the faith in Desdemona which almost survives Iago's insinuations; the agony of jealousy when he gives in to those insinuations, which meant the disintegration of his personality, staked on his faith in that love ('when I love thee not, / Chaos is come again', 3.3.91–2). Hazlitt often praised Kean for the combined expressivity of voice, facial expression, and embodiment, and so he did with Othello (as in his 1814 review: Howe, 5.189); but with Othello he also memorably remarked the expressivity that was often compromised by drink:

In the third act of Othello, his voice in the farewell apostrophe to Content, took the deep intonation of the pealing organ, and heaved from the heart sounds that came on the ear like the funeral dirge of years of promised happiness. (Howe, 5.210)

The usual judgements of Kean's voice—that it was 'harsh', or 'hoarse'; 'like a hackney-coachman's at one o'clock in the morning', said Hunt (Houtchens, 114)—are clearly judgements by conventional standards; but for those with ears to hear, as Hazlitt here indicates, there are virtues greater in the poetic hierarchy than mellifluous delivery. With Kean there were meanings resonant with the whole context of utterance. One of the most remarkable theatrical reviews of the Romantic era is Keats's discussion of Kean, of whom Keats's examples show he had seen a good deal. In relation to Kean's delivery Keats explores the idea that 'a melodious passage of poetry is full of pleasures both sensual and spiritual'. He translates Kean's vocal sounds into their meanings:

When he says in *Othello*, 'put up your bright swords for the dew will rust them', we feel that his throat has commanded where swords were as thick as reeds. From eternal risk, he speaks as though his body were unassailable. Again, his exclamation of 'blood, blood, blood!' is direful and slaughterous to the deepest degree, the very words appear stained and gory. His nature hangs over them, making a prophetic repast.[72]

With much more to the same effect: 'The sensual life of verse springs warm from the lips of Kean.' That Keats should admire Kean is no surprise: Kean is the so-called 'Cockney School' of poetry—Keats and other outsiders, including Hunt and extending to Hazlitt—transferred to the stage. But Keats's point here is general: it lies not in the specific meanings the imaginative listener (Hazlitt, Keats) can 'translate' from Kean's vocal sounds but in the kind of imaginative resonance suggested by such translations. Those who heard Kean did not need to think in Keats's terms to hear what Keats essentially heard—a voice full of emotional and imaginative resonances present independent of any ability to suggest their meanings. 'Harsh' to unattuned ears, Kean's voice was complex music to others. The actor George Vandenhoff described his performance of Othello's final speech as having tones, rhythms, rests, and dynamics 'as if he spoke it from a musical score'.[73] Of the same passage Hazlitt wrote that 'it struck on the heart and the imagination like the swelling notes of some divine music' (Howe, 5.189). Like Hazlitt, what Keats heard was a voice that resonated with the whole context of character and situation, a voice that was the organ of an ultra-vivid personality, filled to the fullness of its great capacity with the entire matter of the drama in the most intensely imagined terms.

Unlike Kemble and Siddons, Kean left few documentary traces about his views of acting or his particular roles. Such evidence as he offered is equivocal. 'There is no such thing as impulsive acting', he told Garrick's widow: 'all is premeditated and studied beforehand'. But also, 'I forgot the affectations of the art and relied upon the emotions of the soul'.[74] Probably there is here no real paradox. Like Siddons, Kean planned carefully; like Siddons, careful planning released him to participate moment by moment in the passions of the drama, which he did, in his most notable roles with apparent recklessness. He therefore seemed, as G. H. Lewes remembered him, 'a stormy spirit uttering itself in tones of irresistible power'.[75] This onstage being, combined with the offstage character of passions which could in the days of his greatness be controlled and directed into this art but which ultimately overwhelmed him, made him a theatrical archetype of the Romantic artist.

With texts often radically adapted, including the incorporation of extensive non-Shakespearean material; realistic scenery changing the mode and pace of the drama; and performance in huge auditoria which adversely affected the style of presentation, the mode of acting, and the relation of the audience to the actors, there is much about the performance of Shakespeare in the major Romantic-period theatres antithetical to the kind of theatres for which Shakespeare wrote. Among the great Romantic critics this prompted at worst 'pain, disgust and indignation', at best the feeling that Shakespeare was not for the theatre. Nevertheless, Kemble, Siddons, Kean, and others of their contemporaries are rightly seen as 'great Shakespeareans'. Alien as any contemporary theatre would find their mode of performance, what would one not give to see performances that so great a commentator as Hazlitt judged (of Kemble's Macbeth) 'the best... that we have seen', (of Kean's Othello) 'the finest piece of acting in the world', and (of Siddons in any role) 'an event in every one's life'? What would one not give to hear the voices so praised for their expressive delivery by Coleridge and Keats; to see performers so celebrated by their contemporaries, from the patrician tastes that memorialized Kemble and Siddons in grand portraits to the popular audiences that purchased Siddons knick-knacks and memorabilia, huzzaed to the echoes Kemble's farewell, and delighted in Kean as one of their own?

The art of the stage, though it 'fleets away like a shadow', leaves material traces from which it can be in part resurrected; but, copious as these are for Romantic theatre, they are also in crucial ways 'inadequate to portray what the rapt spectator has seen and heard'.

Major Critical Writings; Editions, Scholarship and Translations; the English Stage

1759–65: Gotthold Ephraim Lessing (with C. F. Nicolai and Moses Mendelssohn), *Letters concerning the newest Literature.*

1762: Johann Georg Hamann, *Aesthetics in a Nutshell.*

1762–6: Christoph Martin Wieland, translation of twenty-two Shakespeare plays into German (mainly in prose, based on the Warburton edition of 1747).

1765: Samuel Johnson, edition of Shakespeare, in eight volumes, with critical *Preface* (the culmination of a series of eighteenth-century editions bearing on Romantic-period editing and scholarship: Rowe, 1709; Pope, 1725; Theobald, 1733; Hanmer, 1743–4; Warburton, 1747). Revised by George Steevens, 1773 and 1778 (including Malone's first chronology of Shakespeare's plays).

1766: George Steevens, *Twenty of the Plays of Shakespeare . . . printed in Quarto during his life-time, or before the Restoration,* in four volumes.

1767–8: Edward Capell, edition of Shakespeare in ten volumes, the first edition to be based directly on the First Folio and the early Quartos.

1767–9: Lessing, *Hamburg Dramaturgy.*

1769: David Garrick's 'Shakespeare Jubilee' in Stratford-upon-Avon, an early attempt to celebrate Shakespeare as the national poet.

1769–92: Jean-François Ducis, adaptations for performance in French prose of six Shakespeare plays (*Hamlet,* 1769; *Othello,* 1792).

1770–4: Charles Jennens, editions of five individual plays with full collation of textual variants, *King Lear, Macbeth, Othello, Hamlet, Julius Caesar.*

1771: Goethe, *Shakespeare's Birthday.*

1773: Herder, 'Shakespeare' (1771) in *German Character and Art.*

1773–8: Bell's edition of Shakespeare, using adapted texts as performed in the Theatres Royal of Drury Lane and Covent Garden (often used as a basis for later productions, including those of John Philip Kemble).

1775–82: Revision and completion by Johann Joachim Eschenburg of Martin Wieland's translation in thirteen volumes.

1776: Voltaire, *Letter to the Académie française*. Retirement of David Garrick (died 1779).

1776–82: Pierre Le Tourneur, prose translation of Shakespeare into French, in twenty volumes.

1779–83: Edward Capell, *Notes and Various Readings to Shakespeare*, in three volumes.

1780: Edmund Malone, two volumes supplementary to Johnson–Steevens, 1778, including Brooke's *Romeus and Juliet*; a text of the Sonnets based on Q1 (1609); the narrative poems; and seven apocryphal plays from the Third Folio.

1782: First successful appearance of Sarah Siddons at Drury Lane (after a brief and unsuccessful season with David Garrick, 1774–5).

1783: First appearance of John Philip Kemble in London, at the Theatre Royal Drury Lane (30 September, as Hamlet); appointed actor-manager, 1788.

1785: Siddons's first London performance as Lady Macbeth.

1786: Kemble, *Macbeth Reconsidered* (revised and extended, 1817).

1787: Malone, *A dissertation on the three parts of King Henry VI*.

1789–1803: The Boydell Shakespeare Gallery, original paintings by major British artists, exhibited in a specially built public gallery, Pall Mall, London; published in an engraved edition, with text overseen by George Steevens, 1791–1803.

1790: Malone's first edition of Shakespeare, in ten volumes, including the first documentary Life of Shakespeare and a History of the English Stage, similarly based on documentary evidence, about the contexts and conditions in which Shakespeare worked.

1793: George Steevens's first independent edition of Shakespeare, in fifteen volumes.

Ludwig Tieck, essay on the Boydell Gallery; also *Shakespeare's Handling of the Supernatural* (published 1796).

1795: Friedrich Schlegel, *On the Study of Greek Poetry* (published 1797).

1795–6: Goethe, *Wilhelm Meister's Apprenticeship*.

1796: Friedrich Schlegel, *On Goethe's Wilhelm Meister*.

A. W. Schlegel, 'On William Shakespeare' (in Schiller's *Die Horen*).

1797: Friedrich Schlegel (with A. W. Schlegel and Novalis), *Critical [Lyceum-] Fragments*; *Athenaeum-Fragments*, 1798; *Ideas*, 1800.

1797–1801: A. W. Schlegel, translation of sixteen Shakespeare plays in blank verse.

1800: Tieck, *Letters on Shakespeare*.

Friedrich Schlegel, *Dialogue on Poetry.*

Germaine de Staël, *On Literature* (English translation, 1803).

1801: François René de Chateaubriand, *Shakespere or Shakespeare.*

1803: John Philip Kemble moves to the Theatre Royal Covent Garden.

1807: Charles and Mary Lamb, *Tales from Shakespeare, designed for the use of young persons.*

1808: A. W. Schlegel, *Lectures on Dramatic Art and Literature*, delivered in Vienna; published 1809–11; French translation, 1813; English translation, 1815.

Kemble appointed actor-manager of the Theatre Royal Covent Garden.

1809: 'Old Price' riots at the Theatre Royal Covent Garden.

1810: A. W. Schlegel, translation of *Richard III* in blank verse (his last Shakespeare translation).

1811: Coleridge's first public lectures on Shakespeare, with further series including substantial discussions of Shakespeare in 1812–13 and 1818–19.

Charles Lamb, 'On the Tragedies of Shakespeare considered with reference to their fitness for stage representation' (revised 1818).

1812: Official retirement of Sarah Siddons from the stage (though with various later performances, by royal request, or to support actors who were members of her family).

1813: Germaine de Staël, *Germany* (completed in French, 1810, but publication banned; first published in English while de Staël was in exile in England).

Goethe, *Shakespeare without End* (completed and published 1826).

1814: London debut of Edmund Kean at Drury Lane, as Shylock (26 January).

Beginning of Hazlitt's career as a theatrical reviewer.

1817: Coleridge, *Biographia Literaria.*

Hazlitt, *The Characters of Shakespeare's Plays.*

Farewell performance and retirement from the stage of John Philip Kemble (23 June).

1817–20: Discussions of and comments on Shakespeare in Keats's Letters.

1818: Hazlitt, *A View of the English Stage.*

1818–29: Hegel lectures on Aesthetics, including on Tragedy, in Heidelberg and (from 1820) in Berlin (published posthumously, 1835).

1821: Malone's second edition of Shakespeare, posthumously revised from his papers by James Boswell Jr, in twenty-one volumes, supplemented by new documentary materials.

François Guizot (with Amédée Pichot), revised edition of Le Tourneur's translation, with introduction and prefaces by Guizot.

1823: Thomas De Quincey, 'On the knocking at the gate in *Macbeth*'.

1823, 1825: Stendhal, *Racine and Shakespeare*.

1825–33: Dorothea Tieck and Wolf Heinrich Baudissin complete A. W. Schlegel's translation, with overall editing by Tieck.

1827 (September): English acting company including Edmund Kean, Charles Kemble, William Charles Macready, and Harriet Smithson begins a season of performances of Shakespeare in Paris, to great acclaim.

1827 (October): Victor Hugo, 'Preface' to *Cromwell*.

1829: Alfred de Vigny, translation of *Othello* (in verse) staged at the Comédie-Française (published with a preface, 'A Letter to Lord ***', 1830).

1830: Hector Berlioz, Overture, *The Tempest*; first of a series of works based on Shakespeare including the dramatic symphony *Roméo et Juliette* (1839), and the opera *Béatrice et Bénédict* (1862).

1832: Anna Jameson, *Characteristics of Women, Moral, Poetical, and Historical* (later known as *Shakespeare's Heroines*).

1833: Final London performances and death of Edmund Kean.

1836: Heinrich Heine, *The Romantic School*.

Chateaubriand, *Essay on English Literature* (a book).

1838: Heine, *Shakespeare's Girls and Women*.

1843: Tieck's staging of *A Midsummer Night's Dream* in Potsdam with Mendelssohn's incidental music.

Eugène Delacroix, *Hamlet* lithographs.

1844: Théodore Chassériau, *Othello* engravings.

1859–65: François-Victor Hugo, complete translation of Shakespeare (in prose), published in fifteen volumes.

1864: Victor Hugo, *Shakespeare*.

Notes

CHAPTER 1

1. *To Criticize the Critic* (London: Faber, 1965), 19. The observation has been given currency in a misquotation ('distinctive' for 'instinctive') by Frank Kermode as an epigraph to his *Selected Prose of T. S. Eliot*. Where quotations are not referenced in the Introduction, references can be found in the chapters in which issues raised here are more elaborately developed, which also give further details about the writers introduced here allusively.
2. T. M. Raysor (ed.), *Coleridge: Shakespeare Criticism* (1930), 2nd edition, 2 vols. (London: Dent, 1960), 2.129–30.
3. 'On Gusto', *The Complete Works of William Hazlitt*, The Centenary Edition, 21 vols., ed. P. P. Howe (London: Dent, 1930–4), 4.77–80 (77).
4. *The Collected Poems of Wallace Stevens* (New York: Knopf, 1954), 183.

CHAPTER 2

1. See James Engell, 'Coleridge, Johnson, and Shakespeare: A Critical Drama in Five Acts', *Romanticism: The Journal of Romantic Culture and Criticism*, 4.1 (1988), 22–39.
2. 'Shakespeare Criticism I: from Dryden to Coleridge', *A Companion to Shakespeare Studies*, ed. Harley Granville-Barker and G. B. Harrison (Cambridge, MA: Harvard University Press, 1934), 299.
3. See Coleridge's letter of 28 February 1819, T. M. Raysor (ed.), *Coleridge: Shakespeare Criticism* (1930), 2nd edition, 2 vols. (London: Dent, 1960), 2.261–4. References to Coleridge's Shakespeare criticism throughout are to Raysor. The standard scholarly edition of Coleridge's literary lectures is that of R. A. Foakes (ed.), *Lectures 1808–1819: On Literature*, 2 vols., Bollingen Series LXXV (London: Routledge, 1987); *The Collected Works of Samuel Taylor Coleridge*, ed. Kathleen Coburn with Bart Winer, vol. 5. Though a superb edition, this is difficult to use: the material on individual plays is not collected together (as it is in Raysor), and Foakes follows Coleridge in giving only references for quotations. Foakes's *Coleridge's Criticism of Shakespeare: A Selection* (Detroit: Wayne State University Press, 1989) is excellent but limited in scope. For a recent edition see *Coleridge: Lectures on Shakespeare (1811–1819)*, ed. Adam Roberts (Edinburgh: Edinburgh University Press, 2016).

4. See Foakes (ed.), *Lectures 1808–1819*, 1.172.

5. On Coleridge's predecessors who anticipated both his attack on the classical unities and his modes of character analysis see David Nichol Smith (ed.), *Eighteenth-Century Essays on Shakespeare* (1903), 2nd edition (Oxford: Clarendon Press, 1963).

6. On the contested issue of the influence on Coleridge of A. W. Schlegel, especially on the development of his idea of organic form, see Coleridge's letter of 1811 (Raysor, 2.184–91), his note of 1819 (Raysor, 1.16–17), and the discussion in Foakes, *Lectures 1808–1819*, 1.lix–lxiv.

7. 'On the Principles of Genial Criticism', in *Biographia Literaria*, ed. J. Shawcross, 2 vols. (Oxford: Oxford University Press, 1907), 2.232. Cf. that power 'which unites a given *all* into a whole that is presupposed in each of its parts', *Biographia Literaria*, ed. James Engell and W. Jackson Bate, *The Collected Works of Samuel Taylor Coleridge*, vol. 7, 2 vols. (London: Routledge, 1983), 2.62. For this idea in Coleridge's Shakespeare criticism, see Raysor 1.188 and 2.63.

8. *Biographia*, ed. Engell and Bate, 2.16–17.

9. Cf. notes for a lecture on *Venus and Adonis* on the power 'of combining many circumstances into one moment of thought to produce that ultimate end of human Thought, and human Feeling, Unity, and thereby the reduction of the Spirit to its Principle & Fountain, who alone is truly *one*', *The Notebooks of Samuel Taylor Coleridge*, ed. Kathleen Coburn, 4 vols. (London: Routledge, 1957–90), 3.3247.6.

10. Raysor, 1.40. For other instances of this opening keynotes-and-epitome effect as 'an induction or tuning for what is to follow' (Raysor, 1.119), see Raysor, 1.37–8 and 2.230.

11. *Notebooks*, ed. Coburn, 3.2971.

12. See Raysor, 2.105, on additions (supposed by Coleridge non-Shakespearean) by 'the clown . . . called in to lighten the representation'.

13. This, from what became the Essay on Method IV (*The Friend*, 1818), appears only in the extended version in the *Encyclopaedia Metropolitana*: see Alice D. Snyder (ed.), *Coleridge: Treatise on Method as published in the Encyclopaedia Metropolitana* (London: Constable, 1934), 32. Coleridge was not the first to use the word 'psychological', but his note here on 'this *insolens verbum*' (strange and unfamiliar word) is an indication of the novelty of the conceptions with which he was dealing.

14. Foakes (ed.), *Lectures 1808–1819*, 2.151.

15. 1933; reprinted in Knights, *Explorations* (London: Chatto, 1947).

16. As in Jerry Brotton, *This Orient Isle: Elizabethan England and the Islamic World* (London: Allen Lane, 2016).

17. *Table Talk*, July 1827, ed. Carl Woodring, *The Collected Works of Samuel Taylor Coleridge*, vol. 14, 2 vols. (London: Routledge, 1990), 2.61.
18. Letter of 3 January 1812 on Coleridge's lecture on *Hamlet* of the previous day (Raysor, 2.181–2).
19. 'Shakespeare, or the Poet', *Representative Men*, ed. Wallace E. Williams and Douglas Emory Wilson, *The Collected Works of Ralph Waldo Emerson*, vol. 4 (Cambridge, MA: Belknap Press, 1987), 117.
20. *The Friend*, 7 December 1809, ed. Barbara E. Rooke, *The Collected Works of Samuel Taylor Coleridge*, vol. 4, 2 vols. (London: Routledge, 1969), 2.217; repeated in *Biographia*, ed. Engell and Bate, 2.185.
21. Raysor, 2.96; cf. 2.130 and *Biographia*, XIV (quoted above), on the Imagination as a power that 'reveals itself in the balance or reconciliation of opposite . . . qualities: . . . the individual, with the representative'.
22. *Notebooks*, ed. Coburn, 1.943.
23. *The Friend*, ed. Rooke, 1.448–57 (457).
24. *Biographia*, ed. Engell and Bate, 2.185.
25. *'The Birth of Tragedy' and Other Writings*, ed. Raymond Geuss and Ronald Speirs, Cambridge Texts in the History of Philosophy (Cambridge: Cambridge University Press, 1999); *The Birth of Tragedy*, §17.
26. *Treatise on Method*, ed. Snyder, 35.
27. *Preface to Shakespeare* (1765), *The Yale Edition of the Works of Samuel Johnson* (New Haven: Yale University Press, 1958–), vols. 7–8 (1968), *Johnson on Shakespeare*, ed. Arthur Sherbo, 7.79.
28. Raysor, 1.114–17, 1.176–83, and 2.257–8. Coleridge discussed the same issue in a letter of 13 May 1816: *Collected Letters*, ed. Earl Leslie Griggs, 6 vols. (Oxford: Clarendon Press, 1956–71), 4.641–2.
29. *Biographia*, ed. Engell and Bate, 2.6; and cf. 2.134.
30. For Hazlitt's youthful admiration of Coleridge see 'My First Acquaintance with Poets', *The Complete Works of William Hazlitt*, The Centenary Edition, 21 vols., ed. P. P. Howe (London: Dent, 1930–4), 17.106–22. All references to Hazlitt are to this edition. That Hazlitt did not think well of Coleridge's lectures on Shakespeare is evinced by a conversation recorded by J. P. Collier in 1811: see Stanley Jones, *Hazlitt: a Life: from Winterslow to Frith Street* (Oxford: Clarendon, 1989), 64–5.
31. 'On the Periodical Essayists', Howe, 6.92.
32. Oscar Wilde, *The Critic as Artist, Plays, Prose Writings, and Poems*, ed. Isobel Murray (London: Dent, 1975), 33–4.
33. Details of Hazlitt's reworking of his reviews in the *Characters* are given in Howe, 5.391–408. The reviews themselves were reprinted, sometimes with revisions, in *A View of the English Stage* (1818), Howe, vol. 5, and in their original magazine forms in Howe, vol. 18.

34. See, for example, his review of Edmund Kean's Lear: Howe, 18.331–8.
35. Howe, 4.190. For Hazlitt's accounts of 'the miserable medley' acted for
    Richard III, and a comparable treatment of *Antony and Cleopatra* incorp-
    orating parts of Dryden's *All for Love*, see Howe, 4.300–3 and 5.190–1.
36. Howe, 5.221–4 (222). Hazlitt here gives details of what he finds less
    effective in the theatre than in reading, but his judgement remains
    equivocal: 'If the oracle does not speak quite intelligibly, we yet perceive
    that the priest at the altar is inspired with the god, or possessed with a
    demon' (223).
37. References to Keats's letters are to *The Letters of John Keats, 1814–1821*,
    ed. Hyder Edward Rollins, 2 vols. (Cambridge: Cambridge University
    Press, 1958), 1.203. Borrowings from Hazlitt are noted in its annotations.
    Keats's annotations of Hazlitt's *Characters of Shakespeare's Plays* are printed
    in *The Poetical Writings and Other Works of John Keats: The Hampstead
    Edition*, ed. Harry Buxton Forman, rev. Maurice Buxton Forman, 8 vols.
    (New York: Scribner's, 1939), 5.280–90.
38. 'Mr Kean', *The Champion*, 21 December 1817; Buxton Forman,
    5.227–32.
39. 'The inexplicable mystery of sound': T. S. Eliot, 'To Walter de la Mare',
    Collected Poems (London: Faber, 1962), 233.
40. See, for example, his annotation of Titania's 'the middle summer's spring',
    A Midsummer Night's Dream, 2.1.82; Buxton Forman, 5.268–9. Keats's
    annotations (complete, with some markings) are collected in Buxton
    Forman, 5.268–79.
41. Keats explores the contrast and gives an instance in a letter to
    J. H. Reynolds (Rollins, 1.223–4). What Keats admires here is Shake-
    speare's lightness of touch: Jacques (*As You Like It*, 2.1) is seen as a
    Wordsworthian figure, laboriously moralizing upon Nature, the dramatic
    context as a satire of this heavy-footed tendentiousness.
42. *John Keats* (Cambridge, MA: Harvard University Press, 1963), 233–63.
    Bate's account is still a reference point for more elaborately historicized
    readings: see Nicholas Roe, *Keats and the Culture of Dissent* (Oxford:
    Clarendon Press, 1997), 231.
43. See the sonnet, 'On sitting down to read *King Lear* once again'; Buxton
    Forman, 4.76–7.
44. See Helen E. Haworth, 'Keats's copy of Lamb's *Specimens of English
    Dramatic Poetry*', *Bulletin of the New York Public Library*, 74 (1970),
    419–27, and especially Keats's praise of a comment on Shakespeare by
    Lamb as 'the most acute deep sighted and spiritual piece of criticism ever
    penned' (422).

45. References are to *The Works of Charles and Mary Lamb*, ed. E. V. Lucas, 7 vols. (London: Methuen, 1903–5), 1.99, 108.

46. See 'Shakespeare's Improvers' (Lucas, 1.321–3), in which Lamb excoriates adaptations of *Coriolanus*, *Timon of Athens*, and *Macbeth*.

47. 'G. F. Cooke in *Richard III*', Lucas, 1.36–8. See also Lamb's letter to Robert Lloyd, 26 June 1801, *The Letters of Charles and Mary Anne Lamb*, ed. Edwin W. Marrs, Jr, 3 vols. (Ithaca: Cornell University Press, 1975–8), 2.7–10.

48. In offering as a good 'criterion of genius, – whether it progresses and evolves, or only spins upon itself', Coleridge contrasts 'Charles Lamb's exquisite criticisms of Shakespeare with Hazlitt's round and round imitations of them', *Table Talk*, ed. Woodring, 2.183. Cf. Coleridge's praise of Lamb's 'just and original criticism, expressed with all the freshness of originality' in *Biographia*, ed. Engell and Bate, 2.79.

49. 'Scraps of Criticism' (Lucas, 1.373–5); 'villain' in its movement from social meaning ('churl' in its status sense, and so 'outsider') to its normal modern moral sense.

50. Marrs (ed.), *Letters*, 2.36.

51. Cf. Walter Pater, 'Charles Lamb', in *Appreciations* (London: Macmillan, 1889), 107–26.

52. 'On the knocking at the gate in *Macbeth*', *Thomas De Quincey*, ed. Robert Morrison, 21st-Century Oxford Authors (Oxford: Oxford University Press, 2019), 91.

53. Nietzsche, *The Birth of Tragedy*, ed. Geuss and Speirs, §1, 14.

54. See Robin Hamlyn, 'The Shakespeare Galleries of John Boydell and James Woodmason', in Jane Martineau et al., *Shakespeare in Art* (London: Merrell, 2003), 97–113.

55. For a list of the folio plates (with reproductions) and the illustrations of the edition see Walter Pape and Fredrick Burwick (ed.), *The Boydell Shakespeare Gallery* (Bottrop: Peter Pomp, 1996), 205–96. No complete list of the paintings was made. By the time of the Boydell sale they numbered 167.

56. E. V. Lucas (ed.), *The Letters of Charles Lamb*, 3 vols. (London: Dent, 1935), 3.394.

57. Fuseli's extant Shakespeare paintings and drawings number about forty items related to sixteen different plays, created between *c.*1760 and the year of his death: see Gert Schiff, *Henry Fuseli, 1741–1825* (London: Tate, 1975), 58–73. Nine of Fuseli's Shakespeare paintings (six of them now lost) were created for Boydell. On the critical-exploratory Shakespeare paintings of Fuseli's friend and artistic associate William Blake (1757–1827), affirming a Romantic idea of the Imagination and with their

intense visualization of poetic imagery, see my 'Chaucer, Spenser, and Shakespeare' in Sarah Haggarty (ed.), *William Blake in Context* (Cambridge: Cambridge University Press, 2019), 173–83 (178–83).

58. As in Jan Kott, *Shakespeare our Contemporary*, trans. Bolesław Taborski, preface by Peter Brook (London: Routledge, 1967).

59. For Nietzsche on *Macbeth* see *Daybreak* (*Morgenröte*), IV, §240. Fuseli's review of Boydell's 'magnificent scheme', published anonymously in *The Analytical Review* (May 1789, 107–12), is explicit about his intention of a sublime-heroic (proto-Nietzschean) Macbeth in this painting (111).

60. See Marcia Pointon, 'Representing *The Tempest* in Boydell's Shakespeare Gallery', Pape and Burwick (ed.), *The Boydell Shakespeare Gallery*, 103–12.

61. For a political reading of Jameson in relation to the Reform Bill see Judith Johnston, *Anna Jameson: Victorian, Feminist, Woman of Letters* (Aldershot: Scolar Press, 1997), ch. 3.

62. Letter of 6 September 1863, *The Collected Works of Gerard Manley Hopkins*, vols. 1 and 2, *Correspondence*, ed. R. K. R. Thornton and Catherine Philips (Oxford: Oxford University Press, 2013), 1.45–6.

63. Anna Murphy Jameson, *Shakespeare's Heroines [Characteristics of Women: Moral, Poetical, and Historical]*, ed. Cheri L. Larsen Hoeckley (Peterborough, ON.: Broadview, 2005), 55. References in the text are to this edition using Jameson's title, *Characteristics*.

64. See Christy Desmet, '"Intercepting the Dew-Drop": Female Readings and Readers in Anna Jameson's Shakespeare Criticism', in *Women's Re-Visions of Shakespeare*, ed. Marianne Novy (Urbana: University of Illinois Press, 1990), 41–57.

65. *Characteristics*, 55. Cf. the claim made more specifically in relation to Lady Macbeth: 'sympathy is in proportion to the degree of pride, passion, and intellect, we may ourselves possess' (*Characteristics*, 361).

66. Unlike Jameson's, Elizabeth Inchbald's views on Shakespeare have no proto-feminist interest. These are given in prefaces to twenty-four Shakespeare plays in the first five volumes of her collection, *The British Theatre* (London: Longman, 1806–9), and reflect conventions of Restoration and eighteenth-century criticism, to which Inchbald refers copiously. Selections from Inchbald are included in Ann Thompson and Sasha Roberts (eds.), *Women Reading Shakespeare 1660–1900* (Manchester: Manchester University Press, 1997).

67. See Stanley Wells, '*Tales from Shakespeare*', *Proceedings of the British Academy*, LXXIII (1987), 125–52.

68. Letter to Coleridge of 23 October 1802; *Letters*, ed. Marrs, 2.81.

69. See 'Witches and Other Night-Fears', Lucas, 2.65–70.

70. See *The Diary, Reminiscences, and Correspondence of Henry Crabb Robinson*, ed. Thomas Sadler, 3 vols. (London: Macmillan, 1869), 1.349. The diary gives a more complex sense of Lamb's view than the *Tales*, distinguishing between Lady Macbeth's voluntary actions and her involuntary nature: 'though while awake she is a monster, she is a woman in her sleep'.

CHAPTER 3

1. 'Etwas über William Shakespeare bei Gelegenheit *Wilhelm Meisters*' (On William Shakespeareoccasioned by *Wilhelm Meister*), in Hansjügen Blinn (ed.), *Shakespeare-Rezeption: die Diskussion um Shakespeare in Deutschland. II. Ausgewälte Texte von 1793 bis 1827* (Berlin: Schmidt, 1988), 92.

2. *Poems* (1815), *Essay Supplementary to the Preface*; *The Prose Works of William Wordsworth*, ed. J. B. Owen and Jane Worthington Smyser, 3 vols. (Oxford: Clarendon Press, 1974), 3.69.

3. For Coleridge's protest against Wordsworth's comments see Raysor, 2.244–5, and Raysor's discussion, 1.xxvi–xxviii. For Coleridge's tribute to A. W. Schlegel see Raysor, 2.126.

4. Widely viewed as a summation of this line of thought in German criticism is Friedrich Gundolf, *Shakespeare und der deutsche Geist* (Berlin: Bondi, 1911, 2nd edition, 1914).

5. Blinn (ed.), *Shakespeare-Rezeption . . . I. Ausgewälte Texte von 1741 bis 1788* (Berlin: Schmidt, 1982), 70–2 (72).

6. See Coleridge, *Biographia*, ch. 2, a discussion of genius in which he distinguishes between its operation in the worlds of art and intellect and in the world of action, for which Napoleon is his contemporary and monitory example: *Biographia*, ed. Engell and Bate, 1.30–7.

7. Fuseli, *Lectures on Painting, Delivered at the Royal Academy* (London: Johnson, 1801); First Lecture, 6.

8. Manifestations of the idea in the later eighteenth century are often traced to Edward Young, *Conjectures on Original Composition*, 1759 (translated into German in 1760), and William Duff, *An Essay on Original Genius*, 1767. An influential statement of the idea in Germany is that of Kant, *Critique of Judgement* (1790), §46. For a characteristic formulation in England see Coleridge, 'On Poesy or Art' (1818), in Shawcross (ed.) *Biographia*, 2.253–63. For the idea in relation to Shakespeare see Jonathan Bate in Penelope Murray (ed.), *Genius: the History of an Idea* (Oxford: Blackwell, 1989), 76–97.

9. *'The Hamburg Dramaturgy' by G. E. Lessing: A New and Complete Annotated English Translation*, trans. Wendy Arons and Sara Figal, ed. Natalya Baldyga (London: Routledge, 2019). For the German text see Lessing,

Werke, ed. Herbert G. Göpfert et al., 8 vols., (Munich: Hanser, 1972); *Hamburgische Dramaturgie* in vol. 4, ed. Karl Eibl.

10. Cf. 'How many things would seem incontestable in theory had not genius succeeded in proving the opposite by fact', *Laocoön*, trans. Edward Allen McCormick (1962; Baltimore: Johns Hopkins University Press, 1984), §4, 25.

11. See the account of his work in Friedrich Schlegel, 'Concerning the Essence of Criticism' (1804), in Jochen Schulte-Sasse et al. (ed. and trans.), *Theory as Practice: A Critical Anthology of Early German Romantic Writings* (Minneapolis: University of Minnesota Press, 1997), 268–77.

12. Shakespeare appears in §11 (his handling of the supernatural); §15 (*Romeo and Juliet*, *Othello*; praise of Christoph Martin Wieland's translations, 1762–6); §§69–70 (discussion of his mixture of tragic and comic); §73 (discussion of Christian Felix Weisse's *Richard III* with comment on Shakespeare as a model); §80 (the implications for theatrical imagination of the minimal scenery and continuous action in Shakespeare's theatre); §81 (Shakespeare as the embodiment of Aristotle's view of tragedy).

13. Occasionally Lessing's view of the theatre as a morally educative secular pulpit leads him to compromise this engagement of the passions with a moral detachment with which modern readers can hardly sympathize: *Othello* is a primer of jealousy from which 'we can learn . . . how to avoid it' (§15 ¶6)–a remnant of the moralism of eighteenth-century criticism which is not a consistent feature of Lessing's discussions.

14. For Goethe's praise of Hamann as 'the brightest mind of his day' see his conversations with Friedrich Müller (18 December 1823); and on Hamann as a father of German literature see his *Italienische Reise*, Naples, 5 March 1787. For Friedrich Schlegel on Hamann ('this immensely wise and profound thinker, this seer') see 'Auszüge aus Hamanns Briefen an F. H. Jacobi, 1813', *Kritische Neuausgabe*, ed. Hans Eichner (Munich: Schöningh, 1961), 8.628; cf. 'with his divinatory profundity [Hamann] stood alone in the literature of his time', *Kritische Neuausgabe*, 6.378.

15. For the German text of the *Aesthetica* see Hamann, *Sämtliche Werke*, ed. Josef Nadler, 6 vols. (Vienna: Herder, 1949–57), 2.195–217. Translations can be found in H. B. Nisbet (ed.), *German Aesthetic and Literary Criticism* (Cambridge: Cambridge University Press, 1985; trans. Joyce P. Crick); Gwen Griffith Dickson, *Johann Georg Hamann's Relational Metacriticism* (Berlin: de Gruyter, 1995); J. M. Bernstein (ed.), *Classic and Romantic German Aesthetics*, Cambridge Texts in the History of Philosophy (Cambridge: Cambridge University Press, 2003; also Crick's translation); and Hamann, *Writings on Philosophy and Language*, ed. Kenneth Haynes, Cambridge Texts in the History of Philosophy (Cambridge: Cambridge

University Press, 2007). References in the text are to Crick's translation in Nisbet (ed.).

16. Hamann, *Briefwechsel*, ed. Walter Ziesemer and Arthur Henkel, 6 vols. (Frankfurt: Insel, 1955–79), 2.415.22–3; to Herder, 23 May 1786.

17. *From my Life: Poetry and Truth*, trans. Robert R. Heitner (Princeton: Princeton University Press, 1987); vols. 4–5 of *Goethe: Collected Works*, 12 vols., ed. Victor Lange et al., Part III, Book xii, 4.380–1.

18. Isaiah Berlin, *Three Critics of the Enlightenment: Vico, Hamann, Herder*, ed. Henry Hardy (Princeton: Princeton University Press, 2000), 269. On system building as an obstacle to truth see *Briefwechsel*, 1.431.30 (to J. G. Lindner, 12 October 1759) and 6.276.15 (to F. H. Jacobi, 18 February 1786).

19. *The Letters of William Blake*, ed. Geoffrey Keynes, 3rd edition (Oxford: Clarendon Press, 1980), 8.

20. *Socratic Memorabilia*, II; Dickson, *Relational Metacriticism*, 391; Nadler (ed.), *Sämtliche Werke*, 2.73. The discussion of Socratic ignorance constitutes the whole second section of the work.

21. *Socratic Memorabilia*, Nadler (ed.), *Sämtliche Werke*, 2.68; Dickson, *Relational Metacriticism*, 386.

22. See *Marginalia*, 2 November 1803, and *Table Talk*, 14 May 1833, in Foakes (ed.), *Coleridge's Criticism of Shakespeare*, 30–2. On eighteenth- and nineteenth-century attempts to evade the sense of the sonnets addressed to a 'lovely boy' (Sonnet 126), see Peter Stallybrass, 'Editing as Cultural Formation: the Sexing of Shakespeare's Sonnets', James Schiffer (ed.), *Shakespeare's Sonnets: Critical Essays* (New York: Garland, 1999), 75–88.

23. Johann Gottfried Herder, *Selected Writings on Aesthetics*, ed. and trans. Gregory Moore (Princeton: Princeton University Press, 2006), 297. For the German text see Herder, *Werke*, vol. 2, *Schriften zur Ästhetik und Literatur 1767–1781*, ed. Günter E. Grimm (Frankfurt: Deutsche Klassiker, 1993). 'Shakespeare' is frequently collected in and contextualized by anthologies of German criticism of the period, as in H. B. Nisbet (ed.), *German Aesthetic and Literary Criticism*; David Simpson (ed.), *The Origins of Modern Critical Thought: German Aesthetic and Literary Criticism from Lessing to Hegel* (Cambridge: Cambridge University Press, 1988); and Timothy J. Chamberlain (ed.), *Eighteenth-Century German Criticism* (New York: Continuum, 1992).

24. 'A Correspondence on Ossian and the Songs of Ancient Peoples' (1773), published with 'Shakespeare' in *Von deutscher Art und Kunst*; Nisbet (ed.), *German Aesthetic and Literary Criticism*, 154–61 (156).

25. 'On German Architecture', *Essays on Art and Literature*, trans. Ellen von Nardoff and Ernest H. von Nardoff (Princeton: Princeton University Press, 1986), 3–10; vol. 3 of *Goethe: The Collected Works* in 12 volumes. Goethe's argument about the misvaluation of Gothic by standards of classical architecture is analogous to Herder's argument about Shakespeare.

26. Pater, *Studies in the History of the Renaissance* (1873), including 'Winckelmann' (1857), ed. Matthew Beaumont (Oxford: Oxford University Press, 2010); and *Appreciations* (London: Macmillan, 1889). Ricks, *Essays in Appreciation* (Oxford: Oxford University Press, 1996).

27. Friedrich Schlegel, *Athenaeums-Fragmente*, 216; *Dialogue on Poetry and Literary Aphorisms*, trans. Ernst Behler and Roman Struc (University Park: Pennsylvania State University Press, 1968), 143.

28. *Wilhelm Meister's Apprenticeship*, trans. Eric A. Blackall with Victor Lange (Princeton: Princeton University Press, 1989); vol. 9 of *Goethe: Collected Works* in 12 volumes, Book IV, ch. 13, 146. Discussions of Shakespeare and *Hamlet* are scattered throughout Books III to V of the novel's eight books: see primarily III.9, 11, IV.3, 5, 13–16, V.4–6, 9, 11–12. For the German text see Goethe, *Sämtliche Werke nach Epochen seines Schaffens: Münchener Ausgabe*, vol. 5, ed. Hans-Jürgen Schings (Munich: Hanser, 1988).

29. For this and Goethe's later essay (1815), see *Goethe on Shakespeare/Goethe über Shakespeare*, a parallel text edition, trans. Michael Hofmann and David Constantine, with an essay by Rüdiger Görner (London: Globe, 2010).

30. *From my Life: Poetry and Truth*, trans. Robert R. Heitner, Part III, Book 13, 428.

31. Twenty-two plays, 1762–66 (all but *A Midsummer Night's Dream* in prose). The translation was revised and completed, 1775–82, by Johann Joachim Eschenburg (all but *Richard III* in prose), making it the first complete translation of Shakespeare into German, standard before the translations of August Wilhelm Schlegel (from 1797; seventeen plays by 1810; the translation completed under the supervision of Ludwig Tieck, 1825–33; see note 37).

32. 'Shakespeare once again', in *Essays on Art and Literature*, trans. Nardoff and Nardoff, 166–74. On Heufeld's rewriting and Schröder's two rewritings, in which (besides other major changes of plot and characterization) Hamlet lives to rule Denmark, see Simon Williams, *Shakespeare on the German Stage. Volume 1: 1586–1914* (Cambridge: Cambridge University Press, 2004), 69–81. On the Schiller/Goethe reworking of *Macbeth* (1800), and Goethe's rewriting of *Romeo and Juliet* (1812), making both

plays conform more to criteria of French neoclassicism, see Williams, 94–104.

33. Raysor, 2.31. Cf. Coleridge's doubts expressed about a speech in *Coriolanus*: 'I cherish the hope that...becoming wiser, [I] shall discover some profound excellence in what I now appear to myself to detect an imperfection' (Raysor, 1.81).

34. 'On Goethe's *Meister*', Bernstein (ed.), *Classic and Romantic German Aesthetics*, 281.

35. *Lectures on Dramatic Art and Literature*, trans. John Black (1815), rev. A. J. W. Morrison, London: Bohn, 1846. Page references are to this edition. For the German text see A. W. Schlegel, *Kritische Schriften und Breife*, ed. Edgar Lohner, 7 vols. (Stuttgart: Kohlhammer, 1962–74; *KS*); *Vorlesungen* in vols. 5 and 6. For Schlegel's revisions during the 1830s, which explain how the English text of 1815/1846 came to be different from that of the *Kritische Schriften*, see Roger Paulin, *The Life of August Wilhelm Schlegel, Cosmopolitan of Art and Poetry* (Cambridge: Open Book, 2016), 302–14.

36. For a full account of the impact on the English Romantics of Schlegel's Lectures see Thomas G. Sauer, *A. W. Schlegel's Literary Criticism in England, 1811–1846* (Bonn: Grundmann, 1981).

37. The translation was completed 1825–33. What became known as the Schlegel–Tieck translation was largely completed by Wolf von Baudissin (twelve plays) and Tieck's daughter Dorothea (five plays), with original work by Tieck on just two plays with some general oversight of the whole.

38. *Kritische Schriften*, 1.88–122, 123–40. Both essays are printed (abbreviated) in Blinn (ed.), *Shakespeare-Rezeption*, 2.92–101, 109–22. The essay prompted by *Wilhelm Meister* has not been translated. The essay on *Romeo and Juliet* was translated by Julius Charles Hare, 'A. W. Schlegel on Shakespeare's *Romeo and Juliet*; with remarks upon the character of German criticism', *Ollier's Literary Miscellany*, 1 (1820), 1–39.

39. On 'true and faithful translations, which endeavour in expression and versification to rise to the height of the original', cf. Schlegel's discussion of the problems of reading Greek drama in translation, *Lectures on Dramatic Art*, 47–9.

40. For an account of the Schlegel–Tieck translation in the history of German Shakespeares, see Werner Habicht, 'The Romanticism of the Schlegel-Tieck Shakespeare and the History of Nineteenth Century German Shakespeare Translation', in Dirk Delabastita and Lieven D'hulst (ed.), *European Shakespeares: Translating Shakespeare in the Romantic Age* (Amsterdam: Benjamins, 1993), 45–54.

41. Cf. Schlegel's repudiation of the Garrick ending of *Romeo and Juliet* (also deplored by Coleridge) in which Juliet wakes after Romeo has taken the poison but before he dies: 'There is a degree of shock above which everything that is added either turns into torture or slides off the mind without any effect' (*KS*, 1.135).

42. *Athenaeum Fragments*, 204 (by A. W. Schlegel); *Friedrich Schlegel's 'Lucinde' and the Fragments*, trans. Peter Firchow (Minneapolis: University of Minnesota Press, 1971), 189.

43. For Schlegel's account of irony in relation to Shakespeare, 'a sort of secret understanding with the select circle of the more intelligent of his readers or auditors', see *Lectures on Dramatic Art*, 368–70. Unlike Friedrich Schlegel, however, he limits its application: 'whenever the proper tragic enters anything like irony immediately ceases' (370).

44. See, for example, Paulin, *Life*, 312–13. Schlegel's association with the anti-Napoleonist Germaine de Staël makes this only more probable.

45. See especially the critique of Karl Solger in *Erwin: Four Dialogues on Beauty and Art* (1816), in Kathleen M. Wheeler (ed.), *German Aesthetic and Literary Criticism: the Romantic Ironists and Goethe* (Cambridge: Cambridge University Press, 1984), 127–50: 'on the summit of art . . . [his example is Shakespeare] opposites must be so reconciled that the thought of one-sidedness will no longer lay hold of us' (148).

46. *On the Study of Greek Poetry*, trans. Stuart Barnett (Albany: State University of New York Press, 2001). This translation, based on the 1st edition (1797), incorporates in its annotation elements of a revised text Schlegel prepared for a collection of his writings published 1822–25. The Foreword added in 1797 (to the main text completed in 1795), a partial retraction of the essay's critique of modern (post-classical) writing, reaffirms the work's fundamental distinction between Sophoclean and Shakespearean tragedy ('poetic types that are opposed to one another in almost all their aspects', 100), but replaces the earlier term for the Shakespearean, 'philosophical', with 'interesting' (Ger. *interessant*), as a better opposite to the Sophoclean 'aesthetic' (objective, disinterested). For the German text see Friedrich Schlegel, *Kritische Neuausgabe*, ed. Ernst Behler et al., 35 vols. (Munich: Schöningh, 1958–2006); I. *Studien des klassischen Altertums*, ed. Behler, 1979, 205–367.

47. See, for example, Schlegel's place alongside Derrida in Ernst Behler, *Irony and the Discourse of Modernity* (Seattle: University of Washington Press, 1990).

48. Hans Eichner, *Friedrich Schlegel* (New York: Twayne, 1970), 26.

49. *Critical [Lyceum] Fragments*, 7; *'Lucinde' and the Fragments*, trans. Firchow, 143–4. All quotations from the fragments are from this

translation. For the German texts of the fragments, and of the companion
essay 'On Incomprehensibility' ('Über die Unverständlichkeit'), see the
Kritische Neuausgabe, II. *Charakteristiken und Kritiken I (1796–1801)*, ed.
Hans Eichner, 1975.

50. *Dialogue on Poetry and Literary Aphorisms*, trans. Behler and Struc, 155
(translation modified). Quotations from the *Dialogue* are from this translation. For the German text see *Kritische Neuausgabe*, II. *Charakteristiken
und Kritiken I*, ed. Eichner (349). The whole discussion of variety of
response and the individual reader in this part of the *Dialogue* is relevant.

51. Schlegel, *Literary Notebooks: 1797–1801*, ed. Hans Eichner (London:
Athlone, 1957), §71, 26. Selections of these Notebooks are translated in
Schulte-Sasse et al., *Theory as Practice*, 329–35.

52. *Geschichte der Poesie der Griechen und Römer* (1798); *Kritische Neuausgabe*,
I. *Studien des klassischen Altertums*, 499.

53. *'Lucinde' and the Fragments*, 175–7. For Shakespeare's implied presence in
AF 116, cf. *AF* 147: 'Shakespeare's universality is like the centre of
romantic art.' For his implied presence in *LF* 108 and *AF* 121, cf. the
development of *LF* 108 in relation to Shakespeare in 'On Incomprehensibility' (Firchow, *'Lucinde' and the Fragments*, 265–8).

54. 'Concerning the Essence of Critique' ('Von Wesen der Kritik', 1804),
Schulte-Sasse et al., *Theory as Practice*, 268–77 (272). For the German text
see *Kritische Neuausgabe*, II. *Charakteristiken und Kritiken II (1802–29)*,
ed. Eichner, 1975.

55. *'Lucinde' and the Fragments*, 267–8.

56. 'Adagia', *Opus Posthumous*, ed. Samuel French Morse (New York: Ran-
dom House, 1957), 171.

57. Caroline's contribution to August Wilhelm's *Romeo and Juliet* essay, as
evinced by their correspondence, leads to her being named as joint author
in some modern publications: see Blinn (ed.), *Shakespeare-Rezeption*,
2.109. For views of women and the feminine in the Schlegel group see
Schulte-Sasse et al., *Theory as Practice*, 359–462, 'Towards a Theory of the
Feminine', to which might be added 'a catechism of reason for noble-
minded women', *AF*, 364 (by the group's philosopher, Schleiermacher).

58. 'Ein Roman ist ein romantisches Buch' (A novel is a romantic book):
Dialogue, 101.

59. 'Briefe über Shakespeare' (1800), in Tieck, *Kritische Schriften: zum ersten-
male gesammelt*, 4 vols. (Leipzig: Brockhaus, 1848–52; reprinted Berlin:
de Gruyter, 1974), 1.141.

60. 'Briefe über Shakespeare', *Kritische Schriften*, 1.159.

61. 'Goethe und seiner Zeit', *Kritische Schriften*, 2.185.

62. Tieck's Shakespeare criticism available in English includes parts of 'Shakespeare's Treatment of the Marvellous' (trans. Louise Adey) in Jonathan Bate (ed.), *The Romantics on Shakespeare* (London: Penguin, 1992), 60–6; part of the essay on *Romeo and Juliet* in the Variorum edition of Horace Howard Furness (Philadelphia: Lippincott, 1899), 448–51; part of the essay on *Hamlet* (trans. LaMarr Kopp) in Oswald LeWinter (ed.), *Shakespeare in Europe* (1963; Harmondsworth: Penguin, 1970), 92–111; and extracts from critical writings and letters bearing on Shakespeare in Kathleen M. Wheeler (ed.), *German Aesthetic and Literary Criticism*, 115–24, 153–8. For German texts of most of these, and the essay on the Boydell Gallery, see *Kritische Schriften*, 1848–52. For a modern edition see Tieck, *Schriften*, ed. Manfred Frank et al., 12 vols. (Frankfurt: Deutscher Klassiker, 1985–91; five volumes only published); vol. 1, *Schriften 1789–1794*, ed. Achim Hölter, 1991, contains the essays on Shakespeare and the marvellous and the Boydell Gallery engravings. On Tieck's contribution to the 'Schlegel-Tieck' translation, see note 37.

63. See Kathleen Wheeler, 'Coleridge's friendship with Ludwig Tieck', in Donald Sultana (ed.), *New Approaches to Coleridge: biographical and critical essays* (London: Vision, 1981), 96–109. For 'astonishing' see Coleridge, *Letters*, ed. Griggs, 4.744.

64. *Das Buch über Shakespeare: Handschriftliche Aufzeichnungen*, ed. Henry Lüdeke (Halle: Niemeyer, 1920). This contains Tieck's five draft plans and commentary (some brief, some extended) on twenty-one plays. For an account of the book and its contexts in English (and a variety of other Tieck Shakespeareana) see Roger Paulin, *Ludwig Tieck: A Literary Biography* (Oxford: Clarendon Press, 1985).

65. 'Über Lady Macbeth' (1825), *Nachgelassene Schriften*, ed. Rudolf Köpke, 2 vols. (Leipzig: Brockhaus, 1855; repr. Berlin: de Gruyter, 1974), 2.154–8.

66. 'Bemerkungen über einige Charaktere im *Hamlet*, und über die Art, wie diese auf der Bühne dargestellt werden konnten', *Kritische Schriften*, 3.243–98.

67. 'Observations on the Character of Hamlet' (1823), in LeWinter (ed.), *Shakespeare in Europe*, 101.

68. See Williams, *Shakespeare on the German Stage*, 173–81.

69. See Peter Brook, *The Empty Space* (London: McGibbon, 1968); *The Shifting Point: 1946–1987* (New York: Harper, 1987); and *Evoking Shakespeare* (London: Nick Hern, 1998; rev. as *Evoking (and forgetting!) Shakespeare*, 2002).

70. See Williams, *Shakespeare on the German Stage*, 183–5. Mendelssohn's Overture was written earlier (1826), but the incidental music was commissioned specifically for Tieck's 1843 production.

71. Hegel's writings on tragedy are collected by Anne and Henry Paolucci, *Hegel on Tragedy* (Garden City, NY: Anchor, 1962). The translations used by the Paoluccis are now superseded. For the most important texts see Hegel, *Aesthetics. Lectures on Fine Art*, trans. T. M. Knox, 2 vols. (Oxford: Clarendon Press, 1975; the two volumes paginated continuously). This edition is used for references and quotations above. Knox's translation is based on the second edition of the reconstruction of Hegel's lectures by his student Heinrich Gustav Hotho, 3 vols. (Berlin: Duncker, 1842–3; repr. 1965). For a standard German text of Hegel see *Gesammelte Werke*, ed. Walter Jaeschke et al., Rheinisch-Westfälische Akademie der Wissenschaften (Hamburg: Meiner, 1968–).

72. Ida Benecke, *Heine on Shakespeare: a translation of his notes on Shakespeare's heroines* (London: Constable, 1895). For the German text see Heine, *Sämtliche Werke*, Düsseldorfer Ausgabe, ed. Manfred Windfuhr et al., 16 vols. (Hamburg: Hoffmann und Campe, 1975–97); vol. 10, *Shakespeares Mädchen und Frauen und kleinere literaturkritische Schriften*, ed. Jan-Christoph Hauschild, 1993.

73. 'Hegel's Theory of Tragedy', *Oxford Lectures on Poetry* (London: Macmillan, 1909). Bradley's account is drawn from a range of sources, the most important of which is *Aesthetics*, III.C.C.3(c).

74. The Ghost asserts Gertrude's adultery (1.3.42–57); that adultery provides one ground of the murder's aims (3.3.55); Hamlet suspects or fears that Gertrude shares the guilt of Clytemnestra (3.4.28–9); and Gertrude regards herself as deeply guilty (3.4.88–91; 4.5.17–20).

75. See Mark William Roche, *Tragedy and Comedy: a systematic study and a critique of Hegel* (Albany: State University of New York Press, 1998; §4, 'On the Drama of Reconciliation'); and Rowan Williams, *The Tragic Imagination* (Oxford: Oxford University Press, 2016; ch. 3, 'Reconciliation and its discontents: thinking with Hegel').

76. For a wide-ranging discussion of Hegel and Shakespeare see Jennifer A. Bates, *Hegel and Shakespeare on Moral Imagination* (Albany, NY: SUNY Press, 2014). For a discussion of Hegel's crucial idea that Shakespeare's characters are 'free artists of their own selves' (*Aesthetics*, 1228) see Ewan Fernie, *Shakespeare for Freedom: why the plays matter* (Cambridge: Cambridge University Press, 2017).

77. Siegbert Prawer, *Heine's Shakespeare: A Study in Contexts* (Oxford: Clarendon Press, 1970), 4–7.

78. Compare the yet more precise prophecy of Nazism in Heine's preface to the French edition of *Lutetia: The Romantic School and Other Essays*, ed. Jost Hermand and Robert C. Holub, The German Library (New York: Continuum, 1985), 295–301.

79. *Sämtliche Werke*, 8.1, *Zur Geschichte der Religion und Philosophie in Deutschland; Die romantische Schule*, ed. Windfuhr, 401. For an English translation of *Die romantische Schule* (based on the German text) see Hermand and Holub (ed.), *The Romantic School and Other Essays*, 1–127.
80. Hermand and Holub (ed.), *The Romantic School*, 67.
81. *Ludwig Börne*, Hermand and Holub (ed.), *The Romantic School*, 270.

CHAPTER 4

1. On Lessing and Herder see Chapter 2. For Elizabeth Montagu see her *Essay on the Writings and Genius of Shakespeare* (1769; German translation 1771, by the translator of Shakespeare, J. J. Eschenburg; French translation 1777). That the French translation appeared in 1777 made it appear an 'answer' to Voltaire's *Lettre à l'Académie française*, and prompted a response from Voltaire in a second letter to the Academy (1777).
2. For a discussion of Voltaire's writings on drama in context see C. M. Haines, *Shakespeare in France: Criticism, Voltaire to Hugo* (London: Shakespeare Association, 1924), §2. French engagement with Shakespeare from the predecessors of Voltaire to the 1850s is traced in Albert Lacroix, *Histoire de l'influence de Shakespeare sur le théâtre français jusqu'à nos jours* (Brussels: Lesigne, 1856).
3. For accounts of Ducis in context see Marion Monaco, *Shakespeare on the French Stage in the Eighteenth Century* (Paris: Didier, 1974), and John Golder, *Shakespeare for the Age of Reason: the earliest stage adaptations of Jean-François Ducis, 1769–1792*, Studies on Voltaire and the Eighteenth Century (Oxford: Voltaire Foundation, 1992).
4. From the *Lettres Philosophiques* (1728–30), first published (in English) as *Letters concerning the English Nation* (1733). For Voltaire's collected pronouncements on Shakespeare see Theodore Besterman (ed.), *Voltaire on Shakespeare* (Geneva: Institut et musée Voltaire, 1967; quotation, 44). For discussion of these see Michèle Willems, 'Voltaire', Roger Paulin (ed.), *Great Shakespeareans*, vol. 3, *Voltaire, Goethe, Schlegel, Coleridge* (London: Continuum, 2010), 5–43.
5. For the French text of *De la littérature* see de Staël, *Oeuvres*, ed. Catriona Seth (Paris: Gallimard, 2017). References are to this edition. For a complete translation see *A Treatise on Ancient and Modern Literature*, 3 vols. (London: Cawthorn, 1803). For a selection in modern translation see de Staël, *Politics, Literature, and National Character*, ed. and trans. Morroe Berger (New York: Doubleday, 1964; abridged without indications of abridgement); and for a selection in unabridged translation, *Major Writings of Germaine de Staël*, trans. Vivian Folkenflik (New

York: Columbia University Press, 1987). For excerpts from the chapter on Shakespearean tragedy see Barry V. Daniels (ed.), *Revolution in the Theatre: French Romantic Theories of Drama* (Westport, CT: Greenwood, 1983).

6. *De la littérature* was first announced as *De l'influence des révolutions dans les lettres* (Seth, 1506). For de Staël's main discussion of Shakespeare in *De la littérature* see I.xiii, Seth, 138–48, and for comments on his flexibility of style as a (partial) model for new writing, II.v, Seth, 253.

7. For the French text of *De L'Allemagne* see Simone Balayé, ed., 2 vols. (Paris: Garnier-Flammarion, 1968; references are to this edition by volume and page number); for a complete translation, *Germany*, 3 vols. (London: Murray, 1813). For a selection in modern translation see de Staël, *Politics, Literature, and National Character*, ed. Berger (abridged), and (unabridged) *Major Writings*, trans. Folkenflik, and Daniels (ed.), *Revolution in the Theatre*. For a lively biography see J. Christopher Herold, *Mistress to an Age: a Life of Madame de Staël* (London: Hamish Hamilton, 1959).

8. Schlegel's Vienna lectures appeared in 1814 in a French translation by de Staël's cousin and first biographer, Albertine Necker de Saussure.

9. *De l'Allemagne*, 2.20; contrast *De la littérature*, ed. Seth, 144.

10. For discussion of Shakespeare in *De l'Allemagne* see especially 2.xv, 'De l'art dramatique'.

11. *Mercure de France*, April 1801; reprinted in Chateaubriand, *Oeuvres complètes*, 27 vols. (Brussels, 1826–31), vol. 21, *Mélanges littéraires*.

12. See the textual apparatus of the modern scholarly edition, *Essai sur la littérature anglaise et considerations sur le génie des hommes, des temps et des révolutions*, ed. Sébastien Baudoin (Paris: Société des textes français modernes, 2012), especially 260–77 (quotation from 249). The *Essai* was translated as *Sketches of English Literature: with Considerations on the Spirit of the Times, Men, and Revolutions*, 2 vols. (London: Henry Colburn, 1836).

13. References are to the republication of the introduction and prefaces in *Shakespeare and his Times* (London: Bentley, 1852; here 143), published concurrently with the French edition, *Shakespeare et son Temps: étude littéraire* (Paris: Didier, 1852). Both contain the duc de Broglie's 'Shakespeare en France' (1830), written in response to performances of *Othello* translated by Alfred de Vigny at the Comédie-Française (1829). For selections from Guizot's introduction see Jonathan Bate (ed.), *Shakespeare and the Romantics* (London: Penguin, 1992), 203–17.

14. On contemporary police censorship of sex in Shakespeare, see *Shakespeare and his Times*, 311 (de Broglie on Bianca's 'indecent equivoques and disgusting obscenities', necessarily cut from Vigny's *Othello*).

15. On *Hamlet* and *Macbeth* see *Shakespeare and his Times*, 172, and cf. the preface to *Hamlet*, 211; on *Julius Caesar* see 174. While Guizot concedes

that the Porter's jokes should be accommodated 'to the taste... of our age', in the translation he omits only the joke about erections: *Oeuvres complètes de Shakespeare*, 13 vols., (Paris: Ladvocat, 1821), 3.257–8.

16. From an autobiographical fragment written *c*.1820. Stendhal, *Oeuvres complètes*, ed. Victor Del Litto and Ernest Abravanel, 50 vols. (Levallois-Perret: Cercle du bibliophile, 1967–74); *Vie de Henry Brulard*, vols. 20–1, 21.444. References to Stendhal are to this edition by volume and page number.

17. 21.83. For other major expressions of love and admiration see Stendhal's *Journal littéraire*, *Oeuvres complètes*, 33.245, 248, 296 and 34.321–4.

18. *Racine et Shakespeare*, *Oeuvres complètes*, vol. 37. English translation, *Racine and Shakespeare*, trans. Guy Daniels (New York: Cromwell-Collier, 1962). Whether *On Molière, Regnard, and other matters* should be treated as part of *Racine et Shakespeare* is uncertain. It is given as an appendix by Del Litto and Abravanel but incorporated by Daniels and in Michael Crouzet (ed.), *Racine et Shakespeare (1818–1825): et autres textes de théorie romantique* (Paris: Champion, 2006). It is discussed here as integral to Stendhal's view of Shakespeare, with references to the text in *Oeuvres complètes*. For Stendhal's account of the debacle that prompted *Racine et Shakespeare*, see 37.140–1.

19. 37.99, 247–8; cf. 'declamation... is the eloquence of that indifference that pretends to be burning faith' (37.148).

20. *Du rire* (On laughter), VIII, 'De la moralité de Regnard', 37.239–41.

21. *Souvenirs du théâtre anglais à Paris* (Paris: Gaugin, 1827) memorialized the visit with accounts of the principal actors and famous scenes (in English and French) from *Romeo and Juliet*, *Hamlet* and *Othello*.

22. For the French text see Victor Hugo, *Oeuvres complètes: Critique*, ed. Jean-Pierre Reynaud (Paris: Laffont, 1985). For a modern translation see Daniels (ed.), *Revolution in the Theatre*, 151–91. References are to this translation.

23. *Oeuvres complètes: Critique*, 11.

24. See *De l'Allemagne*, 2.27 (which compares and contrasts the acting styles of French, German, and English actors).

25. *Shakespeare*, 1864; *Oeuvres complètes: Critique*, 419 ('Art, like religion, has its "Ecce homo"' [Behold the man; John 19:5]).

26. In using Shakespeare's subtitle as his title Vigny emphasized his assumption that 'Moor' means Arab: Vigny, *Oeuvres complètes*, 2 vols. (Paris: Gallimard, 1986); vol. 1, ed. François Germain and André Jarry, *Poesie. Théâtre*, 593.

27. Vigny worked from the Folio text but may have been influenced by changes made in English productions of the period: see Jarry, *Oeuvres complètes*, 1.1347–68. It is difficult to separate what was acted on the first

night, what was suppressed thereafter, and what Vigny restored from Shakespeare in the published version (1839): see, for example, on Act 4, scenes 1–4 (omitted in 1829), *Oeuvres complètes*, 1.1405. The different versions led Vigny himself into some confusion, as is evident from contradictions about the handkerchief (*Oeuvres complètes*, 1.1417). For a selective account of Vigny's changes see Margaret Gilman, *Othello in French* (Paris: Champion, 1925), 99–109.

28. *Oeuvres complètes*, 1.547.
29. *Oeuvres complètes*, 1.396–414. For an English translation see Daniels, *Revolution in the Theatre*, 211–28. The historic importance of Vigny's translation is made clear by the duc de Broglie, 'Shakespeare en France' (1830): see above, note 13.
30. Hugo, *Théâtre*, ed. Raymond Pouilliart (Paris: Garnier, 1979), 311, 313.
31. See Baudelaire's objections to politicizing criticism generally and specifically to the Paris celebrations of the 300th anniversary of Shakespeare's birth, designed, he argues, in part to promote Hugo's book: 'Anniversaire de la naissance de Shakespeare' (letter to *Le Figaro*, 14 April 1864), *Oeuvres complètes*, ed. Claude Pichois, 2 vols. (Paris: Gallimard, 1975–6), 2.225–30.
32. II.v, 'The Minds and the Masses'; *Oeuvres complètes: Critique*, 389–97.
33. II.iv.2; *Oeuvres complètes: Critique*, 381.
34. II.i.4; *Oeuvres complètes: Critique*, 347.
35. *Oeuvres complètes de Shakespeare*, 15 vols. (Paris: Pagnerre, 1859–65). The volumes, widely available only in later versions which misrepresent Hugo's conception of the edition, can be consulted online: https://fr.wikisource.org/wiki/Livre:Shakespeare_-_%C5%92uvres_compl%C3%A8tes,_traduction_Hugo,_Pagnerre,_1865,_tome_1.djvu. For Victor Hugo's account of how the translation began as an occupation for exile see *Oeuvres complètes: Critique*, 247.
36. Hugo's is fundamentally the view found in contemporary editions such as *The New Oxford Shakespeare: The Complete Works*, ed. Gary Taylor et al. (Oxford: Oxford University Press, 2016). Hugo's innovation with the texts of *Hamlet* is not, however, worked through the edition as a whole. He does not present separate Quarto and Folio texts of the play most crucial to modern changes of editorial practice, *King Lear*.
37. *Memoirs of Hector Berlioz*, trans. David Cairns (London: Gollancz, 1969; corrected edition, Frogmore: Panther, 1970), ch. 18, which gives an account of the devastating effect on Berlioz of performances of *Hamlet* and *Romeo and Juliet*.

38. *Hector Berlioz: New Edition of the Complete Works*, ed. Hugh Macdonald et al. (Kassel: Bärenreiter, 1967–94); vol. 18, *Roméo et Juliette*, ed. D. Kern Holoman, 1990.

39. *Memoirs*, trans. Cairns, 105, excepting Garrick's ending from a general anathema on such changes as 'an inspired discovery, incomparable in its pathos'.

40. See *The Journal of Eugène Delacroix: a selection*, ed. Hubert Wellington, trans. Lucy Norton, 2nd edition (Oxford: Phaidon, 1980); entry for 28 November 1853. For the French text see Eugène Delacroix, *Journal*, ed. Michèle Hannoosh, 2 vols. (Paris: José Corti, 2009).

41. The fifteen paintings (some now lost) include two versions of *Hamlet sees the Ghost of his Father*, three of the *Death of Ophelia*, and six of *Hamlet and Horatio in the Graveyard*. Each of the single painted subjects is similar in composition to the corresponding lithograph, 5, 8, 9, and 11 above. For details see Lee Johnson, *The Paintings of Eugène Delacroix: a Critical Catalogue*, 7 vols. (Oxford: Clarendon, 1981–2000).

42. The identification of the assumed character as Hamlet, though disputed, is endorsed by the Musée Delacroix (which owns the painting), but contested by Johnson, vol. 1, §40.

43. For details see Loys Delteil, *Delacroix, the graphic work: a catalogue raisonné* (1908), trans. and rev. Susan Strauber (San Francisco: Wofsy Fine Arts, 1997), §103–18. The 1843 sequence can be viewed online: https://www.maitres-des-arts-graphiques.com/-EXB.Hamlet.html.

44. See, for example, Paul de Saint Victor writing of the 1864 publication in *La Presse*: 're-read *Hamlet* alongside the lithographs ... and the drama will take on new life, breathe from and be illuminated by their novelties' (Arlette Sérullaz and Yves Bonnefoy, *Delacroix and Hamlet*, Paris: Éditions de la Réunion des musées nationaux, 1993, 11).

45. David Gervais, 'Delacroix' *Hamlet*', *Cambridge Quarterly*, 13 (1984), 40–70 (52).

46. Jay M. Fisher, *Théodore Chassériau: Illustrations for Othello* (Baltimore: Baltimore Museum of Art, 1979).

47. See the comments of Baudelaire in 'The Salon of 1845', *Art in Paris, 1845–1862: Salons and other exhibitions reviewed by Charles Baudelaire*, trans. Jonathan Mayne (Oxford: Phaidon, 1965), 1–32 (14).

48. See Marc Sandoz, *Théodore Chassériau, 1819–1856: Catalogue raisonné des peintures et estamps* (Paris: Arts et métiers graphiques, 1974). For colour reproductions of the paintings see Stéphane Guégan, Vincent Pomarède, and Louis-Antoine Prat, *Théodore Chassériau (1819–1556): The Unknown Romantic* (New Haven: Yale University Press, 2002).

49. That these performances were heavily cut is evident from *Othello... conforme aux représentations données à Paris* (Paris: Vergne, 1827). Gilman (*Othello in French*, 91) estimates that less than half the full text was performed.

50. See Sandoz, *Chassériau*, §§122 and 124 on the influence of the singer Maria Malibron, a famous Desdemona, on Chassériau's later *Othello* paintings.

51. Golder, *Shakespeare for the Age of Reason*, 265.

52. Sandoz, *Chassériau*, §119 (1849), and cf. §120; Guégan et al., *Chassériau*, §196.

53. Sandoz, *Chassériau*, §§122–3 (1849) and §124 (1852).

54. 'Shakespeare et les français', *Nouvelles réflexions sur le théâtre* (Paris: Flammarion, 1959), 116.

CHAPTER 5

1. For a survey of the main editions discussed here see Andrew Murphy, *Shakespeare in Print: A History and Chronology of Shakespeare Publishing* (Cambridge: Cambridge University Press, 2003). On the editorial, scholarly, and critical issues up to the end of the eighteenth century see the introductions to the separate volumes of Brian Vickers (ed.), *Shakespeare: The Critical Heritage*, 6 volumes (London: Routledge, 1974–81).

2. For opposite views of Malone's originality, based on different theoretical perspectives, see (stressing breaks with the past) Margreta de Grazia, *Shakespeare Verbatim: the Reproduction of Authenticity and the 1790 Apparatus* (Oxford: Clarendon Press, 1991), and (stressing continuities) Marcus Walsh, 'Edmond Malone', in *Great Shakespeareans*, ed. Peter Holland and Adrian Poole, 18 vols. (London: Continuum, 2010–13), vol. 1, *Dryden, Pope, Johnson, Malone*, ed. Claude Rawson, 2010, 160–99. Walsh's view is congruent with that of Simon Jarvis, *Scholars and Gentlemen: Shakespearean Textual Criticism and Representations of Scholarly Labour, 1725–1765* (Oxford: Clarendon Press, 1995), and Peter Martin, *Edmond Malone: Shakespearean Scholar. A Literary Biography* (Cambridge: Cambridge University Press, 1995).

3. Rowe's 1709 edition was reprinted in facsimile (with Curll's 1710 Sonnets [see below] as 'Vol. VII'), with an introduction by Peter Holland (London: Pickering & Chatto, 1999).

4. *Preface* (to his edition of Shakespeare, 1765), *Johnson on Shakespeare*, ed. Arthur Sherbo, volumes 7 and 8 of the Yale edition of *The Works of Samuel Johnson* (New Haven: Yale University Press, 1968), 7.51–113 (96).

5. In the Romantic period Sonnets 1 to 126 were assumed to form a group addressed to a young man. For a challenge to this view, pointing out how relatively few of the poems use gender-specific terms of reference, see Paul Edmondson and Stanley Wells, *Shakespeare's Sonnets*, Oxford: Oxford University Press, 2004, especially 28–36.

6. See the comments of George Steevens on Sonnet 20: 'It is impossible to read this fulsome panegyric ... without an equal mixture of disgust and indignation'; and Malone's uneasy defence: 'such addresses to men, however indelicate, were customary in our author's time' (Malone, *Supplement* [to Johnson–Steevens, 1778], 1780, 1.596). Cf. the views of Coleridge in a marginal annotation about the Sonnets addressed to his son Hartley (*Marginalia*, ed. Whalley, I.41–3): in Shakespeare's plays there is 'not even an allusion to that very worst of all possible vices' (same-sex sexual love between men); and his *Table Talk*, 14 May 1833: 'these sonnets [1-126] could only have come from a man deeply in love with a woman'.

7. Pope's 'Preface' as printed in *The Plays and Poems of William Shakespeare*, edited by Edmond Malone [and James Boswell, Jr], 21 vols. (London: Rivington et al., 1821), 1.13. Referenced in the text as 'Boswell–Malone'.

8. On Pope as an editor of Shakespeare see Simon Jarvis, *Great Shakespeareans*, vol. 1, *Dryden, Pope, Johnson, Malone*, 66–114. For a defence of Pope's use of aesthetic criteria in editing see A. D. J. Brown, 'The little fellow has done wonders', *Cambridge Quarterly*, 21 (1992), 120–49.

9. Peter Seary, *Lewis Theobald and the Editing of Shakespeare* (Oxford: Clarendon Press, 1990), vii. Cf. R. B. McKerrow (a leading figure in early twentieth-century 'New Bibliography'), who saw Theobald as 'in many ways ... the true founder of modern Shakespearian scholarship', 'The Treatment of Shakespeare's Text by his earlier Editors, 1709–1768', *Proceedings of the British Academy*, XIX (1933), 89–122 (109).

10. *Double Falsehood, or The Distressed Lovers*, 'by William Shakespeare', ed. Brean Hammond (London: Arden, 2010).

11. Famous successes include *Henry V*, 2.3.17 (Mrs Quickly on the death of Falstaff), ''a babbled of green fields' (F, 'a Table of greene fields'), and *Macbeth*, 1.7.6, 'this bank and shoal of time' (F, 'Banke and Schoole'). Notable failures include *The Tempest*, 5.1.88–92, 'Where the bee sucks there lurk I' (F, 'there suck I'): as a spiritual being (Theobald argued), Ariel could not be supposed to take in food; 'On a bat's back I do fly, / After sunset merrily' (F, 'after summer'), emended on the grounds that bats do not migrate.

12. See Marcus Walsh, *Shakespeare, Milton, and Eighteenth-Century Literary Editing: the beginnings of interpretive scholarship* (Cambridge: Cambridge University Press, 1997), ch. 2.

13. *Miscellaneous Observations on the Tragedy of Macbeth*, 1745; *Johnson on Shakespeare*, 7.3–45 (45).

14. Examples of Warburton's emendations are discussed by Walsh, *Shakespeare, Milton, and Eighteenth-Century Literary Editing*, 153–4 and 160–3.

15. Thomas Edwards, *A Supplement to Mr Warburton's edition of Shakespeare. Being the Canons of Criticism* (London: Cooper, 1748), 12, 13, 53. Edwards's gifts as a comic ironist made the book a bestseller, with revised editions in 1750, 1753, 1758, and 1765.

16. Peter Seary, 'Styan Thirlby', *Oxford Dictionary of National Biography*, ed. H. G. C. Matthew and Brian Harrison (Oxford: Oxford University Press, 2004; annotation from Thirlby's copy of Warburton now in the Folger Shakespeare Library).

17. On Johnson as a critic and editor of Shakespeare see Freya Johnston, *Great Shakespeareans*, vol. 1, *Dryden, Pope, Johnson, Malone*, 115–59.

18. See Nick Groom's introduction (v–lxix) to the Johnson–Steevens edition of 1778, with Malone's two supplementary volumes (1780; reprinted, London: Routledge/Thoemmes, 1995). All eighteenth-century editions were collaborative in the sense that they included annotations derived from many contributors: see Arthur Sherbo, *The Birth of Shakespeare Studies: Commentators from Rowe (1709) to Boswell-Malone (1821)* (East Lansing: Colleagues Press, 1986).

19. See *Boswell's Life of Johnson*, ed. George Birkbeck Hill, rev. F. L. Powell, 6 vols. (Oxford: Clarendon Press, 1934–40), 4.5: 'If the man would have come to me ... I would have endeavoured to "endow his purposes with words"; for, as it is, "he doth gabble monstrously"'. Cf. a similar comment on Capell's prose by Malone: 'a style manifestly formed on that of the Clown in the comedy under our consideration' (*Measure for Measure*), Boswell–Malone, 2.386.

20. Joseph Ritson, *Cursory Criticisms on the edition of Shakespeare published by Edmond Malone* (London: Hookham, 1792), 35.

21. Note to Horatio's 'Good night, sweet prince', 5.2.359; 1778, 10.412–13 (revised from 1773); cf. his note on the end of 3.4 that after this point 'the character of Hamlet has lost all its consequence' (1778, 10.332). The note to 5.2.359 (a short essay) is reprinted in Steevens's edition of 1793 (15.354–5), with a reference to contradictions by Ritson (see note 22 below) and by Malone in his edition of 1790.

22. 'Shakespearean Scraps', in Charles Marowitz, *The Roar of the Canon: Kott and Marowitz on Shakespeare* (New York: Applause, 2001), 157.

23. See Ritson's *Remarks, Critical and Illustrative, on the Text and Notes of the last Edition of Shakespeare* (that is, Johnson–Steevens, 1778; London: Johnson, 1783), 215–24.

24. Jonson and Beaumont and Fletcher were not included because their plays were already available in collected editions (Beaumont and Fletcher, ed. Theobald et al., 1750; Jonson, ed. Whalley, 1756).

25. Vickers, *Critical Heritage*, 5.33.

26. On the implications of Capell's construction of the printed page see Marcus Walsh, 'Form and Function in the English Eighteenth-Century Literary Edition: the Case of Edward Capell', *Studies in Bibliography*, 54 (2001), 225–41. Walsh discusses how the various elements of Capell's edition work together in *Shakespeare, Milton, and Eighteenth-Century Literary Editing*, 175–97.

27. Each volume is in two parts, hence references I.i, I.ii, II.i, II.ii.

28. For the claim that Steevens is the author of these pieces see Vickers, *Critical Heritage*, 5.51.

29. Alice Walker, 'Edward Capell and his edition of *Shakespeare*', *Proceedings of the British Academy*, 46 (1960), 131–45.

30. Malone reaffirms a biographical view in a new annotation of the sonnet in his edition of 1790 (10.268–9).

31. See Peter Alexander, *Shakespeare's Henry VI and Richard III* (Cambridge: Cambridge University Press, 1929), who argues (against Malone and co-authorship) that the 1594/5 texts are memorial reconstructions of plays written by Shakespeare. Malone's views were re-examined by John Dover Wilson (*2 Henry VI*, Cambridge, 1952), and the issues are still under discussion in the Arden3 edition of *3 Henry VI* (ed. John D. Cox and Eric Rasmussen, 2001).

32. See Brian Vickers, *Shakespeare, Co-Author: a Historical Study of Five Collaborative Plays* (Oxford: Oxford University Press, 2002). The latest Oxford *Complete Works* (ed. Gary Taylor et al., 2016) includes sixteen collaborative plays (including plays of which Shakespeare has usually been supposed sole author).

33. 1790, 1.ii, 1–331. For the sources and content of the life and the History of the Stage as these appeared in Malone's 1790 edition see Samuel Schoenbaum, *Shakespeare's Lives* (Oxford: Clarendon Press, 1970), 177–84, and Walsh, 'Malone', *Great Shakespeareans*, 183–93.

34. The original manuscript is lost. Malone's transcript is therefore the main source of its reconstruction by Joseph Quincy Adams, *Dramatic Records of Sir Henry Herbert* (New Haven: Yale University Press, 1917).

35. For a modern edition see *Henslowe's Diary*, ed. R. A. Foakes (Cambridge: Cambridge University Press, 1961, 2nd edition, 2002). See also

the Henslowe-Alleyn Digitisation Project: https://www.henslowe-alleyn.org.uk

36. *A Letter to the Rev. Richard Farmer, D.D.* (London, 1792), 8–11, in response to Ritson's *Cursory Criticisms*, 1792.

37. For Malone's continuing 'correction' by eighteenth-century standards of syntax see Jarvis, *Scholars and Gentlemen*, 185–7. For Steevens's discussion of 'the muddy reservoir of the first folio', witty defence of latitude in emendation, attack on 'blind fidelity to the earliest printed copies', defence of F2, and demonstration that Malone incorporated many F2 corrections into his own text, see Steevens, 1793, I.xii–xxvii.

38. The pamphlet was reprinted in the 1821 edition with *The Tempest* (15.385–419).

39. The revised chronology has some improbable elements of 1790 now made more probable (*Hamlet*, formerly 1596, now 1600; *Othello*, formerly 1611, now 1604). Still misplaced are *Henry VIII* (1603: like Johnson and Steevens, Malone thought it written before the death of Elizabeth I), *Twelfth Night*, and *Julius Caesar* (both 1607).

40. Letter of January 1804: *Letters of William and Dorothy Wordsworth*, ed. Ernest de Selincourt, revised C. L. Shaver et al., 7 vols. (Oxford: Clarendon Press, 1967–93), vol. 1, *The Early Years*, 422.

41. Tyrwhitt's *Observations and Conjectures upon some Passages of Shakespeare* (Oxford: Clarendon, 1766) was prompted by reservations about the editorial procedures of Johnson. Tyrwhitt's methods as an editor of Chaucer resembled those of Capell with Shakespeare: he prepared his text not from a received version but afresh, from all the manuscripts available to him; as with Malone, the edition's accompanying essay on Chaucer's language and versification is concerned with editing in light of historical usage. On Tyrwhitt and Shakespeare see Sherbo, *Shakespeare's Midwives*, ch. 1.

42. Farmer's pamphlet was also printed complete in the 1793 edition of Steevens and its revision (Reed, 1803). It was expanded by Farmer in a 2nd edition (also 1767) and a 3rd edition of 1789. A 4th edition appeared posthumously in 1821. For extracts see Vickers, *Critical Heritage*, 5.259–79. For eighteenth-century discussions of Farmer see T. W. Baldwin, *William Shakespeare's 'small Latine & lesse Greeke'*, 2 vols. (Urbana: University of Illinois Press, 1944), 1.64–72 (including Malone's doubts about Farmer's conclusions: Boswell–Malone, 2.102–6).

43. See Martin, *Edmond Malone*, 136–8.

44. *The Essence of Malone* (London: Becket, 1800), 13 and 24. Hardinge followed it up with *Another Essence of Malone* in 1801.

45. Of the major Romantic critics of Shakespeare, only Coleridge mentions Malone more than in passing. He refers to Malone's chronology, but was sceptical of the results produced by reliance on external evidence (see *Lecture on Literature, 1808–1819*, ed. Foakes, 2.370–6). In his 1811–12 lectures he also used Malone's Account of the English Stage, but his focus is more in the mode of A. W. Schlegel–setting Shakespeare in the context not of earlier English drama but of European drama from the Greeks to the moderns.

CHAPTER 6

1. Quoted from Gāmini Salgādo, *Eyewitnesses of Shakespeare: First Hand Accounts of Performances 1590–1890* (London: Chatto, 1975), 324; from Theodore Martin, 'An Eyewitness of John Kemble', *The Nineteenth Century*, 7 (February 1880), 276–96 (287), which reports Tieck's accounts of Kemble in several other Shakespearean roles.

2. Heine, *Über die französische Bühne*, 'Sechster Brief', *Sämtliche Werke*, 12.1, 262. Franz Horn was a German academic commentator of the period.

3. *Über die französische Bühne*, 'Siebzehnter Brief', *Sämtliche Werke*, 12.1, 486–8; translated in Prawer, *Heine's Shakespeare*, 35–7. Heine's account has been little noticed. It does not appear in Giles Playfair, *The Flash of Lightning: a Portrait of Edmund Kean* (London: Kimber, 1983), or in the account of Kean by Peter Thomson in Peter Holland (ed.), *Great Shakespeareans*, vol. 2, *Garrick, Kemble, Siddons, Kean* (London: Continuum, 2010), 138–81.

4. For a classic account of Shakespeare production in the period see George C. D. Odell, *Shakespeare–from Betterton to Irving* (1920), 2 vols. (London: Constable, 1963), vol. 2, book 4, 'The Age of Kemble'.

5. For the view that Dorothy Jordan was as significant as Siddons in the presentation of Shakespeare in the theatre of the period see Fiona Ritchie, *Women and Shakespeare in the Eighteenth Century* (Cambridge: Cambridge University Press, 2014), which also discusses the influence of women as critics, editors, and playgoers.

6. For an account of theatrical presentation in London in the period, including staging, see Charles Beecher Hogan, *The London Stage: 1660–1800*, Part 5 (Carbondale: Southern Illinois University Press, 1968), xix–ccxviii.

7. Charles H. Shattuck (ed.), *John Philip Kemble Promptbooks*, The Folger Facsimiles, 11 vols. (Charlottesville: University Press of Virginia, 1974).

8. For the following generation the texts used in performance can most readily be seen in Elizabeth Inchbald's *The British Theatre; or,*

A collection of plays which are acted at the Theatres Royal, Drury Lane, Covent Garden, and Haymarket, . . . from the prompt books, 10 vols. (London: Longman, 1808). Volumes 1–5 are adaptations of Shakespeare (twenty-four plays).

9. The published text defends the work of the arranger-directors partly by invoking Restoration and later adaptations: John Barton and Peter Hall, *The Wars of the Roses* (London: British Broadcasting Corporation, 1970).

10. Kemble published seven acting versions between 1796 and 1814. For a modern publication of the third see *Hamlet: J. P. Kemble 1800*, intro. T. J. B. Spencer (London: Cornmarket, 1971). Details of Kemble's cuts are given in Shattuck (ed.), *Promptbooks*, vol. 2.

11. The music for the play attributed to Purcell in the eighteenth century, and published in the early twentieth-century collected edition of Purcell (Novello, 1912, vol. 19), is considered by modern scholars as of doubtful authenticity.

12. For a facsimile of 1789 see *The Tempest, or The Enchanted Island* (London: British Library, 2011). Shattuck (ed.), *Promptbooks*, vol. 8, contains Kemble's 1807 text.

13. The score for this, and other music written for Restoration productions but in use throughout the theatrical life of the adaptation, can be found in Matthew Locke, *Dramatic Music*, ed. Michael Tilmouth, Musica Britannica 51 (London: Stainer & Bell, 1986).

14. *Music for Macbeth*, ed. Amanda Eubanke Winkler (Maddison, WI: A-R Editions, 2004). This music, formerly attributed to Matthew Locke, actually by John Eccles and Richard Leveridge, was performed into the nineteenth century.

15. For detail of the production with which Kemble opened the new Drury Lane theatre see Joseph W. Donohue, 'Kemble's production of *Macbeth* (1794)', *Theatre Notebook*, 21 (1967), 63–74.

16. The scenic splendour and antiquarian authenticity for which Kemble aimed is difficult to reconstruct fully because little remains of set designs. A range of visual material from which to imagine the theatres and stages of the period is collected in Ian Mackintosh and Geoffrey Ashton, *The Georgian Playhouse: Actors, Artists, Audiences and Architecture 1730–1830* (London: Arts Council, 1975).

17. See Shattuck (ed.), *Promptbooks*, vol. 5; *Macbeth* (1803 version), 19, 24, and 46.

18. Shattuck (ed.), *Promptbooks*, vol. 5; *Macbeth*, 63–4.

19. From a review of John Boaden's *Life of John Philip Kemble* (1825), *The Quarterly Review*, 34 (1826), 196–248 (218–19), excerpted in Stanley Wells (ed.), *Shakespeare in the Theatre: an Anthology of Criticism* (Oxford:

Oxford University Press, 1997), 33–7. For Hazlitt's similar praise of Kemble as 'the best Macbeth (upon the whole) that we have seen' see Howe, 18.341–2. For accounts of Kemble and Siddons see Dennis Bartholomeusz, *Macbeth and the Players* (Cambridge: Cambridge University Press, 1969), 98–141; and Joseph W. Donohue, *Dramatic Character in the English Romantic Age* (Princeton: Princeton University Press, 1970), 253–69.

20. For an account of Kemble's similarly spectacular 1795 production of *King Lear* see David Rostron, in Kenneth Richards and Peter Thomson (ed.), *Essays on the Eighteenth-Century English Stage* (London: Methuen, 1972), 149–70. This was a modified form of Nahum Tate's version, with no Fool and a happy ending in which Lear survives and Cordelia marries Edgar. For the 1808 acting text see Shattuck, *Promptbooks*, vol. 5.

21. Shattuck (ed.), *Promptbooks*, vol. 4: in the 1811 text the scene is printed but struck out; in the 1812 text it is not printed. Kemble evolved his 'improved' Antony as he worked on the production.

22. For an account of Kemble's version and its staging see John Ripley, *'Julius Caesar' on Stage in England and America, 1599–1973* (Cambridge: Cambridge University Press, 1980), 50–73.

23. On the play's problematic social and political resonances in the period see Inchbald's introduction to Kemble's text, *The British Theatre*, vol. 5.

24. Shattuck (ed.), *Promptbooks*, vol. 2; version of 1806. For a reprint of the 1812 text see *Coriolanus, or The Roman Matron* (n.p.: Sagwan, 2018).

25. Letter of 19 June 1817: Peter Holland (ed.), *Coriolanus* (London: Bloomsbury, 2018), 414. For similar audience response to a piece of physical theatre by Sarah Siddons as Volumnia, see Wells (ed.), *Shakespeare in the Theatre*, 37–8.

26. For a contemporary account of the Old Price riots see *Selected Writings of Leigh Hunt*, ed. Greg Kucich and Jeffrey N. Cox, 6 vols. (London: Pickering & Chatto, 2003), 1.107–11. For the riots in their political context see Marc Baer, *Theatre and Disorder in Late Georgian London* (Oxford: Clarendon Press, 1991), 18–36; Jane Moody, *Illegitimate Theatre in London, 1770–1840* (Cambridge: Cambridge University Press, 2000), 62–9; and (with discussion of the cartoons) Jonathan Bate, *Shakespearean Constitutions: Politics, Theatre, Criticism 1730–1830* (Oxford: Clarendon Press, 1989), 42–5.

27. For Kemble and Reynolds see Reiko Oya, *Representing Shakespearean Tragedy: Garrick, the Kembles, and Kean* (Cambridge: Cambridge University Press, 2011). For the contrast of Kemble and Kean see Peter Thomson, *On Actors and Acting* (Exeter: Exeter University Press, 2000), 113–26.

28. *Leigh Hunt's Dramatic Criticism, 1808–1831*, ed. Lawrence Huston Houtchens and Carolyn Washburn Houtchens (London: Oxford University Press, 1950), 68; Hazlitt, Howe, 18.226. For Hunt's fundamental assessment and critique of Kemble see 'The Tragic Actors', Houtchens, *Dramatic Criticism*, 103–4.

29. *Macbeth Reconsidered* (1786), written in response to Thomas Whately's *Remarks on Some of the Characters in Shakespeare* (1785); extended in a second edition, 1817.

30. For full details of these paintings see Kenneth Garlick, *Sir Thomas Lawrence: a Complete Catalogue of the Oil Paintings* (London: Phaidon, 1989), §451b, *Coriolanus at the hearth of Tullus Aufidius* (1798), and §451d, *Hamlet with the skull of Yorick* (1801). Both works were widely distributed as engravings.

31. 'Mr Kemble's Retirement', Howe, 5.376–9.

32. Herschel Baker, *John Philip Kemble: the Actor in his Theatre* (Cambridge, MA: Harvard University Press, 1942), 159.

33. Salgãdo, *Eyewitnesses*, 324.

34. *Dramatic Criticism*, ed. Houtchens, 25.

35. Henry Crabb Robinson, *Diary, Reminiscences and Correspondence*, ed. Thomas Sadler, 3 vols. (London: Macmillan, 1869), 2.387.

36. For contemporary material about Siddons see Gail Marshall et al. (ed.), *Lives of Shakespearian Actors II: Edmund Kean, Sarah Siddons and Harriet Smithson by their contemporaries* (London: Pickering, 2009), vol. 2, *Sarah Siddons*, ed. Lisa A. Freeman.

37. See Philip Highfield et al., *A Biographical Dictionary of Actors, Actresses, Musicians, Dancers,... in London 1660–1800*, 16 vols. (Carbondale: Southern Illinois University Press, 1973–93), 14.1–67. On her visual representation see Robyn Asleson (ed.), *A Passion for Performance: Sarah Siddons and her Portraitists* (Los Angeles: Getty Museum, 1999; revised, 2006).

38. For the complexities of the actress persona, and the degree of self-fashioning possible for actresses in the period, see Robyn Asleson (ed.), *Notorious Muse: the Actress in British Art and Culture, 1776–1812* (New Haven: Yale University Press, 2003).

39. On the importance of Siddons's public persona to the position of women in British public life, and the gendered language used by contemporaries in discussing her acting, see Pat Rogers, '"Towering beyond her Sex": Stature and Sublimity in the Achievement of Sarah Siddons', in *Curtain Calls: British and American Women and the Theatre, 1660–1820*, ed. Mary Ann Schonfield and Cecilia Macheski (Athens, OH: Ohio University Press, 1991), 48–67.

40. Shattuck, *Promptbooks*, vol. 5; text of 1804. For anti-French additions, promptbook, 52.
41. Thomas Campbell, *The Life of Mrs Siddons*, 2 vols. (London: Effingham Wilson, 1834), 1.215–16.
42. James Boaden, *Memoirs of Mrs Siddons interspersed with anecdotes of authors and actors*, 2 vols. (London: Colburn, 1827), 2.61. A contemporary engraving in the British Museum Department of Prints and Drawings (1931,0509.191.+) records the gesture.
43. For a contemporary account of Siddons's performance in both scenes (probably by the friend and associate of Scott, James Ballantyne) see Campbell, *Life*, 2.140–52.
44. The notes of G. J. Bell, published in 'Mrs Siddons as Lady Macbeth', H. C. Fleeming Jenkin, *Papers Literary, Scientific, &c*, ed. Sidney Colvin and J. A. Ewing, 2 vols. (London: Longmans, 1887), 1.45–66, are reported in John Wilders (ed.), *Macbeth*, Shakespeare in Production (Cambridge: Cambridge University Press, 2004). Of paintings the two most famous are those of Siddons reading Macbeth's letter (*c.*1803, artist unknown) and the sleepwalking scene (1814, by George Henry Harlow, Figure 6.4).
45. *Dramatic Criticism*, ed. Houtchens, 72.
46. 'Mrs Siddons', *Visits and Sketches at Home and Abroad*, 1834; in *Shakespeare's Heroines*, 393–408 (395).
47. 'Sonnets on Eminent Characters' (1794–5), *Coleridge. Complete Poems*, ed. William Keach (Penguin: London, 1997), 73.
48. 'To Mrs Siddons', *Selected Poems of Joanna Baillie, 1762–1852*, ed. Jennifer Breen (Manchester: Manchester University Press, 1999), 110–12.
49. Thomas Medwin, *Conversations of Lord Byron*, ed. Ernest J. Lovell, Jr (Princeton: Princeton University Press, 1966), 138.
50. Ed. Mary Margaret Robb and Lester Thonssen (Carbondale: Southern Illinois University Press, 1966). The figures showing Siddons (116–22), collected at the end of the book (plate 11), are reproduced in Asleson (ed.), *A Passion for Performance*, ix.
51. Jameson, *Shakespeare's Heroines*, 403; Campbell, *Life*, 2.209–11.
52. 'Lapis Lazuli'; *Collected Poems of W. B. Yeats* (London: Macmillan, 1950), 338.
53. *Selected Writings*, ed. Kucich and Cox, 1.116.
54. For the theatrical culture in which Kean developed see Moody, *Illegitimate Theatre*. For Shakespeare travesties in this context see Richard W. Schoch, *Not Shakespeare: bardolatry and burlesque in the nineteenth century* (Cambridge: Cambridge University Press, 2002); and for their

'texts', Stanley Wells (ed.), *Nineteenth-Century Shakespeare Burlesques*, 5 vols. (London: Diploma, 1977–8).

55. *Table Talk*, ed. Woodring, 1.40; *Letters*, ed. Griggs, 5.269.

56. 16 March 1825; cf. 17 January 1820: 'said he had frequently three women to "stroke" during performances, and that two waited while the other was served'. *Drury Lane Journal: Selections from James Winston's Diaries, 1819–1827*, ed. Alfred L. Nelson and Gilbert B. Cross (London: Society for Theatre Research, 1974), 107 and 4.

57. *Richard II* Kean performed in an adaptation by Richard Wroughton (London: Miller, 1815), which incorporated material from six other Shakespeare plays to transform the king into a more heroically tragic figure (facsimile, London: Cornmarket, 1970). *Timon* he performed in a cut but not otherwise adapted version by George Lamb (London: Chapple, 1816; facsimile, London: Cornmarket, 1972).

58. On Kean playing Shakespeare's *King Lear* see John Genest, *Some Account of the English Stage from the Restoration in 1660 to 1830*, 10 vols. (Bath: Rodd, 1832), 8.186 (four performances, 1823–4). Genest reports that at the first performance the diminutive Kean's difficulty in carrying the body of Cordelia meant the play closed with unintended comedy. At the same time other actors began reviving Shakespeare's texts of plays usually performed in adaptations: Macready, for example, performed Shakespeare's *Richard III* (not Cibber's adaptation) at Covent Garden in 1820–1: Genest, *English Stage*, 8.107–8.

59. Heine, *Über die französische Bühne*, 'Sechster Brief', *Sämtliche Werke*, 12.1, 262.

60. On *Romeo and Juliet* see Howe, 5.208–11; on *Hamlet* Howe, 5.185–9; on *King Lear*, which prompted Hazlitt's most extensive single review of Kean, Howe, 18.331–8.

61. In Hazlitt's early reviews of Kean he found his ability to become the character he played retarded by the actor's profusion and virtuosity of detail: see Howe, 5.184.

62. On this, and other aspects of his performance, see G. H. Lewes, 'Edmund Kean', in *On Actors and the Art of Acting* (London: Smith, Elder), 1875, 1–11 (11).

63. Heine, *Über die französische Bühne*, 'Siebzehnter Brief', *Sämtliche Werke*, 12.1, 486–8 (487); translated in Prawer, *Heine's Shakespeare*, 35–7.

64. For Hazlitt's discussions of Kean's Shylock see Howe, 5.179–80 (two consecutive reviews) and 4.323–34.

65. This became a famous 'point': see Leigh Hunt's account of a later performance: *Dramatic Criticism*, ed. Houtchens, 112–15 (114).

66. London Green, 'Edmund Kean's Richard III', *The Theatre Journal*, 36.4 (1984), 505–24, reconstructs details of Kean's performance from contemporary reports and later reminiscences. A facsimile of *Oxberry's 1822 edition of King Richard III*, ed. Alan S. Downer (London: Society for Theatre Research, 1959), not used by Green, contains notes on Kean's delivery and movements by the American actor James Hackett.

67. Kean's first Lady Macbeth was Sarah Bartley, whom Hunt called 'a washed-down imitation of Mrs. Siddons': Houtchens, *Dramatic Criticism*, 92.

68. For an account of Kean's Macbeth see Bartholomeusz, *Macbeth and the Players*, 144–51. Marvin Rosenberg, *The Masks of Macbeth* (Berkeley: University of California Press, 1978), records details of performances by Kemble, Siddons, and Kean.

69. Howe, 5.211–21; 18.200–4.

70. Howe, 18.263. For his earlier discussions see Howe, 5.189 (1814) and Howe, 5.338–9 (1816).

71. Houtchens, *Dramatic Criticism*, 201–2. Hunt repeated this judgement variously: Houtchens, *Dramatic Criticism*, 220; *Selected Writings*, ed. Kucich and Cox, 3.105.

72. *The Champion*, 21 December 1817. The review (slightly abridged) is in Wells (ed.), *Shakespeare in the Theatre*, 50–2. For the full text see Keats, *Poetical Writings*, ed. Buxton Forman, 5.227–32.

73. Gail Marshall et al. (ed.), *Lives of Shakespearian Actors II* (London: Pickering, 2009), vol.1, *Edmund Kean*, ed. Jim Davis, 96.

74. Toby Cole and Helen Krich Chinoy (eds.), *Actors on Acting* (New York: Crown, 1954), 299, 298. (In the second quotation 'the art' refers to the art of rhetoric and its conventions of expressive gesture.) Hazlitt makes the same point about Kean's ability to release himself into the passions of the moment as based in study and preparation: Howe, 5.202.

75. *On Actors*, 3.

Further Reading

Chapter 1. Introduction: Making it New

Bibliographical details of primary texts and relevant critical works are given in the notes and are not duplicated here.

English Shakespeare criticism leading up to the Romantic period is well represented by the volumes in the Critical Heritage series edited by Brian Vickers (6 vols., London: Routledge, 1974–81), and the comparable period in German criticism by the volumes edited by Hansjügen Blinn (2 vols., Berlin: Erich Schmidt Verlag, 1982, 1988). For the comparable period in France, see Chapter 4, notes. Writing on Shakespeare in the Romantic period (including some German and French work) can be sampled in Jonathan Bate (ed.), *The Romantics on Shakespeare* (London: Penguin, 1992). The series *Great Shakespeareans*, ed. Adrian Poole and Peter Holland (18 vols., London: Continuum [later Bloomsbury], 2010–13), contains several volumes relevant to the period including discussions of critics (English, German, and French), editors, translators, directors, performers, and composers. The introduction of Shakespeare into European cultures beyond Germany and France can be sampled in Oswald LeWinter, *Shakespeare in Europe* (1963; Harmondsworth: Penguin, 1970), which includes writing from Italy, Russia, Scandinavia, and Spain. Zdeněk Stříbrný, *Shakespeare and Eastern Europe* (Oxford: Oxford University Press, 2000) extends the account into Eastern and Central Europe (predominantly in later periods).

Many of the historic publications referred to in the notes are now available online through the Internet Archive, Project Gutenberg, and similar resources. These include Romantic-period critical books and pamphlets, major translations such as François Guizot's revision of Pierre Le Tourneur (1821), and the translation of François-Victor Hugo (1859–65; until recently the standard French version); also performance texts of individual plays (English and French versions), series of illustrations, and illustrated editions. For the most significant of these, original publication details are provided in the notes. Many English performance texts from the period have also been reprinted, particularly by Cornmarket Press in the 1970s, and by more scholarly publishers recently. Of these the most important are the John Philip Kemble prompt books, ed. Charles Shattuck (Folger Shakespeare Facsimiles), details of which are given in the notes to Chapter 6.

Among the regularly cited books on the national and international transformation of Shakespeare are (leading up to the Romantic period) Michael

Dobson, *The Making of the National Poet: Shakespeare, Adaptation, and Author-ship, 1660-1769* (Oxford: Oxford University Press, 1992), and (going into the Romantic period and beyond) Gary Taylor, *Reinventing Shakespeare: A Cultural History from the Restoration to the Present* (New York: Weidenfeld, 1989). Shorter but distilled, on the same subject of Shakespeare as a national and international figure, are Harry Levin, 'The Primacy of Shakespeare', in *Shakespeare and the Revolution of the Times: Perspectives and Commentaries* (New York: Oxford University Press, 1976), and Jonathan Arac, 'The Impact of Shakespeare', in *The Cambridge History of Literary Criticism: Volume 5: Romanticism*, ed. Marshall Brown (Cambridge: Cambridge University Press, 2000). For a critique of contemporary Shakespeare studies based in Romantic critical practices see Edward Pechter, *Shakespeare Studies Today: Romanticism Lost* (Basingstoke: Palgrave Macmillan, 2011).

On contexts of European history from the French Revolution into the Romantic period and beyond, authoritative are, for cultural history with a European perspective (poetry, music, visual art), Tim (T. C. W.) Blanning, *The Romantic Revolution* (London: Weidenfeld, 2010), and, for material, social, and political history, the first sections of Tim Blanning (ed.), *The Oxford History of Modern Europe* (Oxford: Oxford University Press, 2000). For the social and political contexts in England see Boyd Hilton, *'A Mad, Bad, and Dangerous People?': England 1783-1846*, The New Oxford History of England (Oxford: Oxford University Press, 2006).

Chapter 2. England: Genius with Judgement

On Coleridge, the introductions and annotation of the Bollingen *Collected Works*, published by Routledge and Princeton under the general editorship of Kathleen Coburn, provide the most authoritative and detailed information; particularly *The Friend*, ed. Barbara E. Rooke (2 vols., 1969), which contains the important essay on Method (Volume III, Essay IV), the *Biographia Literaria*, ed. James Engell and W. Jackson Bate (2 vols., 1983), and the *Lectures 1808-1819: On Literature*, ed. R. A. Foakes (2 vols., 1987). The standard text of Coleridge's Shakespeare criticism is that edited by T. M. Raysor (1930; 2nd edition, 2 vols., London: Dent, 1960). The standard book on Coleridge's Shakespeare criticism, M. M. Badawi, *Coleridge: Critic of Shakespeare* (Cambridge: Cambridge University Press, 1973), is superseded by the Bollingen edition materials. Coleridge is among the figures included in Jonathan Bate's widely praised *Shakespeare and the English Romantic Imagination* (Oxford: Clarendon, 1986): this discusses the presence of Shakespeare in the poetry, criticism, letters, and drama of each of the major

Romantic poets, though at times with a strained sense of what might constitute echo or allusion.

For Hazlitt the standard text is The Centenary Edition, 21 vols., ed. P. P. Howe (London: Dent, 1930–4), the annotation of which has not been superseded by later editions. *The Characters of Shakespeare's Plays* appears in vol. 1 of *Selected Writings of William Hazlitt*, ed. Duncan Wu et al., intro. Tom Paulin, (9 vols., London: Pickering & Chatto, 1998). For Hazlitt's *A View of the English Stage* and uncollected theatrical journalism The Centenary Edition remains essential. Excellent annotated selections of Hazlitt are published by Oxford World's Classics (ed. Jon Cook, 1991) and (containing more literary and theatrical material) by Penguin (ed. Tom Paulin and David Chandler, 2000). William Archer and Robert William Lowe (eds.), *Hazlitt on Theatre* (1895) (reprinted Whitefish, MT: Literary Licensing, 2012) contains a selection of his most important writings on acting and actors.

The Letters of John *Keats, 1814–1821*, ed. Hyder Edward Rollins (Cambridge: Cambridge University Press, 1958) is the standard reference edition. Excellent selections from Keats's Letters include those ed. Robert Gittings (with introduction and notes by Jon Mee, Oxford: Oxford University Press, 2002) and ed. Grant F. Scott (Cambridge, MA.: Harvard University Press, 2002). Keats's annotations of Shakespeare are collected in vol. 5 of *Poetical Works and other Writings of John Keats*, ed. H. Buxton Forman, rev. Maurice Buxton Forman (8 vols., New York: Scribner's, 1939).

The standard edition of *The Works of Charles and Mary Lamb* is that edited by E. V. Lucas (7 vols., London: Methuen, 1903–5). Their *Tales from Shakespeare* has been edited for Penguin Classics by Marina Warner (London, 2007). For Lamb's essay on Shakespeare's tragedies as not suited to stage performance a well-annotated source is the *Selected Prose*, ed. Adam Phillips (London: Penguin, 1985). Thomas De Quincey's brief but brilliant 'On the knocking at the gate in *Macbeth*' can be found in *Thomas De Quincey*, ed. Robert Morrison, 21st-Century Oxford Authors (Oxford: Oxford University Press, 2019). A modern collected De Quincey, ed. Barry Symonds and Grevel Lindop, is published by Pickering & Chatto (21 vols., London, 2000–3).

Anna Jameson's *Shakespeare's Heroines*, more properly known by Jameson's own preferred title, *Characteristics of Women: Moral, Poetical, and Historical*, ed. Cheri L. Larsen Hoeckley (Peterborough, ON.: Broadview Press, 2005), also includes Jameson's writings on Sarah Siddons. Writings on Shakespeare by women earlier in the period (Elizabeth Montagu, Charlotte Lennox, Elizabeth Griffith) can be investigated through Elizabeth Eger, *Bluestockings: Women of Reason from Enlightenment to Romanticism* (Basingstoke: Palgrave Macmillan, 2010), and Fiona Ritchie, *Women and Shakespeare in the Eighteenth Century* (Cambridge: Cambridge University Press, 2014), who includes actresses from Hannah Pritchard to Sarah Siddons, and the dramatist and theatrical historian Elizabeth Inchbald.

For the engravings of the Boydell Gallery the editions by Winifred Friedman (New York: Garland, 1976) and (on a more limited scale) A. E. Santaniello (New York: Arno, 1979) offer clear reproductions. *The Boydell Shakespeare Gallery*, ed. Walter Pape and Frederick Burwick (Bottrop: Verlag Peter Pomp, 1996) provides a variety of scholarly perspectives on the project. Peter Whitfield, *Illustrating Shakespeare* (London: British Library, 2013) includes chapters on painting and illustration in France and Germany. More sumptuous (in colour) is Jane Martineau et al., *Shakespeare in Art* (London: Merrell, 2003), which contains chapters on the Boydell Gallery, English theatrical paintings in the Romantic period, and Romantic-period paintings of Shakespearean subjects in Europe.

Chapter 3. Germany: 'Our Shakespeare'

Even more than in English criticism, in German criticism—and thence in modern European criticism and critical theory—Shakespeare occupies a unique position. Because the discovery and understanding of Shakespeare is a major strand of German cultural development in the Enlightenment, *Sturm und Drang*, and Romantic periods, and is central to a whole reorientation of cultural values away from French-dominated neoclassicism to aesthetics more distinctly (in the broadest sense) 'Germanic', the contexts of this development have to an unusual degree prompted the anthologizing of critical texts from this period under titles that stake a claim to its foundational status in German criticism, and often for European and American criticism more widely. An example is David Simpson (ed.), *The Origins of Modern Critical Thought: German Aesthetic and Literary Criticism from Lessing to Hegel* (Cambridge: Cambridge University Press, 1988), an anthology which is made up from three collections more fully representative of the whole period: Kathleen M. Wheeler (ed.), *German Aesthetic and Literary Criticism: the Romantic Ironists and Goethe* (Cambridge: Cambridge University Press, 1984), which, alongside Goethe, includes texts by Friedrich and A. W. Schlegel; David Simpson (ed.), *German Aesthetic and Literary Criticism* (Cambridge: Cambridge University Press, 1984), mainly relevant to Shakespeare for what it includes of Hegel; and H. B. Nisbet (ed.), *German Aesthetic and Literary Criticism* (Cambridge: Cambridge University Press, 1985), including texts by Lessing, Hamann, Herder, and Goethe. At least two other collections of aesthetics and critical theory and practice, which only partially cross over with these in their contents, also have Shakespeare as a major reference point: Jochen Schulte-Sasse et al. (ed. and trans.), *Theory as Practice: A Critical*

Anthology of Early German Romantic Writings (Minneapolis: University of Minnesota Press, 1997), an excellent representation of the Schlegels and their associates, including less well-known material by Dorothea Veit-Schlegel and Caroline Schlegel-Schelling; and J. M. Bernstein (ed.), *Classic and Romantic German Aesthetics*, Cambridge Texts in the History of Philosophy (Cambridge: Cambridge University Press, 2003), which includes Hamann, Lessing, Novalis, and Friedrich Schlegel. Not all the writing in these collections deals directly with Shakespeare, but a great deal of it is concerned with problems of aesthetics or interpretation which are linked to Shakespeare. A classic account of this work, which predates major shifts in modern criticism that have their origins in the 1970s and 1980s, and which therefore reflects on it differently from contemporary viewpoints, can be found in the first two volumes of René Wellek's 8-volume *History of Modern Criticism: 1750–1950* (vol. 1, *The Later Eighteenth Century*; vol. 2, *The Romantic Age*, London: Cape, 1955–). However different the specific reflections, it is indicative that here too Shakespeare appears as a consistent point of reference.

Beyond this ubiquitous presence in Enlightenment to Romantic German culture, many of the major writers engaged with Shakespeare evolved critical principles and practices from their understanding of his work, and in some cases recast that work in ways that state or imply critical principles. Those writers include Lessing, Hamann, Herder, Goethe (and with Goethe, Schiller), the Schlegel brothers, Tieck, Heine, and Hegel. Details of standard editions of these, and of the relevant works in English translation, are given in the notes. Recent surveys of the field are offered by Roger Paulin, *The Critical Reception of Shakespeare in Germany 1682-1914: Native Literature and Foreign Genius* (Hildesheim: Olms, 2003); and John A. McCarthy (ed.), *Shakespeare as German Author: Reception, Translation Theory, and Cultural Transfer* (Leiden: Brill, Rodopi, 2018), the introduction to which, 'The "Great Shapesphere"', concerned with Shakespeare from the 1770s to 1850, is in English.

Simon Williams's *Shakespeare on the German Stage: vol. 1: 1586-1914* (Cambridge: Cambridge University Press, 1990) offers an exemplary treatment of a range of issues concerning translation, adaptation, actors, performance, and the major theatres and their production styles, focussed mainly on the Romantic period (chs. 4–9). Ways in which the Schlegel–Tieck translation registered Shakespeare's formal and tonal diversity, challenged restricted ideas of sophisticated literary language, and acted as a model for new writing in German are discussed by Werner Habicht in Dirk Delabastita and Lieven D'hulst (eds.), *European Shakespeares* (Amsterdam: Benjamins, 1993).

256   *Further Reading*

Chapter 4. France: Revolution and After

As in German culture, in France too Shakespeare was a significant figure in pointing ways to the future. But where Shakespeare's role in Germany was in helping to create a native culture as one aspect of a developing sense of nationhood, in France Shakespeare's role, also cultural, was antithetical: to contribute prominently to the fundamental reorientation of a national culture that had become moribund, the culture of an aristocratic society incongruous with the age of the French Revolution and its aftermath. Voltaire was a crucial figure of the superseded culture. His writings on Shakespeare, culminating in a polemic fundamental to understanding French struggles over Shakespeare in the Romantic period, are collected in Theodore Besterman (ed.), *Voltaire on Shakespeare* (Geneva: Institut et musée Voltaire, 1967). The effect of those writings on versions of Shakespeare that appeared on the eighteenth-century stage in France is evident in the adaptations of Jean-François Ducis, to which John Golder's *Shakespeare for the Age of Reason* (Oxford: Voltaire Foundation, 1992) is a guide.

After Voltaire and the Revolution, views of Shakespeare developed in two waves. A muted revision of Voltaire's neoclassicism can be traced in the writings of Germaine de Staël, one of the most important figures of the age in disseminating new cultural ideas from Germany into a wider European context, first in *On Literature* (*De la littérature*, 1800), above all in *Germany* (*De L'Allemagne*, 1813). De Staël's political activities, both during the years of revolution and later in opposition to Napoleon, and the personal association with A. W. Schlegel which helped make her a conduit for new European ideas, can be studied through a selection of her writings, *Major Writings of Germaine de Staël*, trans. Vivian Folkenflik (New York: Columbia University Press, 1987) or in the biography of J. Christopher Herold, *Mistress to an Age* (London: Hamish Hamilton, 1959). The restoration of the French monarchy in 1815 marked the beginning of a new era and a new view of Shakespeare, with a more complete overthrow of the neoclassicism of Voltaire, first in the pamphleteering of the great Romantic novelist Stendhal, then in the polemic of Victor Hugo. This movement can be sampled in two collections of writings on the theatre: Barry V. Daniels, *Revolution in the Theatre: French Romantic Theories of Drama* (Westport, CT: Greenwood, 1983), and (setting de Staël, Stendhal, Hugo, and the debates about Shakespeare in a wider European context) Michael J. Sidnell, *Sources of Dramatic Theory*, vol. 2, *Voltaire to Hugo* (Cambridge: Cambridge University Press, 1991). Daniels includes discussion by de Staël of the great French tragic actor François-Joseph Talma, important in French productions of Shakespeare in the period. After Hugo, Shakespeare became a central figure in French post-Revolutionary Romantic culture, a presence registered in France more than elsewhere not only in literature but also in music (Berlioz, Gounod) and in the visual arts (Delacroix, Chassériau). As with Schlegel–Tieck in Germany, so the Romantic period in France produced a translation which further naturalized Shakespeare into European culture (François-Victor Hugo, 1859–65). Details of editions of all these writers, their most relevant works in English translation, and musical scores and visual art catalogues are given in the notes.

The Shakespeare anniversary of 1964 prompted a special issue of *Yale French Studies* (no. 33, *Shakespeare in France*), which surveys central aspects of the Romantic-period response with essays on most of the main figures (Voltaire, Guizot, Stendhal, Vigny, Victor Hugo, and Berlioz). One of the most detailed and substantially documented accounts of this history comes from the end of the period of change, Albert Lacroix's *Histoire de l'influence de Shakespeare sur le théâtre français jusqu'à nos jours* (Brussels: Lesigne, 1856). John Pemble's *Shakespeare goes to Paris: How the Bard conquered France* (London: Hambledon, 2005) is a lively (and less scholarly) modern equivalent.

Chapter 5. Editors and Scholars: Inheritances and Legacies

The major Romantic period editions of Edmund Malone (1790; rev. James Boswell Jr, 1821), George Steevens (1793), and Isaac Reed (1803) are all in different ways descendants of eighteenth-century traditions of editing, incorporating elements of the editions dating back to Nicholas Rowe (1709) and Alexander Pope (1725), through Lewis Theobald (1733) to Samuel Johnson (1765). Steevens began by working with Johnson (on revisions of his edition in 1773 and 1778), Malone by adding two supplementary volumes to Johnson–Steevens 1778 (in 1780), and Reed through work with Steevens. The detailed facts of this publication history are given by Andrew Murphy, *Shakespeare in Print: A History and Chronology of Shakespeare Publishing* (Cambridge: Cambridge University Press, 2003). Murphy is also the editor of *A Concise Companion to Shakespeare and the Text* (Oxford: Wiley-Blackwell, 2007), which includes his own essay on Romantic-period editors and scholarship and an extensive bibliography. As well as drawing substantially from the eighteenth century, Romantic-period editing also established the major issues for editing and scholarship developed by the 'New Bibliography' of the early twentieth century. Partly in work outside its mainstream—the editions of Edward Capell (1768, with volumes of annotation, 1779–83) and Charles Jennens (five individual plays, 1770–4)—it also foreshadowed concerns of more recent editorial scholarship: Shakespeare as reviser of his own work; Shakespeare as collaborative dramatist. It shifted editing into a world of professionals—from the dramatist Rowe, the poet Pope, the man of letters Johnson, to scholars for whom editorial scholarship (establishing and annotating Shakespeare's text) was their major preoccupation. The most contested figure of the period, in his relation to eighteenth-century editing, is Malone, for opposite sides on the debate about whom see Margreta de Grazia, *Shakespeare Verbatim: the Reproduction of Authenticity and the 1790 Apparatus* (Oxford: Clarendon Press, 1991), and Peter Martin, *Edmond Malone: Shakespearean Scholar. A Literary Biography* (Cambridge: Cambridge University Press, 1995). Other studies of individual eighteenth-century and Romantic-period editors and editions, and of issues in editing and scholarship, are given in the notes, and see above on the series *Great Shakespeareans*, ed. Adrian Poole and Peter Holland.

Chapter 6. The English Stage: The Age of Siddons

A major shift of emphasis in Shakespeare criticism of the last half-century, part of a move from verbal 'New Criticism' to a more contextually aware historical and political criticism, has been an increasing emphasis on performance studies and the meanings of performance. For a variety of reasons the study versus the theatre, the reader versus the audience as ideal location of meaning, was also a live issue in the Romantic period. Several major critics (Coleridge, Hazlitt, Lamb) expressed anti-theatrical views—though Hazlitt also loved the theatre and saw performance as a mode of interpretation. Anti-theatrical views, in part absolute, were also in part conditional, involved with objections to the common practice, inherited from the Restoration and the eighteenth century, of performing Shakespeare in radically adapted versions. John Philip Kemble, as an intellectual actor-manager working to draw together Shakespeare as high art and as popular culture, by publishing his own theatrical versions, and in association with the theatrical historian Elizabeth Inchbald, gave greater status to the archiving of performance materials. Hazlitt and Leigh Hunt, moreover, particularly raised theatrical reviewing into a literary art which preserved in newly vivid form accounts of particular productions and performances. Aided by the charismatic presence of some of the greatest performers in the history of English theatre and the cultural status given to actors by the theatrical portraits of Reynolds, Gainsborough, Lawrence, Romney, and others, the stage also became a complex site of contested cultural ownership, sometimes with political implications. 'Literary' reviews of performances, archival materials, theatrical memoirs and biographies, the diaries and journals of theatrical professionals and amateurs of the stage: the notes provide details of all this material. For discussions centred on actors, texts, and adaptations, see Linda Kelly, *The Kemble Era: John Philip Kemble, Sarah Siddons, and the London Stage* (London: Bodley Head, 1980), and Joseph Donohue, *Theatre in the Age of Kean* (Oxford: Blackwell, 1975). For discussion of the social and political place of theatre, see Marc Baer, *Theatre and Disorder in Late Georgian London* (Oxford: Clarendon Press, 1991) and Jane Moody, *Illegitimate Theatre in London, 1770-1840* (Cambridge: Cambridge University Press, 2000). For a selection of literary theatrical reviews see Stanley Wells (ed.), *Shakespeare in the Theatre: an Anthology of Criticism* (Oxford: Clarendon Press, 1997), and for complete texts of this journalism, Hazlitt's *A View of the English Stage* (Howe, vol. 5) and *Leigh Hunt's Dramatic Criticism, 1808-1831*, ed. Lawrence Huston Houtchens and Carolyn Washburn Houtchens (London: Oxford University Press, 1950). For essays on Shakespeare in the theatrical criticism of Hazlitt and Leigh Hunt see Stanley Wells, *Shakespeare on Page and Stage: Selected Essays*, ed. Paul Edmondson (Oxford: Oxford University Press, 2016).

Index